BEGGED, BORROWED & STOLEN

True Tales of Thievery from America's Past

JAN BRIDGEFORD-SMITH

LYONS
PRESS

Guilford, Connecticut

An imprint of The Rowman & Littlefield Publishing Group, Inc.
4501 Forbes Boulevard, Suite 200, Lanham, Maryland 20706
www.rowman.com

Distributed by NATIONAL BOOK NETWORK

British Library Cataloguing in Publication Information Available

Library of Congress Cataloging-in-Publication Data Available

Names: Bridgeford-Smith, Jan, author.
Title: Begged, borrowed, and stolen : true tales of thievery from America's past / Jan Bridgeford-Smith.
Description: Guilford, Conneticut : Lyons Press, [2021] | Includes bibliographical references and index. | Summary: "A history of America's greatest heists, hijackings, and holdups"—Provided by publisher.
Identifiers: LCCN 2020042749 (print) | LCCN 2020042750 (ebook) | ISBN 9781493052318 (paperback ; alk. paper) | ISBN 9781493052325 (ebook)
Subjects: LCSH: Theft—United States—Case studies. | Thieves—United States—Case studies.
Classification: LCC HV6658 .B75 2021 (print) | LCC HV6658 (ebook) | DDC 364.16/20973—dc23
LC record available at https://lccn.loc.gov/2020042749
LC ebook record available at https://lccn.loc.gov/2020042750

♾™ The paper used in this publication meets the minimum requirements of American National Standard for Information Sciences—Permanence of Paper for Printed Library Materials, ANSI/NISO Z39.48-1992.

Contents

BEGGED

Kennewick Man

Skeleton Seizure

Seventy years before the banks of the Columbia River disgorged the skeleton christened Kennewick Man, a famous courtroom drama captured national headlines. The Scopes Trial was a clash between traditionalism and modernity. Newspaperman John P. Fort, writing for the Chattanooga News, *framed the showdown as a cage match between lawyers. The headline of his day one column read, "Bryan vs. Darrow, Battle of Giants." He opened with these words: "From puddle to paradise, from Eden to Dayton. The squared ring is ready." But it was the last paragraph that got to the heart of the matter. "Man is here in his own courtroom," mused Fort, "arguing about legal principles only on the surface. In reality, he is arguing about where he came from and where he will go when his span of years allotted to him and his inquiring mind is closed."*

The legal boxing match that pitted Darwin and evolution against God, Adam, and Eve echoed through the struggle over Kennewick Man. Once again, the question at the heart of the drama was this: Which origin story would be honored—the ancient tale recited by elders through countless generations, or the genetic connection revealed by modern technology?

WILL THOMAS AND DAVID DEACY, TWO COLLEGE STUDENTS, WADED IN the shallows of Washington State's Columbia River, spectators at the annual hydroplane races. Suddenly, one of them stumbled over what he thought was a large, round white rock. Within minutes of picking up the offending object, the young men dialed 911—not because of a broken toe but because of the human skull that caused it.

Benton County sheriff's deputies arrived and summoned a dive team to assist with finding additional remains. More bones were discovered and county coroner Floyd Johnson was contacted. After an initial investigation, the coroner and police taped off the area as a crime scene. Not sure of the age of the bones already retrieved or how the victim might have died, Johnson phoned Dr. James Chatters—a forensic anthropologist, archaeologist, and paleontologist—for a consultation, and to assist in the recovery of more bones, if more existed at the site. Unknown to Chatters, he was about to open a Pandora's box of legal, racial, and ethical disputes that would last for nearly twenty years.

The controversy began as a case of mistaken identity.

July 28, 1996, was the day the Benton County Sheriff's office was first notified of the skull in the shallows of the Columbia River near Kennewick, Washington. This section of the waterway was under the management of the US Army Corps of Engineers at the time. When James Chatters joined Floyd Johnson that day, the two men discovered more bones. But it wasn't until July 30 that Chatters applied for and was retroactively granted a permit under the federal Archaeological Resources Protection Act (ARPA) by the Walla Walla District Corps of Engineers. This permit allowed for continued site excavations and removal of any additional remains that might be found. As required, the Walla Walla District office notified local Indian tribes of the bones in case the discovered remains were Native American.

A total of some three hundred bone elements and fragments were removed from the Columbia River site over the next month. Dr. Chatters placed himself as guardian of the bones, carefully photographing, cataloging, analyzing, and assembling the skeletal remains in a lab housed in his garage. Once the bony puzzle was organized, what emerged was an adult male skeleton nearly 90 percent complete.

But whose ancestor had been discovered?

"The completeness and unusually good condition of the skeleton," Dr. Chatters later wrote, "presence of Caucasoid traits, lack of definitive Native American characteristics, and the association with an early homestead led me to suspect that the bones represented a European settler." But that theory started unraveling when Dr. Chatters noticed a projectile (spear) point lodged in the skeleton's upper hip bone. Closer examination using X-rays and CT scans showed that the object's design was consistent, Chatters believed, with a Cascade point, a style that was common in the area thousands of years before the "documented arrival of Europeans in this region," Chatters mused. "We either had an ancient individual with physical characteristics unlike later 'native peoples' or a trapper/explorer who'd had difficulties with 'stone-age' peoples during his travels."

To resolve the mystery, the anthropologist removed a small bit of metacarpal bone and sent it to a lab for radiocarbon dating. What he got back astonished him. Harbored in his garage was a skeleton carbon-dated

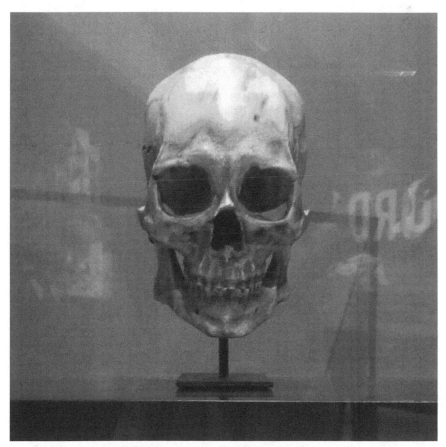

A cast of the Kennewick Man's skull on display at the State Museum of Natural History Karlsruhe. The original fossil belonged to one of the most complete human skeletons of ancient man yet to be found.
COURTESY OF WIKIMEDIA COMMONS

to approximately 8500 BP (scientific shorthand for "before the present year")—a number that translated into bones that were nearly nine thousand calendar years old. If the stone point in the hip wasn't enough to quash the European settler theory, the carbon-dating certainly was.

Dr. Chatters was perplexed. His initial assessment of whose ancestor was assembled on the lab table was obviously wrong. Yet the skull remained confounding since its shape and facial measurements did not align with the skull and facial configurations of any modern North American Indians. The five local tribes—Confederated Tribes of the Umatilla Reservation, Nez Perce, Wanapum Band, Confederated Tribes of the Colville Reservation, and Yakima—didn't share Chatters' doubts or speculations. They were adamant: The skeletal warrior belonged to them. He was the Ancient One, a sacred figure of their origin narratives; the ancestor spoken of in religious stories that had been told from one generation to the next for ten thousand years.

Aaron Ashley, a member of the Umatilla Reservation, said two decades later, "We have oral stories that tell of our history on this land, and we knew, at the moment of discovery, that he was our relation."

Once alerted to the Columbia River discovery, local tribes wanted the Ancient One returned to them for reburial. Armand Minthorn, a leader among the Umatilla, became the Indians' most visible face and voice for their petition to reclaim the skeleton. This demand rested on the federal Native American Graves Protection and Repatriation Act, or NAGPRA. "Sacred human remains are not artifacts," Minthorn claimed in a July 2001 interview with *PBS NewsHour*. He explained, "They are what they are—sacred—and they are our ancestral remains, and they need to be treated as such."

While the Corps of Engineers pondered the Indians' claim of kinship to the Ancient One, Dr. Chatters began a systematic, science-driven investigation of the skeleton. He wrote:

> *I conducted a standard forensic examination and measurements. . . .*
> *All teeth were present at the time of death. This was a male of late*
> *middle age (40–55 years), and tall (170 to 176 cm), slender build.*
> *He had suffered numerous injuries, the most severe of which were*

compound fractures of at least six ribs and apparent damage to his left shoulder musculature, atrophy of the left humerus due to the muscle damage, and the healing projectile wound in his right pelvis. The lack of head flattening from cradle board use, minimal arthritis in weight-bearing bones, and the unusually light wear on his teeth distinguish the behavior and diet of Kennewick Man from that of more recent peoples in the region. The man lacks definitive characteristics of the classic mongoloid stock to which modern Native Americans belong.

Dr. Chatters learned a great deal from the bones in his care. Yet, for the Native Americans, it appeared the scientist had a broader agenda than simply decoding skeletal information. "The Kennewick discovery," Chatters stated, "along with other recent finds in Nevada, may significantly alter conventional views of how, when, and by whom the Americas were peopled." He added: "No matter how long we might study the Kennewick Man, we would never know the form or color of his eyes, skin and hair, whether his hair was curly or straight, his lips thin or full—in short, many of the characteristics by which we judge living peoples' racial affiliation."

It was a curious statement since Dr. Chatters later defied his own comment. He constructed a model of the Kennewick Man skull and then built a face on it—eyes, lips, hair, skin. When he was finished, the anthropologist had produced an uncanny look-alike of Patrick Stewart, *Star Trek*'s Captain Jean-Luc Picard.

The other statement by Dr. Chatters that proved troubling to the Indians was his claim that Kennewick Man and other recent discoveries in Nevada could possibly "alter conventional views of how, when, and by whom the Americas were peopled." This idea—that perhaps different waves of prehistoric peoples from different parts of the globe made it to the Americas—was not original to Dr. Chatters. Several notable researchers in the paleo-disciplines were interested in this possibility. Kennewick Man, if sufficiently studied, might provide the evidence needed to bolster this hypothesis. An undercurrent of real or perceived racializing had infused the debate over the skeleton's lineage.

That an ancient "Caucasoid," possibly of European origin, might be in the mix of earliest immigrants to the New World excited another faction as well—at least long enough to make a couple of newspaper headlines. Members of the American Ásatrú Church, a modern incarnation of ancient Icelandic religious rites based on the worship of Norse gods and goddesses, briefly got involved in the racial competition over the Kennewick remains. The small band threw their support behind Dr. Chatters, fervently hoping the skeleton brimmed with Euro DNA. But, lacking resources to sustain what was shaping up to be a legal fight, the Ásatrú faction quickly bowed out. It's unclear if the church's cameo appearance in the struggle garnered new members for the Nordic congregation.

On August 30, 1996, the Corps of Engineers notified Dr. Chatters that he must stop all study of the bones. Insult was added to injury when the skeleton was removed from Chatters' stewardship, and the bones remanded to a neutral location while the Indians' petition was being evaluated. James Chatters, firmly convinced Kennewick Man had no ties to any current Indian tribes, was piqued. He opined that "if the Corps persists in its refusal to allow additional studies . . . experts will lose the chance to directly examine this rare phenomenon." It was a bitter pill to swallow for Chatters. The Corps also issued a public notice that the remains of the Ancient One were going to be released to the five tribes in accordance with NAGPRA. Passed in 1990, the Native American Graves Protection and Repatriation Act was meant to assist Native Americans in gaining custody of their cultural artifacts and ancestors' remains that were held in the collections of federal agencies or institutions receiving federal funding.

That where the bones were discovered had once been Indian land was certain. An 1851 treaty with the federal government included the excavation site as part of the acreage ceded at the time by tribal leaders. But another aspect of the NAGPRA law was trickier. The tribes needed to show that the Ancient One had a "cultural affiliation" with them for their claims to be respected. Cultural affiliation is defined in the law as "a relationship of shared group identity which can be reasonably traced historically or prehistorically between a present-day Indian Tribe or Native Hawaiian organization and an identifiable earlier group." The evidence can include "geographical, kinship, biological, archaeological, anthropological, linguistic, oral tradition, or historical evidence or other relevant information or expert opinion."

NAGPRA legislation acknowledged that in the case of human remains, meeting the standard of cultural affiliation could be tough. There was some wiggle room allowed when it came to showing "an absolute continuity from present-day Indian Tribes to older, prehistoric remains without some reasonable gaps in the historic or prehistoric record." In other words, cultural affiliation could be demonstrated in different ways, even if there was a gap in the historical record.

The tribes that claimed the Ancient One submitted oral history accounts that leaders said were ten thousand years old. As the Cherokee put it, "We cannot separate our place on earth from our lives on the earth nor from our vision nor our meaning as a people. . . . So when we speak of land . . . [w]e are speaking of something truly sacred." Umatilla spokesperson Armand Minthorn concurred: "I know where my people lived, where they died, where they hunted, where they fished, and where they were buried, because my oral histories tell me that." Anthropologists like Western Washington University's Daniel Boxberger were asked to review the histories for the federal government. In a 2001 *PBS NewsHour* interview, Boxberger said that he "became quickly convinced that there's a collective memory on the plateau that goes back very far. Some of the oral traditions speak of such times as when the land was covered with snow and ice about ten thousand years ago."

Leadership at the Army Corps of Engineers for the Walla Walla District chose to accept this as evidence of cultural affiliation. There was no documentation of any kind to support the idea that Paleoamericans other than the ancient ancestors of Native Americans had ever set foot on that part of the continent.

The decision in favor of the tribes dismayed James Chatters. It was no secret that once the remains were returned, the Indians intended to immediately bury the Ancient One, believing that his soul had already been aboveground too long. Chatters told journalist Lee Hochberg, "It's very easy to say, well, my elders told me. . . . If the Indian tribes believe that every skeleton is sacred and should be back in the ground, does that apply to all of them in the world?"

When Hochberg asked Minthorn, "If a skeleton were found that's 100,000 years old, would that also be your ancestor?" the Umatilla Indian

and curator at the Smithsonian National Museum of Natural History. "We are finding out they were coming thousands of years earlier than we had thought, arriving not just over the Bering Strait but by boats and other means." It was heady stuff, these possibilities. Seductive. Exciting. Native Americans, however, didn't share the exuberance for these origin hypotheses. For them, the Ancient One was personal. It was a sacred issue. Questions of origin were directly related to the obligation of burial. The land they had once inhabited was holy because they were created on it, not arrived from somewhere else. They had always been where they were. *They* were of the land.

In July of 2005, Owsley led a team of twenty scientists that spent ten intensive days at the Burke, measuring, examining, and running tests on Kennewick Man. It wasn't long before a great deal more was known about the Ancient One. Minute details of the bones could be calculated and documented thanks to improvements in scanning technology. Closer scrutiny of the projectile point in the hip revealed it was not a Cascade tip as originally thought. This pointed object was sharp at one end but had a stem at the other. A Cascade tip was sharpened at both ends. And the spear point appeared to have entered the hip from the front, not the back. This injury, while severe, isn't what killed Kennewick Man. "It was a healed injury," said Owsley. "There was no clear indication in the skeleton of cause of death."

In fact, the bones revealed numerous injuries—broken ribs, a leg, and a collarbone—that all marked this hunter as a survivor, a man who was tough as nails.

It took nearly a decade before Douglas Owsley and his team published their research. Much was learned in the investigations, including that Kennewick Man's companions purposely buried him parallel to the river. The erosion that upended his grave exposing the bones had occurred not long before the skull was discovered in 1996. But there was one thing Owsley's team did not establish—a reliable DNA result.

Grinding enough genetic material from ancient bone, enough material to perform genome sequencing, is a challenge. But a lab at Denmark's University of Copenhagen, headed by one of the premier DNA experts in the world, Eske Willerslev, finally overcame this technical obstacle.

Willerslev and his colleagues published their report in June of 2015. "In order to resolve Kennewick Man's ancestry and affiliations," they wrote, "we have sequenced his genome … and compared it to worldwide genomic data, including for the Ainu [an almost extinct population group found in Northern Japan] and Polynesians. We find that Kennewick Man is closer

Jiwoong Cheh of StudioEIS brought the Ancient One to life with this sculpted bust based on the forensic skull reconstruction by Amanda Danning.

to modern Native Americans than to any other population worldwide. Among the Native American groups . . . several seem to be descended from a population closely related to that of Kennewick Man, including the Confederated Tribes of the Colville Reservation (Colville), one of the five tribes claiming Kennewick Man."

The report went on to discount the skull morphology conclusions that suggested Kennewick Man was related to some other modern peoples. "Based on genetic comparisons . . . Kennewick Man shows continuity with Native North Americans over at least the last eight millennia."

In December of 2016, just before he left office, President Obama signed a bill that gave the federal government ninety days to release the remains of the Ancient One, still being held in stewardship at the Burke Museum. The US Army Corps of Engineers formally transferred custody of the skeleton to the State of Washington. Through the state's procedure, the Ancient One was placed into the care of his Native American descendants by museum officials on Friday, February 17, 2017. The following day, two hundred members of the Umatilla, Yakama Nation, Nez Perce Tribe, Confederated Tribes of the Colville Reservation, and the Wanapum Band of Indians buried their ancestor at an undisclosed site near the Columbia River.

Twenty years earlier, in 1998, a congressional panel investigating the dispute between the Indians and the scientists heard this from Armand Minthorn: "We are not worried that study of the remains will change history, or cause us to lose our standing in history. We already know what happened ten thousand years ago." The Ancient One was never placed on public display.

James Armistead Lafayette

Snatching Secrets

At the Valentine Museum in Richmond, Virginia, there hangs a bust-length image of an older man by the artist John Blennerhassett Martin. It was painted in 1824. The subject's smoothly dark complexion is enhanced by a high white collar and ruffle that surrounds his neck like a shimmering nimbus. He wears a midnight-blue coat animated with two parallel rows of brass buttons that march from throat to waist in precise formation. This decoration, along with the garment's stand-up collar, mark the jacket as military clothing. Handsome, even features are set in a long, oval face that starts with a high, broad forehead and tapers gracefully to a narrow, pronounced chin. Gray hair, like a dusting of snow, coats his carefully trimmed Afro. The gentleman conveys an affable expression, his closed lips fixed in a slight smile, but a careful study of the eyes reveals a tired wariness of the kind that comes from too many worldly disappointments. This is a portrait of slave-turned-spy James Armistead Lafayette, an American patriot.

THERE ARE TWO BIRTH YEARS FLOATED FOR JAMES ARMISTEAD LAFAYette, 1748 and 1760. Current research favors December 10, 1748, as the day he was born on the plantation of William Armistead in New Kent County, Virginia. The child's destiny as a piece of property was preordained by having an enslaved mother. James' slave status and race also meant scant information about his life was recorded or preserved. Piecing together a few extant documents, historians speculate James was a laborer in Armistead's tobacco fields. His intelligence and cunning are attested to by his later exploits as a spy, and there are some indications that his master and other slave-owners recognized his intellect even earlier.

When the American Revolution broke out, the enslaved residents of British North America numbered approximately 450,000 men, women, and children of African descent, or roughly 20 percent of the total 2.5 million population. It's no wonder the renowned English writer, Samuel Johnson, observed that the loudest agitation for liberty came from individuals oblivious to their hypocrisy. Slavery was practiced in all thirteen colonies, but the highest concentration of enslaved African Americans was in the Chesapeake area and south. Slave labor in this region was crucial to the social fabric and economies that relied on exports like cotton, tobacco, rice, indigo, and naval stores. New World settlement in the area was only profitable thanks to the early importation of enslaved Black people from Africa and the West Indies.

George Washington proved Samuel Johnson was on the money about hypocrisy. On November 12, 1775, the General decreed that "neither negroes, boys unable to bear arms, nor old men" could enlist in the Continental Army. Leaders of militia units in New England weren't as nervous about Black men with rifles. Before the ban on Black soldiers, historians estimate approximately 5 percent, or about one hundred African Americans fought at Bunker Hill. But fear of armed slave rebellions took precedence in Washington's mind over having enough men to muster an army. He wasn't alone. Members of the Continental Congress also feared armed and trained African Americans. They supported the ban.

British royal governor, John Murray, 4th Earl of Dunmore, had different ideas. He understood the consequences if large numbers of African Americans could be induced to desert the plantations and fight against their white masters and former tormentors. Lord Dunmore released a proclamation, drawn on November 7, 1775, that promised freedom for any enslaved individual who escaped to British custody from a *rebel* master. The operative word here is "rebel," meaning a slave-owner who sided with the Patriot cause. Any enslaved person who fled a Loyalist master was routinely returned by the British to their miserable circumstances. As author Gary B. Nash noted in *The Unknown American Revolution*, Dunmore's proclamation was "more an announcement of military strategy than a pronouncement of abolitionist principles."

However, the royal governor's gambit paid off. Depending on the source, somewhere between three hundred and five hundred enslaved people abandoned their Patriot masters within hours of the proclamation and went over to the British side. Dunmore immediately organized a Black brigade, the Ethiopian Regiment.

At the Battle of Great Bridge, near Norfolk, Lord Dunmore put together a small army that included white Loyalists and Black soldiers from the Ethiopian Regiment. Dunmore's force left their island fort and crossed a bridge that spanned the Elizabeth River. They met with some opposition from Patriots guarding the structure, including a tenacious Black soldier, a freedman from Portsmouth, named William Flora. But Dunmore's force prevailed and an assault was mounted on the Second Virginia Regiment commanded by Colonel William Woodford.

A cunning leader, Woodford had employed a spy, a Black man, to pass bad intel to Dunmore. Based on the spy's misleading information, the British attack was short, bloody, and unsuccessful. Dunmore and his men were forced to retreat to their fort by Woodford's Patriot fighters. Popular legend suggested that when General Washington heard about Woodford's victory, he had to rethink his policy on Black enlistees.

By January 1776, Washington relented somewhat and allowed freedmen "with prior military experience" to serve in the Continental Army. Another exception was made by Washington beginning in 1777 when he allowed all free African Americans to enlist, regardless of experience. The Continental Congress finally recognized that the Patriot cause was hopeless if the colonies failed to meet enlistment quotas. Any black man, free or enslaved, ready to fight, was welcomed.

Of the Southern colonies, only Maryland extended enlistment to Blacks. By 1779, the depleted ranks of the Continental Army became so dire that the nascent Congress took another step. A bounty of $1,000 was offered in South Carolina and Georgia for every enslaved man provided by a slave-owner to the army. But legislators in both colonies were still so riddled with fear that their lives and fortunes would be in peril, they voted down the offer. Given how queasy slaveholders were about arming slaves, James Armistead Lafayette's story is a testimony to his quiet dignity and courage.

By 1781, thousands of African Americans had thrown in their lot with the British in exchange for their freedom. James Armistead, however, petitioned his master for the right to join the Continental Army forces gathered in Virginia under the command of the French soldier, General Gilbert du Motier, Marquis de Lafayette. William Armistead agreed. Despite the dangers of war, James doubtless found his enlistment a welcome respite from the cruel conditions of being a field slave.

Lafayette thought James would make an excellent spy and dispatched him right away to cross behind the British lines. Passing as a laborer in search of work, the Black man roused little if any suspicion within the British encampment. It's likely that James first ingratiated himself with Benedict Arnold's command. The patriot-turned-traitor had joined the British forces just before the siege of Richmond. Wherever he started, James soon worked his way into the headquarters of General Charles Cornwallis. Undoubtedly, he was put to work as a waiter and all-purpose attendant in the camp. The British were no more adept at *seeing* Black servants than slaveholders. Historians surmise that James overheard conversations within the camp and passed the information to "a network of other Black men who would move back and forth between enemy lines."

While Armistead was not privy to Cornwallis's most sensitive papers, he did gain the general's confidence. After all, it made sense that a Black man's interests would ally with the British, who had actively courted their allegiance. In fact, Cornwallis was so convinced that he and James were in accord that he prevailed on him to spy for the British. James accepted and turned double agent.

Fortune began to turn against the world's most formidable army by the fall of 1781. France formally entered the fray on the side of the Continental Army, a move that bolstered the Patriots' spirits, coffers, and forces on land and sea. British troops, on the other hand, were tired and running low on supplies. Cornwallis needed to move his men to Yorktown, Virginia, where he could await British ships carrying desperately needed replenishments.

James realized he had a juicy piece of information when he learned of Cornwallis's impending troop movement. He immediately got a message to Lafayette, who passed it on to Washington. Together, the two commanders planned and executed a strategy that trapped Cornwallis, forcing him to surrender his army, supplies, and weaponry. The capitulation of the British at Yorktown effectively ended the Crown's war on the colonies. It was another year before a treaty was concluded, but the conflict was over.

During the nearly seven years of fighting, an estimated twenty thousand formerly enslaved Black men, women, and children sought refuge behind British lines. They mostly worked in support roles not combat positions. This practice kept Loyalist slaveholders from coming unglued. One consequence of this policy is that far more Black men, about five thousand in total, served as armed soldiers with the Continental Army. On average, these soldiers maintained their enlistments nearly twice as long as white enlistees.

After the war, a number of Loyalist plantation owners in Savannah and Charleston, took their families and their slaves hundreds of miles away. They reestablished their households in Florida and on islands scattered throughout the Caribbean. As for the slaves of Patriots who made it into British protection before November 30, 1782, they were emancipated and restitution paid by the Crown to the slave's owner. To identify which African Americans were eligible for freedom and which weren't, the British verified the names, ages, and date of escape for every Black refugee in their custody. These records were cataloged in what became known as the *Book of Negroes*.

Three thousand Black men, women, and children clutched their "freedom certificates" issued by the British and melted into the 1783 parade of Loyalists exiting from New York for Nova Scotia. It proved a disappointing destination. Though no longer hostage to shackles and whips, the Black émigrés were hampered in their new home by lack of supplies, equipment, and the monetary support they'd been assured awaited them in their new home. After nearly a decade of desperate economic circumstances, almost 50 percent of the once-hopeful settlers abandoned the Canadian province. A few hundred crossed the Atlantic to London, while another 1,200 chose the offer of resettlement in the British colony of Sierra Leone on the African continent. One man whose return to Africa seemed both appropriate and droll was Harry Washington, a former slave owned by George Washington, the newly elected president of the United States. In a turnabout of the kind that seems like a cosmic joke rather than coincidence, Harry Washington was convicted in 1800 of being a leader in a settler's rebellion to overthrow the British colonial authority. The issue? Taxation.

But James Armistead was not among those who dashed toward liberty. Instead, he returned to Kent County, Virginia, and his life of slavery.

Despite his noble service, the Act of 1783 that emancipated slave-soldiers who fought with the Continental Army did not extend to James, a slave-spy. He was forced to petition the Virginia legislature for his freedom. To improve his chances of escaping his onerous status, James solicited assistance from his former commander, General Lafayette. On a visit to Richmond in 1784, the French soldier wrote a letter attesting to his regard for James. "The ex-spy," he wrote, "had rendered 'services to me while I had the honour to command in this state. His intelligence from the enemy's camp were industriously collected and more faithfully delivered. He perfectly acquitted himself with some important commissions I gave him and appears to me entitled to every reward his situation can admit of."

Two years crawled by for James with no action on his petition. Then, in the 1786 autumn session of the Virginia General Assembly, his petition for emancipation, supported by his owner, William Armistead, was granted with these words: "[A]t the peril of his life [he] found means to frequent the British camp, and thereby faithfully executed important commissions entrusted to him by the marquis." Underscoring the commercial rather than human value of slaves, William Armistead received compensation for James from the Commonwealth at the going auction-block price to purchase a comparable man.

Based on Kent County records, James acquired a farm near his former plantation. He married and had at least one son. Ironically, he is also listed as the owner of three slaves. But his economic circumstances were precarious at best. Neither freedom nor land guaranteed stability or opportunity for a Black man. At some point in 1817, the nearly destitute, elderly James petitioned the Virginia legislature once more, this time for monetary relief. Based on his Revolutionary War service, he was awarded a pension of $60 per year from the state for the remainder of his life.

Before he died, James—who years before had adopted the general's last name as his own—had one final, sweet moment with the Marquis. In

1824, the revered general returned to the United States for a celebratory tour of the nation. In Richmond, he spotted James among the cheering crowd. Wading into the scramble of well-wishers, Lafayette, who had survived another revolution in France, embraced the aged Black man who had so generously served a nation that still did not treat him as one of its own.

James Armistead Lafayette died in 1830 or 1832, either in Virginia or near Baltimore, Maryland. He was eighty-four, eighty-two, seventy-two, or seventy years of age, depending on the birth date used. There is but one verified likeness of James, the portrait by Martin that hangs in the Valentine Museum. It's rumored the man appears in a 1783 oil painting by Jean-Baptiste Le Paon and in a ten-foot-high, bronze sculpture tableau based on the Le Paon canvas. Created by Daniel Chester French, the bronze adorns the 9th Street Entrance to Prospect Park in the borough of Queens.

Le Paon's painting, on display at Lafayette College, is titled *Marquis de Lafayette at Yorktown*, and depicts the general beside a horse attended by a Black groomsman, depicted wearing an extravagant feather-decorated hat, and dressed in attire more suitable for a dance than holding a horse on a muddy hill. Scholars are undecided if the groomsman in Le Paon's painting is James. It's quite likely that General Lafayette had more than one African American in his ranks. Or perhaps the artist simply used his imagination to create the figure. The bronze relief also portrays Lafayette standing in front of a horse held by a Black servant. But at least in this rendition, the attendant wears a tricorner hat and is dressed in far more sensible breeches and boots.

As with so much in James's life, whether he is the unnamed man by Lafayette's side is a mystery—a fitting legacy, perhaps, for the double agent. Harriet Beecher Stowe, the writer whose 1852 novel, *Uncle Tom's Cabin*, inspired abolitionist action on both sides of the Mason-Dixon line, called the actions of Black men who served the Patriot cause "far more magnanimous." She eloquently pointed out that "it was not for their own land that they fought . . . but for a land which had enslaved them. . . . Bravery, under such circumstances, has a peculiar beauty and merit."

John Sutter

Stolen Land and Golden Greed

His name is synonymous with the California Gold Rush of 1849—John Augustus Sutter. The precious metal, first discovered on Sutter's baronial-inspired estate, touched off the pivotal event that fast-tracked California to statehood and mythologized the territory's image as a place of golden possibilities. But for California's indigenous peoples, the Gold Rush touched off a horror that lasted into the first decades of the twentieth century and brought the state's Indians to the brink of extinction. Sutter, too, suffered, at the hands of the "forty-niners," the nickname given to the tens of thousands of miners, entrepreneurs, and scalawags who flooded the state in the race for wealth. Perhaps his fate was inevitable—a cosmic reckoning on behalf of the Native Americans whose stolen land had provided his wealth.

HE CALLED HIMSELF CAPTAIN SUTTER AND STYLED HIMSELF AS AN officer and gentleman, but he arrived on American shores to escape arrest and trial for shady dealings and debts. Born in Germany but raised in Switzerland, Johann August Sutter left his five children and wife—after squandering her fortune—in Burgdorf, Switzerland, then anglicized his name to John Augustus Sutter, and departed the European continent from Le Havre, France, in 1834. When he landed in New York City, Sutter was eager to explore the continent. He spoke German, Spanish, and English as well as Swiss French, and had a pioneering spirit. Those attributes worked to his advantage in a land hungry for intrepid European settlers.

A daguerreotype of Sutter taken in 1850 when he was forty-seven years old shows a man with a high forehead, a retreating hairline, and a prominent, straight nose. Great salt-and-pepper sideburns, from top of ear to jawline, frame a broad, unblemished face. The mustache over his upper lip is long enough to twist into a slight, waxy curl at each end. Beneath his lower lip is a small, triangular patch of lighter hair that points to a firm chin. But it's the expression in his light-colored eyes and the tilt of his head which grabs a viewer's attention. His countenance suggests a cast of mind that hovers between calculating and haughty, as if the man is perpetually on the hunt for acquisitions—animal, land, stuff, or people—that meet his standards. It's an impatient soul that gazes out through Sutter's eyes, which may explain what drove his four-year journey to reach northern California.

Restless and energetic, Sutter sojourned in St. Louis, Santa Fe, then Westport, site of present-day Kansas City. From Kansas Territory, he joined a party headed to Fort Vancouver on the Columbia River via the Oregon Trail. Anxious to reach California, Sutter didn't care to stay long in the Northwest Territory, but his timing was all wrong. It was October. Trekking overland to the Mexican-governed territory would have placed him in the mountains as winter set in.

Left with no choice, the determined Sutter elected to use the only other viable route to reach his destination—water. He took a ship bound for the Kingdom of Hawaii. From there, he could catch another boat headed to California. Again, timing was not on his side. Sutter missed the outbound ship and instead lingered in the Kingdom for four months. In desperation, he arranged passage for himself, his hired laborers—eight Hawaiian men and two Hawaiian women—and a bulldog. The boat had to first deliver supplies to the czarist Russian colony of New Archangel (present-day Sitka, Alaska) then to the port settlement of Yerba Buena, where the city of San Francisco developed. The Sutter party set foot on the California coast in July of 1839. On the journey from Hawaii to Yerba Bueana, a number of hopeful, white settlers, joined Sutter, attracted by his vision of an agricultural utopia.

Although most of the territory along coastal California was controlled by approximately one thousand Spanish land barons, huge swaths of inland territory were still controlled by indigenous peoples. Sutter used his Catholic credentials and self-aggrandized military service to worm his way into the landholder's affections. He styled himself as an officer of the Swiss Guard who had escaped the French Revolution, a complete

Captain John Sutter in 1850. He appears to still be in good health and fortune; the discovery of gold on his land had not yet turned his life and finances upside down.

charade since he'd only enlisted in the Swiss Army for a short stint as a very young man. Nonetheless, his army tales and pious talk he was sure would earn him brownie points with the Mexican governor of the territory, Juan Bautista Alvarado.

He was right. Alvarado allowed Sutter and his coterie to settle near present-day Sacramento. After a year, and the announcement that he was a proud, new citizen of Mexico, Sutter wheedled and cajoled Alvarado to grant him a choice parcel of land—48,827 acres, at the confluence of the Sacramento and American rivers. The acreage Sutter claimed, calling it New Helvetia—*Helvetia* being the Latin name for Switzerland—was already inhabited by small tribal groups of California Indians, a key reason for Alvarado's blessing. The governor believed Sutter's presence in the Central Valley meant a bulwark against Indian uprisings in that region, as well as protection against incursions by Russian fishermen and trappers who might be interested in moving their operations south. Czarist Russia, after all, was parked on California's northern border. At least, that's what Sutter told him.

The governor's instincts were on point. Sutter started building a walled, cannon-fortified compound, Fort Sutter, as soon as he'd received permission to settle. Within the perimeter of Fort Sutter's walls were a trading post, Sutter's mansion, as well as other buildings that housed a blacksmith shop, furniture shop, and distillery. An agricultural empire was in the making.

In his first year, Sutter purchased, on credit, five hundred cattle, fifty work and riding horses, and twenty-five breeding mares. The livestock represented the backbone of California farming: the breeding and slaughter of free-range cattle. And Sutter had other ideas on how to exploit the mild climate, rich soil, plentiful wild game, and fishing resources for profit. In the glory years of his sprawling barony, which by 1841 included the Russian-American Company's Fort Ross acreage on the Pacific Coast, John Sutter's endeavors were vast and disparate. He manufactured furniture; distilled wild grape brandy; sold otter and beaver hides; killed and rendered beef and wild game for salable meat, hides, and tallow; fished sturgeon and salmon; cultivated wheat; and had grand produce gardens filled with beans, melons, potatoes, cabbages, peas, corn, parsnips, and lettuce.

A Swedish naturalist and investor, Dr. G. M. Sandels—who once sunk money into a failed Mexican gold mine—visited Sutter in 1843. A conversation with his host that Sandels must have thought revealing was recorded by the doctor in his journal. Given Sutter's thirst for money, it seems believable, but it's not altogether clear why the physician found it memorable:

> Sutter asked, "Doctor, can't you find me a gold mine?"
>
> "Captain Sutter," said Sandels, "your best gold mine is here in this rich soil."
>
> "True, my friend. This good land is all the gold mine I could ever wish."

And it did seem as if the land was golden for Sutter's fortunes kept improving. An accounting of his New Helvetia assets in 1847 revealed acreage equal to "200 square miles, and tallied 160 white males, 47 white females, 5 Hawaiians, 1 black man, 50 Indian males, 15 Indian females, and 10 half-blood children. Sutter also listed 20,000 cattle, 2,500 horses, 2,000 sheep, 1,000 hogs, and 70 mules. New Helvetia operated 3 horse-driven mills (for grinding grain or turning lathes), 2 water mills, 1 sawmill, 1 tannery, 60 houses, and the fort itself."

That he counted people who worked for him as assets, no different than the animals he bought and sold, says so much about the man. Yet Sutter knew how to lure people to work for him. And he was not averse to sharing his bounty with travelers, especially Anglo-Americans looking to permanently settle in the territory. His well-placed compound was often a destination for weary pioneers coming from northern, overland routes. In his memoirs, written years later, Sutter offered an assessment of how his actions had infuriated Alvarado and other government officials: "I gave passports to those entering the country . . . and this [they] did not like. I was friendly with the emigrants of whom [they] were jealous. I encouraged immigration, while they discouraged it. I sympathized with the Americans while they hated them."

This statement reveals the shallowness and political calculations that guided Sutter's benevolence, despite the laudatory comments he received from white émigrés who entered his domain. "At Sutter's," historian Robert Cleland wrote, "immigrants, exhausted and half-starved . . . found shelter, food, and clothing, and an opportunity to learn something of the new land and people to which they had come." John Bidwell, who organized a party of settlers to the territory in 1841, spoke of Sutter, who later employed him, as "one of the most liberal and hospitable of men." This rosy picture of a noble master masked a nefarious reality, however, one that included a private militia, allegations of selling children, sexual assault, and a loathsome perspective on the Indians whose land he inhabited.

Hundreds of mostly Nisenan and Miwok were employed as laborers and craftsmen on Sutter's estate. He traded with them, relied on them for protection, and exploited them. Like all California landholders, he needed the Indians. It was the only way to survive. He dwelled in a region where non-Indians were vastly outnumbered by indigenous peoples, and there was no other labor pool. The Indians were the lifeblood of his rancho and the muscle of his private militia. Sutter used fancied tales of his army experience to impress everyone he met, but the stories were especially helpful in his recruitment of Indians to his paramilitary unit. He dressed his private force in gaudy recycled Russian uniforms acquired when he purchased the Fort Ross site. Compounding the odd, flamboyant scene of uniform-clad Indians marching and drilling in an open field was Sutter himself, bedecked in his own military outfit and calling out commands in German. He puffed and strutted in such a lofty, disdainful manner that one of his contemporaries compared him to the infamous Spanish conquistador, Hernán Cortés, "in his palmist days." Comical as they may have appeared, Sutter effectively used his militia to "compel reluctant Indians to labor in his fields and conscript native workers for other ranchers." He wasn't shy about voicing his sentiments. "Indians," he said, "had to be kept 'strictly under fear' for the benefit of white landowners."

From accounts by people familiar with Sutter's operation, it's clear he was tyrannical toward the Indians he employed. Sutter used "kidnapping, food privation, and slavery" to obtain the Indian workforce he needed. He also bribed and coerced Native chiefs to obtain their cooperation in pushing tribal members to work for him. One of Sutter's Swiss employees at the fort, a man named Heinrich Lienhard, reported that the chiefs "received far better pay than the poor wretches who worked as common laborers, and had to slave two weeks for a plain muslin shirt, or the material for a pair of cotton trousers." Sutter used another well-worn method of keeping his Indian workers in virtual bondage. He paid them with a kind of tin coin that could only be redeemed for goods at his store, a tactic that kept his indigenous workforce entirely dependent on his largesse.

Another grim account of Sutter's abysmal practices comes from Theodor Cordua, a Prussian rancher who leased land from Sutter prior to becoming an overlord on his own large estate. "Those [Indians] who did not want to work were considered enemies. With the other tribes the field was taken against the hostile Indian . . . the villages were attacked usually before daybreak when everybody was asleep. Neither old nor young was spared . . . and often the Sacramento River was colored red by the blood of the innocent Indians." It's likely Cordua's comment is an exaggeration, but there's other, well-documented evidence that Sutter severely punished Indians he believed to be deceitful or rebellious. He was known to send his private armed posse into the hills to find, brutally punish, and return runaways. In the tradition of a feudal lord, he even had Indian laborers executed if they were repeatedly defiant.

Lienhard also witnessed the ordinary privations endured by Indians forced to labor at the fort. He described the workers being imprisoned in a locked chamber: "As the room had neither beds nor straw, the inmates were forced to sleep on the bare floor. When I opened the door for them in the morning, the odor that greeted me was overwhelming, for no sanitary arrangements had been provided. What these rooms were like after ten days or two weeks can be imagined, and the fact that nocturnal confinement was not agreeable to the Indians was obvious. Large numbers deserted during the daytime, or remained outside the fort when the gates were locked."

Another graphic description of the conditions imposed on the Indians was recorded in 1846 by a visitor to Fort Sutter, mountain man James Clyman, who stated: "The Capt. [Sutter] keeps 600 to 800 Indians in a complete state of Slavery and as I had the mortification of seeing them dine I may give a short description. 10 or 15 Troughs 3 or 4 feet long were brought out of the cook room and seated in the Broiling sun. All the Labourers grate [*sic*] and small ran to the troughs like so many pigs and fed themselves with their hands as long as the troughs contained even a moisture."

Sutter's callous treatment extended to trafficking kidnapped Indian children, a practice he admitted to a California historian, Hubert H. Bancroft, during an interview in 1876. Bancroft wrote that "from the first, [Sutter] was in the habit of seizing Indian children, who were retained as servants, or slaves, at his own establishment, or sent to his friends in different parts of the country [Alta California]. But he always took care to capture for his purpose only children from distant or hostile tribes."

If Sutter had any qualms about his treatment of the Indians, he never expressed them. Selling Indian women and children was ubiquitous and considered a usual custom in Sutter's time. But he was an exceptionally active participant in this practice, and his dealings were sufficiently problematic that Governor Alvarado was compelled to step in. His explanation for the intervention was straightforward: "Sutter's conduct was so deplorable that if I had not succeeded in persuading [him] to stop the kidnapping operations, it is probable that there would have been a general uprising of Indians within the Northern district under Sutter's jurisdiction as a Mexican official." That Sutter's activity warranted Alvarado's attention is especially terrifying given how the California Indians were routinely treated by Spanish and Mexican land barons. Within a decade, however, events would upend all the activities, heinous or kind, of the self-proclaimed former Royal Swiss Guard, Captain Sutter.

In the fall of 1847, the captain decided another mill was needed in New Helvetia. He dispatched James Marshall, one of his overseers, to look for a suitable location where the American River could easily be diverted to supply power and begin the building process. One account suggests that Marshall was led to the Maidu village of Coloma by a small contingent of Maidu, Nisenan, and other Indians. When he saw Coloma, Marshall decided it was a fine place to site the mill. He ordered his Indian laborers to begin digging the millrace—the channel that brings a swift current of water to the wheel, the mill's power source.

In one version of the Gold Rush story, it's California Indians who first brought gold nuggets to Marshall's attention in January of 1848. They found the valuable chunks while digging the millrace. For generations, Indians had lived in the foothills of the Sierra Nevada Mountains. They had seen gold before, but since it was neither edible nor wearable, it held no value for them. Marshall and the other white laborers on-site had a very different response.

Another account posits that Marshall, "while inspecting the tail race ... spotted telltale yellow flakes beneath the surface of the rippling water."

Regardless of who first spied the gold, Marshall quickly took the material to Sutter. The captain did a quick test and determined that the shimmery metallic flakes were the real deal—gold! Fearing the discovery's repercussions, Sutter swore Marshall to secrecy. While his instincts were correct about keeping quiet, Sutter's bid for privacy was an improbable gesture. Word of the strike leaked out, sending a shock wave through the

California territory. Californios, the large landholders, pulled their Indian workers and families together and headed for the tumbling streams that snaked through the foothill country adjacent to the Sierra Nevada Mountains. By June of 1848, scores of sailors whose ships were anchored in the bay waters off San Francisco had abandoned their vessels and joined the parade of fortune seekers headed to Sutter's Mill. Gold fever also took hold among Sutter's skilled laborers and farmhands. They turned to prospecting, leaving the captain virtually alone to run his sprawling empire.

In the early days of the Gold Rush, California Indians also mined and panned for the precious metal. Acting governor Richard B. Mason, the territory having been ceded to the United States at the end of the Mexican-American War, estimated in 1848 that over half the miners in California were Indians. At least four thousand indigenous people were working in the goldfields by 1850.

Mining and panning for gold was hot, grimy, and physically taxing. Days were long and for most "forty-niners" the rewards were few.

But the good times soon ended. The *Daily Alta California* reported in 1849, "Whites are becoming impressed with the belief that it will be absolutely necessary to exterminate the savages before they can labor much longer in the mines with security." After California was granted statehood in 1850, the state's first elected governor, Peter Hardeman Burnett, made it a priority to eradicate the state's Indians. In his second annual address to the legislature in 1851, he predicted that "a war of extermination will continue to be waged between the races until the Indian race becomes extinct [...] While we cannot anticipate this result but with painful regret, the inevitable destiny of the race is beyond the power or wisdom of man to avert."

With wave after wave of Anglo-Americans flooding into California after 1848, the Native population experienced a whirlwind of terrors. The list of atrocities is long and depressing, with drearily predictable results. Burned out of their homes, murdered, starved, raped, and forcibly bound into servitude, by the end of the nineteenth century, the Indian population of California had been reduced by 80 percent from pre–Gold Rush days. The treasure was toxic to the very people who had coexisted with it for centuries.

As for Sutter, his non-Indian workers left him for the goldfields, while his Indian laborers fled to the mountains—if they were lucky—once it was evident they were no longer safe anywhere that forty-niners roamed. Newspapers of the time regularly reported on Indians being shot and killed by rowdy Anglos intent on raping their women, or simply for bragging rights. It was only a matter of time before Sutter was left without any workers at all. His past generosity to American émigrés was forgotten, and he was overwhelmed by hordes of squatters that swept in on the Rush.

Ironically, after years of separation, Sutter's family arrived in California only to watch him vainly struggle to hold on to his ranching operations. He went bankrupt over land title litigation by 1852, and was finally forced to sell New Helvetia to cover his debts. In 1858, he was sued by a loosely connected squatters' group, the Settlers' Association, over the last of his Mexican-granted land. Sutter lost the court fight. In desperation, he moved to a property called Hock Farm with his wife and sons. This, his last toehold in northern California, went up in smoke when an arsonist torched the property in 1865.

Luckily for Sutter, he managed to squeeze out a pension of $250 per month from the California legislature that lasted from 1862 to 1878, but he never got past the financial disaster visited on him by the gold strike at Sutter's Mill. Though he petitioned the US Congress on a regular basis for a financial settlement, his request was never acted on. An appeal, filed with the US Supreme Court, went nowhere. John Augustus Sutter died penniless, in a Washington, DC, hotel room, in 1880, while visiting the capital to make another plea for financial relief.

There are many people who regard Sutter as an unfortunate but important figure in the history of the West. And just as many people have dismissed Sutter's lethal treatment of the Indians as not unusual for the time. But here's the point: In an official capacity placed upon him by the state, Sutter was responsible for maintaining "'the native Indians of the different tribes . . . in the enjoyment and liberty of their posses-sions, without molesting them . . . [or] making war upon them in any way without previously obtaining authority [from] the government.'" By every measure, the man failed in his duty.

During the first years of the Gold Rush, approximately one hundred thousand Native Americans died from disease, starvation, and murder. By 1873, a mere thirty thousand indigenous people were left in the state. "It's called a genocide. That's what it was. A genocide. [There's] no other way to describe it, and that's the way it needs to be described in the history books," said California governor Gavin Newsom on February 18, 2019. His remarks were delivered at a blessing ceremony for a Native American heritage center. In a rare win for the Indians, California presently has the largest Native American population in the country, with 109 federally recognized tribes calling it home.

Interred in Lancaster County, Pennsylvania, Sutter is far from the land that made him wealthy—and then left him a pauper.

Panning for gold remains legal in most of California's rivers and streams.

Schillinger v. United States

Cast in Concrete

East of London, England, across the King's Ferry Bridge that spans The Swale, sits the Isle of Sheppey. The burg of Sheerness sits on the island's northern coast, where the Thames River meets the sea, and at the edge of the village sits the Ship on Shore pub. Next to the tavern is an odd, fortress-like structure called the Grotto. Closer scrutiny reveals the eccentric building as a folly constructed from mismatched shore stones, mortar, and curiously rounded cement blocks. In 1848, a small ship called Lucky Escape *ran out of luck and foundered in stormy seas close to Sheerness. The boat carried a cargo of barrels loaded with Portsmouth cement, a concoction first patented by a British masonry man, Joseph Aspdin. Coastal guards patrolling the beach waded into the choppy waters and recovered the vessel's load, including the barrels. A resourceful lot, the men allowed the contents of the wooden containers to harden, removed the barrel stays, and used the cement blocks to build themselves a formidable shelter, useful against the elements. The American, John J. Schillinger, never raised a pint in the Sheerness pub, but he was keenly aware of Portsmouth cement, the most commonly used ingredient in concrete—the material that made Schillinger a legal landmark.*

CONCRETE. IT SEEMS SO BORING, SO ORDINARY, SO *DRAB*. DESPITE ITS long history—seriously, this stuff built the Roman Empire—nations haven't gone to war over it and governments haven't toppled for lack of it. In the modern world, the hard material is *so* everywhere—sidewalks and skyscrapers, bridges and highways, houses, cathedrals, dams and swimming pools—that it's second only to water as the most widely used substance on Earth. In addition to all its structural versatility, at the end of the nineteenth century it was concrete that supported a doctrine near and dear to every Federalist's heart—sovereign immunity. Concrete's rise as a legal star began with a patent application filed in 1870, then revised and reissued in 1875, by John Schillinger. He made the application based on an innovative process he developed for pouring sidewalks:

I form the concrete by mixing cement with sand and gravel, or other suitable material, to form a plastic compound. . . . While the mass is plastic, I lay or spread the same on the foundation or bed of the pavement, either in moulds or between movable joists . . . to form the edges of the concrete blocks.

What's innovative isn't the concrete, it's that each cement block was separated from neighboring blocks. The method was simple, low-cost, and effective. Schillinger put tar paper or an equally non-porous material against the edge of a poured block to create a watertight barrier—a joint. Before the next cement block was poured, the edge of the plastic mold that formed the block was put tight against the tar paper. This technique was repeated for each section until the desired walkway length was reached. The result was a pavement where the heaving or cracking of one cement block didn't affect adjacent sections. It also allowed removal and replacement of damaged or heaved blocks without tearing up an entire sidewalk. Okay, it's not the internet but it *was* revolutionary in the masonry world.

Schillinger explained the breakthrough this way in his application:

What I claim as new, and desire to secure by letters patent, is: 1) A concrete pavement laid in detached blocks or sections, substantially in the manner . . . described; 2) the arrangement of tar-paper, or its equivalent, between adjoining blocks of concrete, substantially as and for the purpose set forth.

Within two years of being granted a patent, Schillinger went to court to defend his innovation. The 1877 case illustrates the breaches poor Schillinger continuously confronted. Here's what happened. Judge Shipman of the Circuit Court for the Southern District of New York issued an order that stopped another concrete manufacturer named Gunther, who

34

was not licensed by Schillinger to use his patented process, from laying pavement that used separate blocks of concrete—made by creating edges in the material as it was forming—and then placing tinfoil, not tar paper, between the joints of his blocks. Gunther's method produced the same result as Schillinger's using essentially the same method. Judge Shipman ruled tinfoil block making was *clearly a patent infringement.* With that ruling, the case was then referred to a court-appointed "master" who had to compile a report for the judge on how many tinfoil blocks of concrete Gunther had laid so an appropriate cash settlement could be ordered. While this report was being prepared, Schillinger filed *another* complaint with Judge Shipman against Gunther, this time alleging that the wily contractor had used a trowel to cut the concrete into blocks, again creating a joint that allowed the block to be easily removed without disturbing its neighbors.

Rather than go through another hearing to decide if the trowel was or wasn't an infringement, Shipman allowed the trowel complaint to be "attached" to the tinfoil investigation. But wait, there's more. When the master's report was completed, Gunther, the trowel-tinfoil-concrete violator, appealed the damages he was ordered to pay. The case went to Judge Samuel Blatchford of the US Second Judicial Circuit (US Court of Appeals for the Second Circuit) in October of 1878. The *only* issue Judge Blatchford decided on this go-round was whether the method of estimating the damages was fair. He ruled in favor of the method. He didn't rule on whether Judge Shipman was right or wrong in his decision to allow trowel block making to be lumped in with the tinfoil block making.

In August of 1879, the lucky Judge Blatchford had Schillinger and Gunther once more on his docket. This time, the judge wasn't having it. He was adamant that Judge Shipman had settled the trowel-made, foil-made dispute, period. Both methods were an infringement of Schillinger's patent. Round one of the sidewalk fights went to Schillinger and Judge Shipman. But that was just the beginning of the sidewalk's lengthy litigation story.

Simply put, if a concrete manufacturer wasn't licensed by Schillinger, but nonetheless used the concrete block process for constructing a sidewalk, that manufacturer or contractor could be sued for patent infringement. Concrete walks, however, were—and are—omnipresent across the nation. With so many walkways, what were the odds that any particular builder, mason, or manufacturer would be outed and prosecuted? A Supreme Court decision answered that question in 1889. In the case of *Hurlbut v. Schillinger*, a paragraph in the opinion starts with, "The Schillinger patent has been before *several* of the circuit courts of the United States, and also before this Court, for adjudication." The list that followed was impressive. Cases involving the Schillinger patent had been tried before six circuit courts in the following districts: the Southern and Northern Districts of New York, the Southern District of Ohio, the Districts of Oregon and California, and the Supreme Court of the District of Columbia. Most of the circuit court cases ended up being appealed at least to the next level. And before the *Hurlbut* case, two other Schillinger cases, *California Artificial Stone-Paving Co. v. Molitar* and *California Paving Co. v. Schalicke*, had been appealed all the way to the Supreme Court. Finally, there is *the* Supreme Court case, *Schillinger v. United States*, which guaranteed that John J. Schillinger's legal legacy would be as solid as the concrete he used.

The Schillinger patent's first Supreme Court appearance, *California Artificial Stone-Paving Co. v. Molitar*, occurred in 1885. Skipping to the end, in this situation the Supreme Court dismissed the case because the questions it was being asked to resolve were confusing, and there wasn't enough information for a decision on anything. Also, how the case arrived at the Supreme Court was based on an appeal procedure—a certificate of division of opinion—that faded out in 1911. And just to be clear, there is no guarantee that the following summary would be allowed in a court of law, or on a bar exam. Here's how the case unfolded.

The California Artificial Stone-Paving Company was the only entity licensed in the state of California to use the patented Schillinger method. In 1881, California Paving brought a lawsuit that charged Charles A. Molitar had used the patented Schillinger process to produce concrete blocks. California Paving believed Molitar should be stopped. The company also wanted Molitar to reimburse California Paving for any payment he'd received as a direct result of purchase or use of those unauthorized concrete blocks. It went to trial. The lawsuit ended with a guilty verdict for Molitar. He was ordered to stop making concrete blocks using the Schillinger process and pay damages based on what he'd already earned from the illegal blocks he'd produced. But wait, there's more.

California Paving went back to the trial judge in 1883 with a charge that Molitar had violated the court order from 1881. The rumpus was over pavement constructed by Molitar in Redwood City, California. Molitar denied the charge, saying the concrete blocks he used for that pavement were made by a different method than Schillinger's patented one. The trial judge agreed with Molitar. Strike one. California Paving appealed. The appellate hearing ended with the two judges unable to agree on several issues, so the trial judge's decision could stand while the case was kicked to the Supreme Court based on the legal procedure known as a certificate of division of opinion. Strike two against California Paving.

After looking over the legal tangle, the Supreme Court dismissed the case because it wasn't clear from the record what the points of disagreement were between the appellate judges. Also, the questions handed to the court to resolve were too broad and the information too scanty. The Supreme Court's written decision stated the certificate of division process can be used "only when 'a question' has occurred on which the judges have differed, and where 'the point' of disagreement may be distinctly stated. It cannot be resorted to for the purpose of presenting questions of fact, or mixed questions of fact and law, or a difference of opinion on the general case."

There was more: "[W]e do not know," wrote the justices, "what was the precise interpretation of the patent in 1881. Without that information, there was no way to conclude if the new pavement, constructed in Redwood City, is an infringement or not." Finally, "If the judges disagree," the justices opined, "there can be no judgment of contempt; and the defendant must be discharged." The written statement ended with a bit of advice for California Paving and the lower courts: *Be careful*. In other words, Molitar couldn't be held in contempt of a court order because the two appellate court judges disagreed, which meant the trial judge's decision in favor of Molitar was upheld. Don't be alarmed if you're confused. Basically, the Supreme Court's decision was this: California Paving should bring a new lawsuit against Charles A. Molitar rather than continue arguing in court about contempt charges. *Strike three. California Artificial Stone-Paving Co. v. Molitar* was done. Phew.

But, California Paving lived to fight another day. They didn't have to wait long. The company's new legal skirmish started in 1886.This time the case was *California Artificial Stone-Paving Company v. Schalicke.* It was the same story. California Paving alleged that Schalicke had committed a patent violation. The courts at the circuit level found in Schalicke's favor. California Paving appealed to the Supreme Court for a review of the determination. In this situation, the justices referred to the 1875 language of the patent, and cited other lawsuits about Schillinger's patent. The justices' written decision focused on Schillinger's explanation in his patent application: "What I claim as new, and desire to secure by letters patent, is: 1) A concrete pavement laid in detached blocks or sections, substantially in the manner shown and described. 2) The arrangement of tar paper or its equivalent between adjoining blocks of concrete substantially as and for the purpose set forth." The decision of the court continued: "The evidence in the present case [Schalicke] shows that the defendant, during the process of making his pavement, marked off its surface into squares." The next statement is the *key* issue: "But the question is whether he [Schalicke] to any extent divided it into blocks, so that the line of cracking was controlled . . . and so that a block could be taken out and a new one put in its place without disturbing or injuring an adjoining block."

This complete separation of one block from another was *crucial* to any questions of patent infringement. The decision highlighted Schillinger's 1875 statement—that his patent *did not* cover a slab of concrete made without inserting anything, either temporary or permanent, between the joints. The line that Schalicke trowled on is cement slabs, "was only for ornamentation, and produced no free joints between blocks." In other words, the pavement did not include "detached blocks or sections." The Supreme Court's decision affirmed the circuit court's decision. Schalicke was *not guilty* of patent infringement. California Paving had a no good, very bad run with Supreme Court appeals. It was not the end, however, for Schillinger. Next on the Supreme Court's docket was *Hurlbut v. Schillinger,* 1889.

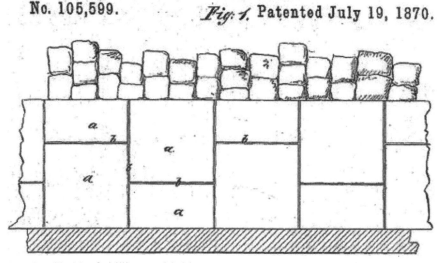

J. J. SCHILLINGER.
CONCRETE PAVEMENT.

No. 105,599.

Fig. 1. Patented July 19, 1870.

Drawing filed by Schillinger with his patent application to illustrating the innovative concrete walkway "system" he wanted protected. This schematic became well-known in many courtrooms across the country.

In this case, Schillinger and a man named Salisbury—who held the exclusive license in Illinois to use the Schillinger method—filed a patent infringement suit against Hurlbut. Salisbury died before the lawsuit was decided, but in 1884, his widow, Olive Salisbury, pursued the litigation on behalf of her husband's estate. On May 15, 1884, the court entered an order that Hurlbut stop the manufacture of his concrete blocks. The court said Salisbury held an exclusive right on a valid patent and Hurlbut had committed patent violations. An independent auditor was appointed by the court to prepare a report of the profits and damages directly related to use of the Schillinger method that Hurlbut had on his books in the period between August 26, 1882, and May 20, 1884.

Sound familiar? Based on the auditor's report, the court ordered Hurlbut to pay Salisbury's widow $2,836.36. Hurlbut appealed the decision to the Supreme Court. To read the written decision in this case is a snoozer because most of what's included repeated the Schalicke decision, *except* this one has a different outcome.

Hurlbut, the justices concluded, used a process that violated Schillinger's patent. In fact, the decision said that Hurlbut's decoration-only defense didn't hold water. He claimed he only used a trowel to "give to the pavement the appearance of flagging," but the justices disagreed. The Court's decision stated: "the evidence is entirely clear that the cut was made sufficiently deep . . . to make such a separation . . . into blocks as would compel any . . . crack to follow the line of the cut . . . thus the object of Schillinger's invention was attained."

Another line of defense Hurlbut used was that Schillinger's method wasn't *inventive or novel*, so the patent was bogus. Mr. Hurlbut's attorney cited other cases that involved different patents and walkways to prove that Schillinger's method wasn't original. The Court concluded this argument was, to put it bluntly, *baloney*. The cases cited were not relevant to the situation.

Finally, the justices thought the lower court's figure on what Hurlbut owed Schillinger and Salisbury was appropriate. Bing. Bang. Boom. Case closed. Schillinger prevailed. One line, however, near the beginning of the five thousand–word decision makes clear where the verdict will land: "The invention of Schillinger was a very valuable one." With those words, Hurlbut's concrete goose was cooked.

Here's a bit of backstory about how these three patent cases—Molitar, Schalicke, and Hurlbut—which don't seem to pose a constitutional question, got to the Supreme Court. The short answer is that the American court system was organized differently in the late nineteenth century. Like every other branch of government, the judicial branch has changed and rearranged over the past two centuries. Some courts have completely disappeared while other courts have been added. Which court hears what type of case has also changed, and the kind of legal questions entertained by the US Supreme Court have also transformed through time. Today, those patent infringement cases would not appear on the Court's docket.

But there was a Schillinger case, the last of its kind, that came to the nation's highest court, which touched on a fundamental principle, a doctrine, that guides how the US Constitution delineates powers between the legislative and judicial branches. *Schillinger v. United States* was litigation with important consequences. The appeal was argued in front of the justices on October 9 and 10, 1894, and the Court's decision was issued on November 19. The case came from the US Court of Claims, which was abolished in 1982 and reconstituted as the US Court of Federal Claims.

Established in 1855, the Court of Claims had three judges who held lifetime appointments. Their job was to review cases that involved money claims against the federal government. Before this court came into existence, any financial claims against the federal government from a private person or entity had to be made through an application to Congress. You can imagine how well *that* worked. From it's inception, the Court of Claims only settled cases that involved money owed based on a federal law, a federal regulation, or a federal contract, a crucial stipulation.

The issue the Supreme Court pondered in *Schillinger v. United States* was the concept of *sovereign immunity*; that is, the United States cannot be sued *without its consent*. This chapter of the Schillinger saga involved the Architect of the Capitol (AOC), an office that was founded in 1793 when the cornerstone of the Capitol building was laid. The AOC is responsible for the development and care of buildings, monuments, gardens, and art on what is known as the Capitol Hill campus. In 1875, the AOC commissioned Frederick Law Olmsted, the great nineteenth-century landscape and urban-park guru, to draw up plans and specifications for a bid proposal to construct a pavement on the Capitol grounds. In the bid specifications, Olmsted wrote, "The pavement to be laid with free joints, in the best manner, the courses running diagonally, and arranged around the curved parts to the satisfaction of the said Fred Law Olmsted." G. W. Cook won the bid and the AOC signed a contract with him for the project. Nowhere in the proposal or contract was there any mention of Schillinger or his patent.

There was a statement in the contract that read, "in the event of any legal proceedings being taken by other parties against the contractor of the United States for the infringement of any patent or claimed patent during the execution of the work, the contractor shall hold the United States harmless." That sentence might hint at the Schillinger patent, but it's a stretch. Anyway, Cook won the contract with a bid of 28.5 cents per square foot. Other bidders who were exclusively licensed to use the

Schillinger method bid at forty-five cents per square foot. The work was completed by Cook, and he got paid for it between 1875 and 1881.

The Schillinger contractors who lost out were furious. They brought a case to the Court of Claims alleging that the United States owed them damages for "wrongful use" of the Schillinger method by Cook. The Court of Claims told the petitioners there was no contract "expressed or implied on the part of the government for the use of such patent, and on that ground dismissed the petition as outside of the jurisdiction of the court." The disappointed contractors took their beef to the Supreme Court.

After review, the majority opinion was written by Justice Samuel Blatchford who had moved up from his prior position on the US Court of Appeals for the Second Circuit. Blatchford—who by this time could probably recite the Schillinger patent by heart—concluded that the Court of Claims *only* had jurisdiction to decide matters that fell within the limits set by Congress. First, a claim must be based on "the Constitution of the United States or any law of Congress except for pensions, or upon any regulation of an executive department, or upon any contract, expressed or implied, with the government of the United States, or for damages, liquidated or unliquidated, in cases not sounding in tort." Stop here. That little legal phrase, "not sounding in tort," is hugely important. A tort is a civil suit against a person or organization because he, she, or it *directly caused harm* to the party bringing the lawsuit. (This is a *rough* definition. Consult a lawyer if you think you have a case sounding in tort. Back to *Schillinger*.)

The heart of the Supreme Court ruling is spelled out in the statement, "That this action [Schillinger's claim] is one sounding in tort is clear." In other words, the Schillinger contractors, the plaintiffs, should have brought a civil lawsuit against Mr. Cook. Their demand for money did not belong in front of the Court of Claims. Why? Justice Blanchford spelled out the reason this way: the plaintiffs charged the government with "wrongful appropriation." This meant the federal government made a "promise, either express or implied," that a patented process, with the patent-holder's consent, was to be used in the sidewalk project. Then, the government didn't *pay for the right to use the patent*. Yes, the finer points of the law can make your eyes cross and break the brain. And there's more.

In this situation, Congress *didn't direct or imply* that the Schillinger patent was to be used. "No officer of the government directed its use, and the contract which was executed by Cook did not name or describe it. There was no recognition by the government or any of its officers of the fact that in the construction of the pavement there was any use of the patent, or that any appropriation was being made of claimants' property." In other words, the government assumed everything was hunky-dory with how the pavement was being constructed. It's the good old "hear no evil, see no evil, speak no evil" defense strategy.

Supreme Court Associate Justice David Josiah Brewer, who served on the august court from 1890 until his death in 1910, wrote the majority decision in the landmark case, *Schillinger v. United States*.

From start to finish, there was no agreement between the Schillinger folks and *the government* about using the Schillinger method for making concrete blocks. And here's the wrap-up: "[T]here was no suggestion of a waiver of the tort, or a pretense of any implied contract, until *after* the decision of the Court of Claims that it had no jurisdiction over an action to recover for the tort." Translation: The Court of Claims was correct. Schillinger had no case against the government.

You would think there's nothing more to say on why the Court of Claims made the right call, but Justice Blatchford lobbed another reason into the mix. Even *if* Cook had violated patent law, the United States government had not snatched the patent for its own use. Schillinger and company needed to take up their beef directly with Cook, not the government.

To be fair, two justices did disagree, and a dissenting opinion was written that stated the AOC knew full well Cook would use Schillinger's patented method to build a pavement "with free joints." However, in 1875 when the proposal went to bid, the patent hadn't yet been tested in a court case, so the AOC went ahead with Cook, even though Schillinger protested the bid award at the time it was made.

The Court of Claims (and successor courts) have been called "the people's court," and praised as an example of a "fundamental principle of the United States Constitution that individuals have rights against the government." *Schillinger v. United States* showed that those rights can also be limited by that same government. And so it was that the *sovereign immunity principle* was upheld by the Supreme Court—and anchored in concrete.

Edison, Tesla, and Westinghouse

The War of the Currents

Tillie Ziegler had seen it before. Bill was passed out and snoring like a hog. He'd gone on a helluva binge the night before. Came home smelling of rotting food, sweat, dirt, and alcohol. Likely the man had drunk up all the pennies he earned selling bruised, decaying vegetables from his pushcart. Hardly made enough as it was to keep a roof over their heads. Well, she'd give him a piece of her mind when he finally woke from his stupor.

And that's just what Matilda Ziegler did when her common-law husband, William Kemmler, crawled out of bed. It was a Thursday, March 29, 1888, still chilly days in Buffalo, New York. Whatever Tillie said or did, she provoked Kemmler into a rage. He accused her of stealing his money so she could run off with one of his drinking buddies. When the screaming match between the couple reached a crescendo, Kemmler left the house and headed to his barn. When he returned to the argument, he carried a hatchet. This time, he would win the argument with Tillie for good. After repeatedly striking her with his weapon, Matilda Ziegler lay in a bloody heap. She was very dead. William Kemmler went to a nearby house, where he announced to his neighbor that he had just killed his girlfriend. A swift trial ended with Kemmler convicted of first-degree murder. He was sentenced to death—and earned a place in American history.

H. M. Stevens told his story to a *New York World* reporter in the spring of 1899. It was a warning.

When the accident happened, Mr. Stevens was the superintendent of the Middlesex Lighting Company in Lowell, Massachusetts. During a routine inspection of the company's power plant in the summer of 1895,

Superintendent Stevens slipped on a greasy spot near a "thirty-five-light dynamo," an electricity power generator. Plunging forward, Stevens fully expected to smack his face on the floor. To save himself, he impulsively reached out and grabbed the nearest stable object to regain his balance. He "unwittingly grabbed with either hand the positive and negative brushes of the machine. Having completed a circuit, 1,500 volts of electric current coursed through his body. Shocked unconscious, Stevens slumped over the machine, hands still grasping the brushes, and remained a human wire for some seconds before his unmoving weight and gravity mercifully dropped him to the floor." He looked rigid. Dead. A coworker suggested moving his stiff body outside and placing him on damp ground.

Slowly, Stevens regained consciousness, gasping for breath and unable to speak. It took four hours of whiskey and deep massage before he was moved back to his room at the St. Charles Hotel.

Newspapers across the country carried Stevens's tale. It was important because New York State was about to carry out the nation's first criminal execution—in the electric chair. William Kemmler, the condemned man, was appealing the method of his death as a violation of the US Constitution—cruel and unusual punishment. Asked about the wisdom of death by electric shock, Stevens said, "Do I believe in killing a man by electricity? . . . No, I do not. I don't believe the profession knows enough about electricity yet to warrant them attempting to kill a man with it. All electricians know that different men are differently affected by electricity. . . . I think it's a risky thing to try to execute this Kemmler by electricity. The science is not far enough removed from the experimental stage as yet."

Events would eventually prove Stevens right. In the meantime, the odious Mr. Kemmler was needed to prove a point that had nothing to do with the US Constitution and everything to do with egos and big business. Kemmler's destiny as a human test subject had been set in motion nearly a decade earlier, on November 4, 1879, when Thomas Edison filed his patent for an incandescent lightbulb.

Edison's humble creation, "an electric lamp using 'a carbon filament or strip coiled and connected . . . to platina contact wires,'" was the first step in a contest that blossomed into a war over what type of current, direct or alternating, would be generated to light the buildings and streets of America. The competition got seriously under way in 1886, when George Westinghouse installed his first commercial electrical system in Buffalo, New York. In 1881, the rivalry had taken a turn toward vicious and bloody. Writers, historians, and filmmakers call it "the war of the currents," but "war of the hot dogs" is closer to the mark.

Thomas Edison, Nikola Tesla, and George Westinghouse are the most widely known names linked to America's electrification battle. But there were other men in the fight, some sinister, and a few, honorable. As to the victims of this war, except for William Kemmler, their names are unrecorded. They were mostly dogs, a few calves, and a horse. Topsy—a circus elephant that fought back when abused and suffered an electrical death for her sins—was *not* part of this conflict. She's often named as a sacrifice, murdered by Edison to prove a point. *Total urban legend.* Topsy was a martyr to human ignorance, not to Edison's ego. When the poor elephant was put to death in 1903, the battle over alternating or direct current had been settled for a decade.

Understanding the potential of electricity to change the world was the bond shared by Tesla, Westinghouse, and Edison. Where they disagreed was in the details—the place where the devil always dwells. More than accolades were at stake; there was big money on the table.

Edison and Westinghouse were capable businessmen as well as inventors. For them, a discovery was only counted a success if it could be turned into a marketable, unique product or process that could be defended if a patent dispute erupted with a competitor. And patent disputes *always* erupted between competitors. Nikola Tesla, the other principal in the electricity drama, was like a zebra running with horses—he was an inventor of a different stripe. As one writer said, "He was an artist. . . . His medium is not pigment, his medium is not clay. His medium is electricity." Edison labeled him "a poet of science" though he didn't mean it as a compliment.

Tesla's American odyssey began on June 6, 1884, when the twenty-eight-year-old Serbian immigrant arrived in New York City. In his pants pockets, he carried only pennies and poems. He found Manhattan exceedingly ugly. "What I saw," Tesla wrote, "was rough and unattractive. Is this America, I asked myself in painful surprise?" A cultured, educated man who spoke several languages, Tesla stood out in a crowd. At six-foot-two and a modest 140 pounds, he was beyond slim. The young man cut a dapper figure, always neatly dressed, "fastidious and courtly." He was good-looking with fine features—a narrow, aquiline nose, high cheekbones, straight brows, and a full mouth topped by a trim mustache. In describing Tesla, his contemporaries often called him "elegant" with "amazing blue eyes that people noticed."

Despite his poverty, Tesla was sure his fortunes would change in the United States. His confidence came from a precious item—a letter of recommendation addressed to the man he most admired, Thomas Alva Edison. He also carried plans and a prototype of an invention he was sure Edison would embrace: a motor that could efficiently run using AC—alternating current. It promised to solve one of the most formidable drawbacks to the DC—direct-current—delivery system that Edison's Electric Light Company employed.

Tesla's route to Edison's office took him over the very streets beneath which the world's first electric grid was buried—eighty thousand feet of copper conductors that fed electricity to a fifty-one-square-block area in Lower Manhattan. It was a daunting accomplishment, one Edison

Always impeccably groomed, Nikola Tesla was handsome, charming, and brilliant. He had no difficulty attracting equally handsome, charming, and brilliant women, but none of his romances ever ended in marriage.

needed to resurrect his reputation, which had been fading, as America's premier inventor.

Edison's public unveiling of a useful incandescent lightbulb was held on New Year's Eve, 1879. Unfortunately, the demonstration fell a bit flat since he had made too many audacious promises about electric lighting up to that point. Almost two years earlier, he boldly pronounced that once he perfected his bulb, every room in every home in all of America would be bathed in an electric glow. It wasn't surprising, then, that his New Year's demo got snarky reviews in the press. The *Saturday Review* went with this comment from a British electrical expert: "What a happy man Mr. Edison must be! Three times within the short space of eighteen months he has had the glory of finally and triumphantly solving a problem of world-wide interest. It is true that each time the problem has been the same, and that it comes up again after each solution, fresh, smiling, and unsolved, ready to receive its next death-blow." Ouch.

A gaggle of engineers still thought "an electric light to be a mathematical impossibility, something like a perpetual motion machine." One member of that posse labeled Edison "'a fraud, a willful deceiver of the public' who was interested only in booming his stock price." Oops. *Puck*, a humor magazine, offered this charming defense of the inventor: "'Edison is not a humbug. He is a man of a type common enough in this country—a smart, persevering, sanguine, ignorant, show-off American. He can do a great deal and he thinks he can do everything.'" Yikes.

Mr. Edison was sorely rankled by the smug remarks. To overcome his critics, he announced early in 1880, his intention to build a commercial lighting station in Manhattan. It would be the first in the country to generate electric power for interior lighting. It was a savvy, and risky, move. If he was successful, Edison knew the New York press would trumpet his achievement. If the venture failed, he'd be pilloried. And likely, bankrupt.

It took eighteen months before financing, permits, and a host of technical problems were put in order. Edison was forced to fund the manufacturing of parts needed for the project with his own money. At last, in the spring of 1881, Edison's crews started the tedious work of burying the wires that would carry electric current generated from a single, coal-fired power station located on Manhattan's Pearl Street. This buried-wire design added more time and cost to the project. Cobblestones had to be pried up, trenches dug, wired cables laid, cobblestones replaced—all work that was halted when winter arrived.

Edison remained undeterred. His scheme to build out an underground system was driven by two concerns: First, he wanted to preserve the integrity of the wiring—a massive headache when wires, tethered to unreliable poles, crisscrossed over streets exposed to wind, weather, and hundreds of other wires. Second, he had hyped the public-safety angle of a buried grid. A few high-profile fatal accidents involving high-voltage equipment had made newspaper headlines. Warnings of the dangers electric lighting posed had gotten attention in the press. Edison's company, Edison Electric, pointed with pride to their underground layout, which prevented direct-current wires from becoming tangled in the mass of high-voltage cables that fed the city's streetlamps. Buried wires would ensure that no high-voltage power would be accidentally transmitted into homes and offices.

Edison's eventual confrontation with George Westinghouse relied on the argument that high-voltage current was deadly. But on September 4, 1882, the day Edison Electric Light's Pearl Street power station came online, the battle with Westinghouse was still years away.

In the middle of that September afternoon, Thomas Edison, decked out in a frock coat and white derby, stood in the offices of his Wall Street bankers, Drexel, Morgan & Company, surrounded by reporters and board members of Edison Electric. This was the test, the capstone event of the incandescent light project he had started four years earlier. At exactly 3:00 p.m., the senior electrician closed the switch at the Pearl Street station sending an electric current into the street where it buzzed through fourteen miles of underground wiring that served fifty-nine customers, who controlled 1,284 lamps. In the banking office of J. P. Morgan, Thomas Edison kept his eye on the time, and at 3:00 p.m., he walked over to the wall where a switch, controlling a large, electric chandelier, was installed. With a flourish, he flipped the switch. And there was light.

At first, it was an underwhelming display. There were pockets of dimly glowing light, visible though not glittering. But as the afternoon melted into evening, the glass globes that held Edison's incandescent dream clearly signaled America's future. They shone brightly in the gathering gloom, small points of brightness like glowing fireflies flitting across a dark and silent meadow. Edison glowed as well. He had reclaimed his celebrity status as an innovator.

The day Nikola Tesla stepped off the boat and made his way to Edison's New York City office, the Pearl Street power station had been lighting buildings on the lower end of lower Manhattan for nearly two years. Edison's lighting system worked, but it had a serious drawback—direct current.

Karl Berggren, professor of electrical engineering at MIT, explains electrical current as simply the flow or stream of charged electrons. In a direct-current system, the electrons move from a generator over a wire to their destination—a light fixture or motor—and then return to the generator in a continuous loop. But as the electrons travel along the wire, energy is lost, rather like a runner who slows the longer he runs. For Edison's design to be an effective system, a generating station couldn't be much beyond a mile from whatever fixture or machine it was supposed to power.

Tesla had the answer to this limitation—alternating current. Berggren explains this type of current as "an oscillating repetition—the current flowing in a positive direction and . . . the alternate cycle where the current moves in a negative direction. This back-and-forth is what gives AC its name." In other words, there's a wavelike motion, similar to the ocean tide's ebb and flow, which creates a surging effect and allows current to travel much longer distances and still reach the destination with enough energy from the churning electrons to power the intended destination. But there was a problem with AC in the earliest days of electric lighting. No one had yet designed a motor that could efficiently use that type of current. Tesla had solved the motor problem, at least on paper, in 1882.

On his first meeting with Edison, he sincerely believed the world-famous inventor would embrace his solution and move to AC technology. Tesla desperately wanted Edison as a mentor and business partner. Ushered into the great inventor's presence, he handed him the letter of recommendation from his former employer. Tesla had worked as an engineer in the Edison company's Paris branch, which produced lamps and other components for the Edison electric light system. "Meeting Edison," the young immigrant said, "thrilled me to the marrow." Tesla was hired on the spot, but it was a mismatch from the start.

Even in his late thirties, Edison looked like a smooth-cheeked, rumpled schoolboy. A reporter, one of the dozens that interviewed him at his Menlo Park lab, described his appearance: "Pants baggy and unpressed, vest flying open, coat stained with grease, hands discolored by acid." He survived on pie, coffee, chewing tobacco, cigars, and catnaps. Partial deafness caused him to look dour in most photos. He scowled in concentration when listening to something or someone. But when he talked about his inventions, his expression relaxed and he transformed into a gleeful storyteller.

When Edison first revealed his rudimentary incandescent bulb in 1878, journalist William Croffut dubbed him the Wizard of Menlo Park, a nickname that stuck for the rest of his life—and beyond. He was folksy, plainspoken, and ambitious, driven to leave his mark on the world. Thomas Alva Edison, a self-taught, self-made, wildly successful workaholic, mirrored the American spirit—at least to his admirers. Because of his Horatio Alger rags-to-riches story, and prodigious output of new ideas, Americans began to see themselves as a nation of inventors. Edison's years of pursuing incandescent light ended in triumph. He had bent an irascible force of nature to his will and then safely delivered it to people's homes. To the public, Edison and electricity were synonymous. He believed it, too.

But if Edison was coffee and apple pie, Tesla was champagne and caviar. Eloquent and university-educated, Tesla spoke eight languages and held his own in discussions on literature, philosophy, and the arts. He possessed what has been referred to as an imagistic cognition or imagistic knowledge, which means he recalled everything he read with exquisite clarity, by "seeing" a mental image of the words or illustrations *on the page*. His scientific revelations were also image driven. In his mind, he "saw" vivid pictures of the solutions to particular technical, engineering and design dilemmas. His inventions first appeared in his consciousness as richly detailed visions. He was fond of posh accommodations, quality clothing, beautiful women, and fine food. Like Edison, he slept little, and nothing was more important to him than his work. But his brilliance and refinement was tinged with oddness. Obsessiveness was his constant companion. In his autobiography, written when he was sixty-three, he said: "I had a violent aversion against the earrings of women. . . . The sight of a pearl would almost give me a fit. . . . I would not touch the hair of other people except, perhaps, at the point of a revolver. I would get a fever by looking at a peach and if a piece of camphor was anywhere in the house it caused me the keenest discomfort. . . . I counted the steps in my walks and calculated the cubical contents of soup plates, coffee cups and pieces of food—otherwise my meal was unenjoyable. All repeated acts or operations I performed had to be divisible by three and if I missed I felt impelled to do it all over again, even if it took hours." Tesla's phobias sometimes hampered him and certainly hampered any prospects of long-term romance.

For Edison, energy research was all about application, product development, and commercialization. He attacked problems, looking for solutions using a trial-and-error method. Tesla, an educated engineer, guided his research based on theory and mathematics. Edison was a hands-on inventor, Tesla, an imaginative futurist.

Edison Machine Works was Tesla's first job with Edison. It didn't end well. Nikola claimed the supervisor at the shop offered him a $50,000 bonus if he could improve the generators that powered Edison's lighting system. Tesla accepted the challenge. He was at the shop every day and most of the night, working on Edison's machines. But Edison's goodwill toward the young engineer—whom he once commended for having a work ethic that exceeded any of Edison's other assistants—evaporated when Tesla told him the key to improved delivery of electricity was alternating current. He had designed a motor, he told Edison, that could make AC work. Edison wasn't interested. He had sunk too much of his own wealth, sweat, and reputation into his DC system and had no intention of retrofitting or redoing it. He complimented Tesla on his brilliance but told him he was wasting his time on alternating current. There was no future in it. After six months of tinkering with generators, Tesla quit. When he asked for his bonus, the supervisor laughed. The bonus line was just a figure of speech, a joke. Embarrassed, discouraged, and heartbroken that Edison had dismissed his ideas, Tesla struck out on his own.

Despite being clueless about winning over investors and attracting funding, Tesla set up his own lab, convinced capital would flow in his direction once the right people were introduced to his ideas. Sound naive? Maybe, but in the 1880s, Americans—consumers, investors, businessmen, and politicians—were giddy for light. Tesla attracted two New Jersey businessmen, Robert Lane and Benjamin Vail, who were interested in developing an electric lighting business. The three men formed the Tesla Electric Light Company to produce arc lighting equipment. Tesla worked on patenting designs for the venture, but the partnership unraveled after a year. Lane and Vail insisted Tesla wanted too much money for his work. They cut him loose and confiscated his patents.

Cheated and broke, Tesla was once again emotionally crushed, penniless, and alone. He spent the winter of 1885–1886 as a ditchdigger. "There were many days," he said, "where I didn't know where my next meal was coming from." But America was in the throes of a technology boom. It was the land of opportunity for a man like Tesla.

His fortunes changed before despair broke him. Two investors, Alfred S. Brown and Charles F. Peck, heard about Tesla, the engineer who had once worked with Edison. Electric power, and all things related to its development, was the new American gold rush. They wanted to get in on the action. Nikola Tesla was in business once more. The Tesla Electric Light Company moved to 89 Liberty Street, Manhattan, and the young engineer got to work designing and testing new motors and generators. He finally filed a patent in 1888 for the induction motor, which operated on alternating current, the idea he'd carried in his head for six years.

Tesla was invited to demonstrate his invention at the American Institute of Electrical Engineers. Not bad for a man whose most recent work history was digging trenches. His fortunes continued to improve. George Westinghouse, another hard-charging businessman who had invented his way into a fortune, was impressed by Tesla. When the two men struck a deal, Westinghouse transformed Tesla's work into a stunning commercial success.

Westinghouse was an entrepreneur and industrialist who made his first fortune in railroads. He designed and patented an air brake system for trains, then organized a manufacturing operation to produce the

George Westinghouse Jr. in 1884, age forty-two, just as he was taking on Thomas A. Edison for control of America's electrical future.

system. With the financial backing of a few wealthy railroad men, George formed the Westinghouse Air Brake Company in 1869, built a plant in Pittsburgh, and within a decade cornered the worldwide air brake market for passenger trains. Soon, he was looking around for the next challenge.

In his book *Edison and the Electric Chair*, Mark Essig recounts a story, attributed to Edison's secretary, about why Westinghouse got into the electricity business. "When Westinghouse tried to interest Edison in a steam engine he had invented, Edison supposedly replied, 'Tell Westinghouse to stick to air brakes. He knows all about them. He doesn't know anything about engines.' Westinghouse, so the story goes, decided to avenge the insult by competing with Edison." Nice bit of gossip, but Essig points out the better explanation is that Westinghouse, after a visit to Edison's lab, saw the wealth potential in electricity.

Once he decided to move into the business, Westinghouse hired an expert in electric power systems, William Stanley. Together they designed a power scheme and in 1884 began doing one-off installations of lighting systems, mostly in homes and single buildings. But it didn't take Westinghouse long to realize his tweaked system couldn't compete head-to-head with Edison's; they were too similar, and Edison had too big a jump on the direct-current market.

In a bold move, Stanley and Westinghouse switched it up, and in 1885 began work on an electric power system that used alternating current. If it worked, electricity could be transmitted along thin copper wires—crucial, since copper was expensive—over long distances from power source to destination without losing energy. Transformer technology was key to stepping up voltage at the power source, then pulling it back before the current entered a building. Too much power pushing the current and lighting fixtures blew, wires sizzled, and fire erupted. Ugly.

By November 1886, Westinghouse and Stanley were ready to install a commercial alternating-current system that could safely distribute a low-voltage current to homes and offices. Buffalo, New York, was the site they selected. In a rather improbable twist, while Westinghouse was installing an electrical system to improve peoples' lives, a Buffalo dentist named Alfred Southwick was experimenting with electricity as a means of death.

America had social reform fever at the end of the nineteenth century. Crime and punishment were high on the list. David B. Hill, governor of New York State, announced in 1885 that hanging as a method of criminal execution belonged, like the plague, to the Dark Ages. When it came to State-sanctioned killing, he wanted an alternative that was science-based. Southwick was pleased by Hill's words. He saw an opportunity to apply his execution experiments with animals to the challenge of capital punishment. Friendly with a state senator, Daniel McMillan, Southwick pressed the idea of a death penalty commission authorized by the legislature, to study the issue of science-based death.

In 1886, Southwick's lobbying paid off. The death penalty commission was created to recommend a kinder, gentler method for carrying out executions. Three commissioners were appointed: Southwick, Elbridge Gerry, and Matthew Hale. Elbridge Gerry, commission chair, was the social issues heavyweight in the group, wedged between a dentist and an undistinguished Albany lawyer. A wealthy man whose grandfather was an original signer of the Declaration of Independence, Gerry was a philanthropist and activist. He served as counsel to the American Society for the Prevention of Cruelty to Animals and founded the New York State Society for the Prevention of Cruelty to Children. Clout, social and political, was in his DNA.

Like Scrooge in Dickens's *A Christmas Carol*, ghosts of crime and punishment past, present, and future haunted the death penalty commission. And there was the press, always circling, ready to pounce on any information from the commissioners that could be infused with lurid details and fear factor. When Edison and Westinghouse got drawn into the commissioners' deliberations, it heightened the hoopla surrounding the debate. Yet, the mechanics and morality of shocking a criminal to death was really a one-off battle in the war of the currents, a devious publicity campaign that failed to stop Westinghouse but did push the issue of safety and high-voltage wires into the spotlight.

Edison, Westinghouse, and the electric chair have become so entangled that as the writer and science historian, Mark Essig, pointed out, "[T]wo distinct issues—whether the current was safe enough to use for lighting purposes, and whether it could kill criminals painlessly—became hopelessly confused, and neither received the attention it deserved. . . ." The struggle for dominance in the electric utilities market superseded the good sense and better angels of both Edison and Westinghouse. They were at such a fevered pitch over the AC-DC debate that any situation that hinted at electricity stoked their competitive nerves.

Edison refused to take responsibility—at the time, and for the rest of his life—for being complicit in the development of the electric chair although he was. It was quite a stunning turn, really, for a man who insisted he did *not* support capital punishment. In fact, Tesla and Edison are often tagged as the main antagonists in the electricity fights. They were—sort of. Tesla worked for Westinghouse when the war of the currents was at its height, but he was in the lab. His contribution to the rivalry centered on the patents, filing and fighting over them, that were important to advancing electricity generation, transmission, and delivery technology. He never wavered in his commitment to alternating current as superior to direct current, but in the capital punishment debates and debacles, he's not a major figure. It was a different story with Edison.

The financial stakes were huge in the contest to light up America, but so was pride and reputation, and these feelings ran deep and wide in both Westinghouse and Edison. For all they shared, however, their differences were easy to spot, starting with their appearance. While Edison was clean-shaven, Westinghouse had mutton-chop sideburns that flowed into a bushy mustache. He was a big man, over six feet tall, with a portly torso and a fleshy face. The expression in his eyes was amiable, but the downward tilt of his mustache on either side of his mouth made him look stern as if he were a serious walrus.

The two men also had very different approaches to public attention. Edison not only put his name on all his business endeavors, he *was* the face and voice of his enterprises. Westinghouse, on the other hand, loathed talking to the press or being photographed. "When I want newspaper advertising," Westinghouse said, "I will order it and pay cash." In his mind, the price of public recognition was fending off strangers on the street eager to tell him about this or that great idea, or worse, just wishing to have an inconsequential chat with the great man.

With the successful installation in Buffalo of an alternating-current system, Edison, who had been dismissive of his rival, sat up and took notice of Westinghouse. Still, Edison didn't believe alternating current was the future of electrification, despite the twenty-five new orders Westinghouse had fielded in the wake of Buffalo. But the Wizard of Menlo Park was very familiar with the aggressive marketing and business practices that Westinghouse used to shut out his competition. In April of 1887, Westinghouse moved into the New Orleans power market. He took on Edison Electric by selling his systems at a loss. Salesmen for Westinghouse Electric were like sharks that smelled blood in the water. Edison's systems had glitches. Edison's representative in the steamy city let his boss know that

Westinghouse was besting them in the marketplace. Numbers confirmed the dismal news. Sales for Westinghouse Electric in 1887 had seen a 400 percent increase over 1886—from $200,000 to $800,000. Westinghouse had parlayed his Buffalo coup into sixty-eight central power stations online or under contract in a single year. Edison got antsy.

Back in Buffalo, Alfred Southwick, the dentist who had already researched the use of electricity to euthanize animals, started his animal experiments again in the summer of 1887. Now a commissioner on New York's death penalty panel, he wanted to gather evidence that would convince his fellow commissioners to support electrocution as the most humane option for criminal executions. Buffalo was besieged by packs of wild dogs running the streets, causing endless complaints from residents to the city council. Councilmen set a twenty-five-cent bounty for every wild dog captured and delivered to the city pound. Local boys made quick work of it and the pound was soon inundated with canines. Buffalo's Society for the Prevention of Cruelty to Animals (SPCA) stepped in to manage the pound, which included killing unwanted animals. Shooting was out of the question, and a makeshift gas chamber was unpredictable. Looking for a solution, Southwick's name came up. He agreed to assist.

A demonstration of his method was held, with press invited, on July 16, 1887. Southwick and Dr. George Fell, a local physician, "constructed a pine box, lined it with a zinc plate, and filled it with an inch of water. They ran an electrical line from the nearest arc light cable, connecting one pole to the zinc plate, the other to a muzzle with a metal bit. A small terrier was fitted with the muzzle and led into the box." What happened next was neatly summarized by the *Morning Express*: "A simple touch of a lever—a corpse." Another twenty-seven dogs were similarly dispatched. Members of the SPCA who attended the event were adamant that the process had been quick and painless. (It's not clear what criteria were used to declare a verdict of "painless.")

Despite the experience with the SPCA dogs, Southwick wasn't successful in getting death penalty commission chair Elbridge Gerry on board with electricity-induced death. Gerry favored poison injection. Southwick decided to go to America's foremost authority on electricity, Thomas Edison, for support. He wrote Edison a letter in November of 1887 explaining the commission's charge and requesting information as to the amount of electricity it would take to reliably shock a man to death. Oh, and, one more question: What's the best system to produce the needed power? Edison's reply was fast and clear. He didn't support capital punishment and wouldn't offer an opinion. But Southwick persisted, and in December, sent another letter to Edison. He begged him to divorce the morality of capital punishment, which was a given, and assist the commission's efforts to find a more-humane death for those sentenced to death than dangling from the end of a rope.

Edison was swayed. He wrote to Southwick and said the most compassionate method was one that was quick and painless. Death by electricity could fit that bill. But the crafty Edison didn't stop there. He added fighting words: The most suitable system to deliver the death current "is that class of dynamo-electric machine which employs intermittent currents . . . these are known as 'alternating machines,' manufactured principally . . . by Mr. Geo. Westinghouse, Pittsburgh." And with that, Thomas Edison kicked his rivalry with Westinghouse to another level. "An inventor," he once said, "needs an enemy."

Elbridge Gerry, the commissioner who had resisted the electricity option, was influenced by Edison's letter. The commission members were now unanimous in their support for electricity as the death force to use in criminal executions. In the commission's report, Gerry included draft legislation to that end. While the report offered pseudoscientific-sounding explanations for the recommendation, no real science (a hypothesis tested under controlled conditions) was offered, nor any solid medical evidence for exactly *how* an electric shock ends human life. Doctors debated why death occurred. No matter. The legislature, after some tweaking of Gerry's draft measure, passed the recommended legislation. On June 4, 1888, Governor Hill's signature gave New York the distinction of being the first state to emerge from the Dark Ages of hanging criminals into the modern age of zapping them.

A few curious journalists read the death penalty report. It didn't take a scientist to see the gaps in the information used to justify the final recommendation. None of the experts who weighed in, including Edison, had personally conducted any tests on the killing power of electricity.

Anecdotes of death from an electric shock were not under controlled conditions. There could have been a hundred different reasons death occurred. The dog deaths carried out by Southwick and Fell were not carefully documented, and neither of the perpetrators had a clue as to how electricity worked. Seriously, the entire report was suspect.

A reporter from the *New York World* visited Edison in June of 1888 at his state-of-the-art laboratory complex in West Orange, New Jersey. He was looking for answers as to how and why electricity killed. Edison obliged. He directed two of his assistants, Edward Kennelly and Charles Batchelor, to assemble the equipment needed to do a test execution on a dog. On Thursday, June 21, a dog supplied by the newspaper met his fate in West Orange. Twenty people, including Edison, watched the demonstration.

The killing field consisted of a wooden board placed on the ground. A piece of tin with a wire attached to one corner was placed over the board. The wire was connected to an alternating-current generator pumping out electricity at a force of 1,500 volts. Next to the tin-covered board, Kennelly set a metal pan of water. It was separated from the ground by two strips of rubber and wired to the generator. The idea was simple: When the dog drank from the water, its body would close the circuit between pan and tin plate. This is where the scene turns dreadful. Using a rope tied around the neck of the test dog, Kennelly dragged the struggling animal toward the metal stand. The terrified dog broke free and scrambled for safety but was quickly recaptured. This time, a sturdier rope was used, and the dog was pulled onto the tin by Kennelly. Wisely, the canine refused to drink the water. In another attempt to break free, the dog jumped up, but as it wrestled into the air, one paw hit the pan of water while a back paw was still touching the tin plate. A quick twist, a muffled, lonely yelp, and the "little cur dog fell dead."

The *World* reporter turned to Edison and questioned him on how quickly an electric shock would kill a man. "'In the ten-thousandth part of a second,' Edison replied." He also sketched a crude delivery system for delivering the jolt. It involved handcuffs and metal chains. Then Edison added the tagline that the best results would come from using an alternating-current generator.

At this point, Westinghouse had been steadily chipping away at the drawbacks that hampered an alternating-current system. Alarm had spread through Edison Electric beginning in 1887 when it was evident Westinghouse had made serious inroads into their territory. Early in 1888, a series of accidental deaths happened on New York City streets, involving unsuspecting passersby getting shocked by pole-tangled, high-voltage wiring. Edward Johnson, president of Edison Electric, mailed hundreds of copies of a manifesto titled "Warning from the Edison Electric Light Company" to municipal officials and journalists across the country. Along with claimed violations of patent infringements by Westinghouse and other alternate-current power companies, he charged that alternating current had killed dozens while the Edison system had never resulted in loss of life.

He was right about this, and for an obvious reason: Edison buried his cables. Westinghouse did not; his wires were strung on poles. It was a dangerous practice in crowded urban environments. Westinghouse Electric only buried their cables when they were forced to after New York City, in a fit of frustration after passing an ordinance that required dangerous wiring to be buried, cut down every pole and wire that was damaged and still standing. But that came later. The "Warning" sparked a backlash from alternating-current companies. Debates raged in forums sponsored by different electrical societies. The war of the currents was raging full throttle. Westinghouse, realizing it could be a costly confrontation, wrote Edison and proposed they work out a more-amicable relationship. Edison quickly rebuffed the offer, certain he had the upper hand when it came to safety and measuring power usage.

In March of 1888, however, Westinghouse Electric produced its own electric metering to work with an AC system. Westinghouse electricity could be more profitably priced, sold, and billed, knocking out Edison Electric's advantage in this arena. The next move Westinghouse made was the turning point in the competition over whose system would power America.

By spring of 1888, Tesla secured five different patents for an induction motor that could successfully power an alternating-current system. Brown and Peck, the investors behind Tesla Electric Company, had agreed to promote Tesla's inventions and handle his patents. Profits were split between the partners as well as invested into research and development. Tesla's innovative electric motor, patented in May 1888, did not require a commutator—an electrical switch that periodically reversed the current flow produced by a generator—which greatly reduced the servicing and maintenance costs for an AC generator.

Tesla, Westinghouse, and electricity come together in July 1888, when Brown and Peck put together a deal. A contract for Tesla's AC motors and related equipment was worked out with Westinghouse Electric. It called for $60,000 paid in cash and stock plus a royalty of $2.50 for every horsepower produced by each of Tesla's motors. Westinghouse also hired Tesla as a consultant for a year. It turned out the induction motor took several years to perfect before it was viable in commercial use. Meanwhile, Westinghouse was caught in the financial panic of 1890 and had to drastically reduce his company's cash outlay in order to stay afloat. He asked Tesla, in 1891, to be released from the $2.50 clause, which up to that point had been staked against a $15,000 annual royalty paid to Tesla Electric (even though the motor wasn't yet widely in use). Tesla relinquished the royalty clause. He wanted Westinghouse to continue promoting his motor. Finally, in 1897, Westinghouse purchased Tesla's patents outright for a sum of $216,000—a payout worth more than $6.5 million in 2020 dollars.

With Tesla firmly embedded in the Westinghouse camp by the summer of 1888, Edison saw the handwriting on the wall. He was genuinely concerned about the safety hazards he believed were posed by alternating current, but he was wise enough to know that in time, those challenges would be resolved. His own engineers were pressuring him to move to alternating current. It was simply a more-viable system for commercial applications. Edison refused. Instead, he doubled down on his campaign to associate the name "Westinghouse"—and alternating current—with death.

The next phase of animal testing at West Orange, under controlled and meticulously recorded conditions, started that summer, sanctioned by Edison and led by Kennelly. Killing animals outright shifted to investigations of *how much* voltage was needed, with alternating or with direct current, before death occurred. Dogs were subjected to increasing levels of shock using different systems to prove Edison's contention that alternating current had a greater lethality potential than direct current, at the same (or less) voltage.

An excerpt from Kennelly's notebook, where he recorded the results of each shock given to a specific dog, is revealing—and horrid. Among the test animals used in experiments conducted on July 12, 1888, was a black, mixed-breed dog. Kennelly's notes read: "[A]t 300 volts, 'dog howled for about 1 minute & struggled violently'; at 400 and 500, 'dog yelped and struggled'; at 600, 'dog yelped and groaned. Died in 90 seconds.'" It was impossible not to see and hear the suffering imposed on the animals by these trials.

Other entries of the pain inflicted during the experiments are far more repulsive. Edison got his supply of dogs by paying a quarter for each stray brought to the lab. When the number of dogs began to dwindle, he contacted Henry Bergh, president of the national ASPCA, and requested his assistance in procuring dogs from pounds. Bergh refused. There was insufficient proof that death by electric shock was painless. It didn't deter Edison or Kennelly, both of whom were laser-focused on *proving* that alternating current was more lethal, and unpredictable, than direct current.

The animal experiments, public and private, coupled with accidental deaths, triggered this observation in the trade publication, *Electrician*: "'If this sort of thing goes on, with the accidental killing of men and the experimental killing of dogs . . . the public will soon become as familiar with the idea that electricity is death as with the old superstition that it is life.'"

Harold Pitney Brown, a self-made electrical engineer and salesman, waded into the rumpus in early June of 1888. He gained notoriety in the press and public meetings for his fierce opposition, based on its lethal properties, to alternating current. Interested in conducting his own animal experiments to prove his point, he wrote to Edison, who then invited him to use his lab and join Kennelly's research effort. Brown took advantage of the offer. Between Kennelly and Brown, dozens of dogs, at least four calves, and famously, a horse, were exterminated in the pursuit to discredit alternating current.

The mostly widely publicized demonstration of the AC-DC killing contest came in December of 1888, a month before the New York death by electric shock law was to take effect. Brown had arranged for a series of experiments at Edison's lab in West Orange. The press, members of the Medico-Legal Society, and Elbridge Gerry, along with Edison, were in attendance. Alternating current was used on all the animals, larger than a human, killed that day. Four calves and a lame horse were the victims. Each one was felled by a 750-volt shock. Exactly how death by shock was caused still eluded the medical profession—an important detail when a physician was expected to pronounce an executed criminal *dead*. The Medico-Legal Society decided to endorse the use of at least 1,000 and up to 1,500 volts of alternating current for human executions. The hazard implication for city residents wasn't lost. Newspaper stories about December's animal carnage pointed out that power lines, strung like spaghetti over city streets, used twice as much voltage.

Westinghouse was furious. He understood exactly what Edison was trying to do. Since Edison couldn't invent his way to a direct-current system that bested alternating current, he was waging a propaganda campaign. Edison was also going after Westinghouse in the courts over patents. "Westinghouse simply grabbed fifty-four of my patents and started into business, saying that he could sell his manufactures cheaper because he did not have to pay out money experimenting," Edison told the *New York Herald* on October 7, 1889. He added, "Westinghouse used to be a pretty solid fellow, but he has lately taken to shystering."

Edison's crusade to ruin Westinghouse took a particularly devious turn in 1889 when New York State's death-by-shock law took effect. Harold Brown bid on the contract to construct the device, the chair, to be used for executions. He thoroughly rake Westinghouse over the coals every chance he got, all the while holding himself out as a nonpartisan observer. Edison had never publicly admitted he financed Brown's experiments. He also never acknowledged that he materially supported Brown's efforts to vilify his rival; nor did he reveal that he'd supported Brown's lobbying activities for limits on the voltage level AC cables could use, effectively shutting out the system's high-speed, longer-distance advantage. But none of this stayed quiet for long.

On August 25, 1889, the *New York Sun* ran a story headlined "For Shame, Brown! Disgraceful Facts about the Electric Killing Scheme;

Queer Work for a State's Expert; Paid by One Electric Company to Injure Another." The story was drawn from forty-five letters stolen out of Brown's desk. The correspondence detailed Brown's plot with Edison to ruin George Westinghouse, and revealed the extent of Edison's collusion with Brown. It was a sabotage effort that included Edison's treasurer asking Brown to forward AC-bashing pamphlets to Missouri legislators; Edison and Kennelly coaching Brown for his appearance at a hearing on William Kemmler's appeal; and financing Brown's purchase of an AC generator on the sly after Westinghouse refused to sell him one. For his part, desperate to keep his name and generator from being used in conjunction with the electric chair, Westinghouse secretly funded a high-powered attorney to defend the first victim, William Kemmler.

Kemmler, terrified at the prospect of being a human guinea pig, pleaded to be hanged. He never denied that he had killed his mistress, Tillie Ziegler, but he thought his death would be at the end of a rope. His case was appealed to the New York State Court of Appeals, which sided with the lower court's opinion that the New York State law directing death by electrocution was *not* unconstitutional. Game over.

Kemmler's execution, strapped to a chair and wired to a Westing-house generator, took place at Auburn Prison in Auburn, New York, on August 6, 1890. It was a grisly debacle. Electric current had to be administered twice, and there were reports of Kemmler's head bursting into flame. (It was actually the back of his jacket.)

The horror of Kemmler's death didn't prevent the electric chair from gaining in popularity, and Kemmler wasn't the only convicted criminal to meet a dreadful fate because of technical difficulties. If anything, executions gone bad spurred demands for the glitches to be resolved rather than reevaluating the meaning of "cruel and unusual punishment." But practice makes perfect, and in time, the snags were worked out—mostly. (New York State's last criminal execution took place on August 15, 1963, at Sing Sing Prison in Ossining, New York, when convicted murderer Eddie Lee Mays, age thirty-four, was put to death in the electric chair.)

By the end of 1890, the war of the currents was fading. For one thing, the suits and countersuits were costly and time-consuming. City-by-city fights between the big three electric suppliers—Edison

Electric, Westinghouse Electric, and Thomson-Houston Electric, a New England–based company organized in 1882 that grew rapidly throughout the 1880s, took a toll on every companies' resources. When the global financial panic of 1890 took hold, ardor cooled for spending money on litigation, research, and artificially low pricing. Edison remained intransigent about alternating current or mergers with other power companies despite pleas from all directions. Even when presented with financial statements that showed Thomson-Houston's profits were double that of Edison General's, despite comparable sales figures, Edison wouldn't budge.

This photo, taken in the mid-1920s, shows a relaxed Edison, three decades after he lost his bid to power the nation using direct current.

Thomson-Houston management, however, was eager for the deal. Consequently, Edison lost control of his company in 1892 when banker J. P. Morgan joined five other financiers to force a merger between Edison General and Thomas-Houston. Edison, whose name was synonymous with electricity, was left out of the new company's management structure, and his name was erased from the corporate stationery, replaced by "General Electric." With that merger, an industry that formerly had fifteen companies was reduced to just two corporations, General Electric and Westinghouse.

The final defeat of Edison's direct current arrived when Westinghouse low-balled his bid to light the World's Columbian Exposition of 1893. Held in Chicago, the extravaganza celebrated the four hundredth anniversary of Christopher Columbus's arrival in the New World. Westinghouse made no profit on the contract, but oh, when the switch was flipped and the "White City" centerpiece of the Exposition came alive

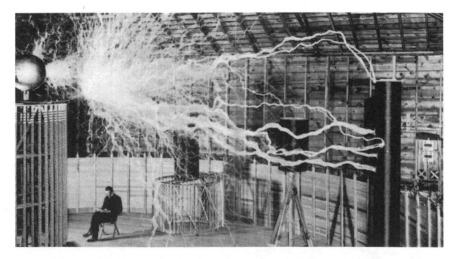

Nikola Tesla at his Colorado Springs lab in December 1899. He appears to be reading seated next to a high voltage generator releasing giant bolts of electricity but the picture was a promo stunt—a double exposure—by photographer Dickenson V. Alley.
COURTESY OF WELLCOME LIBRARY, LONDON. WELLCOME IMAGES, IMAGES@WELLCOME.AC.UK
HTTP://WELLCOMEIMAGES.ORG.

with shining light, it was evident that America was moving into an electric future powered by alternating current.

Serbian immigrant Nikola Tesla attended the Exposition that night. One wonders what he might have been thinking when the lights came on. Given his vivid imagination, perhaps he'd already envisioned the scene and was merely surprised that others were astonished. But he once told a reporter, "I do not think there is any thrill like that felt by the inventor as he sees some creation of the brain unfolding to success. Such emotions make a man forget food, sleep, friends, love, everything." What Tesla never forgot, however, were his dreams of how future innovations might serve humankind. Today, the poet scientist would be pleased to see how his ideas have echoed through more than a century of technology advances.

Ben-Hur

Stolen Storylines

It was the most celebrated novel of the nineteenth century, a book so powerful it seduced a former president into nonstop reading for thirty hours, influenced the faith of millions worldwide, altered the course of American cinema, and forever changed the fortunes of writers. When its plot was pilfered for a fifteen-minute moving picture spectacle, Ben-Hur: A Tale of the Christ, *moved from cultural phenomenon to legal sensation.*

MGM Studios released the third iteration of Ben-Hur with the kind of Broadway red-carpet glitz and flashbulb-popping fanfare that might have made Augustus Caesar drool with envy. This was a go-for-broke blockbuster that cost a swell $15 million to make—$129 million in 2020 dollars. The production had the dubious honor of being the most expensive movie ever made to that point. It was studio exec Joseph Vogel's gamble, a play to keep MGM from taking a swan dive into the bankruptcy abyss. It worked. Domestic gross receipts totaled more than $74 million (over $892 million in 2020 dollars), drawing in revenues nearly five times what it cost to make the film.

This *Ben-Hur* walked away with eleven Oscars, three Golden Globes, and a chariot-full of other awards. It's been honored, reissued, revived, and lauded since it premiered at Loew's State Theatre in New York City on November 18, 1959. Running time was three hours, forty-four minutes, long enough to require an intermission. The length wasn't outrageous, considering the screenplay had to accommodate Lew Wallace's 550-page tome. By every measure, it was a dazzler, a history-making movie.

But the real game-changer was the picture's cinematic ancestor. Released in 1907, the first *unauthorized* adaptation of Wallace's novel was directed by Sidney Olcott for Kalem Pictures. Total running time was fifteen minutes, and that included a chariot race. It was a short film that made a difference in an unlikely arena.

When the video starts, two words, *Ben Hur*, on a title card flicker into view. In less than three seconds, just long enough for the image to register from eyeball to brain, the card fades into blackness. More words appear — "Produced by Kalem Picture Corporation and Directed by Frank Oakes Rose and Sidney Olcott"—then vanish. Another card—"Jerusalem Rebels at Roman Mis-Rule"—materializes, the phrase superimposed over an arch supported by Roman columns. White on black, this interstitial placard looks like it was drawn by a stylus on scratchboard. In less than three seconds, sixteen frames shimmer past. But the next fourteen minutes and fifty-seven seconds seem an eternity.

Rather than an irate mob burning, looting, and throwing stones in rebellious outrage, the costumed crowd on-screen—men in striped tunics and turbans, women in white robes and flowing veils, everyone in sandals—looks like an exercise class searching for meaning. A dozen people pace in tandem to one side of the set. Then, like a bee swarm, the group turns and paces back to where they started. Arms go up. Arms go down. A two-fisted gesture that resembles pounding on a table but without the table completes the choreography. It could be a sign of angry frustration—or hunger.

The back-and-forth sashaying is interrupted when two spear-carrying centurions come on the scene. Why swords are necessary is a mystery, but maybe that's standard. Anyway, the guards close in and start lunging into the crowd, chest-bumping random individuals. It's reminiscent of border collies herding sheep. A nip here, a bark there, and the woolly herd stays in line. Luckily, before any of the mob can be harmed, trumpeters followed by banner-waving attendants and a half-dozen centurions enter, stage left. It's a parade. A toga-wearing gentleman, no helmet, and waving a hand in the air, strolls past the camera. The crowd waves back. Seconds elapse. More waving goes on as the man and his entourage walk leisurely off camera, stage right. The crowd follows. Jerusalem—depicted by a stone wall painted on a sheet, and some potted plants—is calm once more.

Watching this scene of silent, civil unrest with modern eyes, it looks confused and campy. Though it lasts less than two minutes, it feels like twenty. The moving picture's signature moment, "The Chariot Race," staged by firefighters from Brooklyn's 3rd Battery firehouse, lasts only about four minutes. An entry in the 1909 *World Almanac* mentions "twenty-seven members of Brooklyn's Third Battery as the holders of the military endurance record for riding fifty miles in six hours," so clearly horsemanship—at least without the chariot—was an integral part of their training. It seems implausible that a mere one thousand feet of film—for a production staged with borrowed scenery from Pain's Fireworks Company, borrowed costumes from the Metropolitan Opera House, and not a lick of dialogue or narrative—touched off a lawsuit that dragged on for three years.

Moving Picture World, an early cinema trade publication, ran a small announcement in March of 1908 that appeared on page 57 under the headline, "Injunction Asked Against 'The Production of a Roman Spectacle.'" The notice said that Kalem Picture Company and Klein Optical Company were being sued for damages over infringement of property rights.

The plaintiffs asking for an injunction—a stop-doing-what-you're-doing court order—included Harper & Brothers, who owned the copyright to the novel *Ben-Hur*; Marc Klaw and Abraham Erlanger, theatrical producers who held the rights to the stage version of the book; and for added oomph, Henry Wallace, son of Lew Wallace, author of the novel. Henry entered the fray representing the estate of his deceased mother, Susan E. Wallace.

After naming the players in the case, the notice went on: "The complaint alleges that without authority or permission the defendants are producing *Ben-Hur* in moving picture theaters. The production is advertised as, 'A Roman Spectacle,' the pictures, the complaint alleges, being adapted from General Wallace's book. The Court is asked to grant a restraining order while the litigation is pending."

With every showing of the movie, the defendants were projecting stolen property onto a screen—at least, that was the argument of the plaintiffs. But Kalem Pictures and Klein Optical held a different view. The companies' defense strategy turned on a legal loophole they thought

Poster from the Broadway premiere of *Ben-Hur*. Produced by A. L. Erlanger and Marc Klaw, Manhattan Theatre, New York, New York, circa 1899. The play used real horses on treadmills.

could be exploited by hair-splitting. Legal safeguards against film piracy or adapting a written work into a screenplay, without permission, had not kept pace with the rapidly expanding moving picture industry. When the dust settled after the Supreme Court released its 1911 decision in the case of *Kalem Co. v. Harper Bros.*, it happened that the no-budget *Ben Hur* movie had as profound an impact on the film and writing industry as the Wallace novel had on Christendom. Millions of readers believed *Ben-Hur: A Tale of the Christ* carried a mystical power that changed lives. Maybe they were on to something.

Lew Wallace's saga, published in 1880, didn't hit blockbuster status for almost two years—but when it took off, it soared. The book has *never* been out of print. In 1900, it claimed the number-one spot from *Uncle Tom's Cabin* as the nineteenth century's best-selling American novel. By then, thirty-six English-language editions had been issued, along with translations into twenty other languages, including Braille. The only book, besides the Bible, to surpass the novel's numbers in the twentieth century was *Gone with the Wind*, published in 1936.

"If every American did not read the novel," literary historian James D. Hart noted, "almost everyone was aware of it." Selecting *Ben-Hur* as a moving picture subject wasn't random. In 1907, only the Bible exceeded the novel as the most widely read book in the country. And in 1907, Ben-Hur was a name that sold merchandise as well as books and theater tickets. He was the Harry Potter of his time. Kalem Pictures hoped the name would have the same effect on its bottom line.

It took Lew Wallace four years to write his classic saga, a project he plunged into after a chance meeting on a train in the summer of 1876. Wallace, a retired general in the Union Army, was on his way to the Third National Soldiers' Reunion in Indianapolis, an imposing affair attended by thousands of Union veterans ready to rally, reminisce, and march in a parade the *New York Times* reported as "the grandest street display ever seen in the United States." A fellow veteran and popular public speaker, Robert Ingersoll, was on the same train and sought Wallace out. He wanted to discuss his favorite topic with the general—atheism.

Wallace was a man who enjoyed mastering a subject. "I would not give a tuppence," he told a *New York Times* reporter in 1893, "for the

American who has not at least tried to do one of three things . . . paint a picture, write a book, or get out a patent on something." Then he added, "Or, tried to play some musical instrument. There you have the genius of the true American in those four—art, literature, invention, music." This was pure Wallace. He was talking about himself.

Once he realized he was not as familiar as Ingersoll with the Bible and Christianity, Wallace vowed to himself to learn the material. Another man might have simply started with the first words in the Book of Genesis, "In the beginning . . ." and kept reading until he reached the Christian Bible's final verse in the Book of Revelation, "Amen! Come, Lord Jesus! Come now." But the general went a different route. He decided to educate himself by writing a book. After the publication of *Ben-Hur: A Tale of the Christ*, he told an audience in San Francisco that he had "seen the Nazarene. I saw him perform works which no mere man could perform. I have heard him speak. I was at the crucifixion. With *Ben-Hur* I watched and studied him for years." In the writing of his book, Wallace converted himself—from an indifferent churchgoer to an evangelical Christian soldier.

At its core, Wallace's story is a very, very old one: Love triumphs over hate. The finer points are these. Two men, Judah Ben-Hur and Messala, childhood friends, take very different paths. Messala, jaded and cruel, corrupted by wealth and power, personifies good gone wrong. Ben-Hur remains true to his ideals of charity and justice, but he almost gives in to vengeful impulses when he is betrayed by Messala. Judah Ben-Hur pulls back from that abyss and, after a very satisfying victory in a chariot race that leaves Messala a crippled wreck and the audience breathless, he forgives his errant friend. Ben-Hur's compassion is redemptive, not only for himself, but also for Messala.

Interwoven with the saga of Ben-Hur, his family, and Messala is the life story of Jesus of Nazareth. It's through encounters with the Nazarene, and a couple of miracles, that Judah Ben-Hur saves his soul and embraces the Christian message: Jesus is the son of God. The adept braiding of the Jesus/Judah stories lifts the book from a sweeping, historical adventure saga, fun but conventional, and transforms it into an emotionally charged tale of salvation.

Wallace also dropped in other thematic nuggets to sweeten the plot. For an audience just moving beyond the Civil War's mismanaged Reconstruction era, readers living on either side of the Mason–Dixon Line could get behind the novel's manly call to martial exploits, especially when the deeds concluded with acts of Christly charity rather than Old Testament retribution.

And for a nation on the brink of a Gilded Age, there's Judah Ben-Hur's riches-to-rags-to-riches journey. Though Judah's decency is tested, he is also hugely, handsomely, wildly rewarded with earthly treasure for his steadfast faith in God, a motif echoed in today's prosperity gospel. This theme of wealth as a reward for goodness and hard work was a staple ploy in the novels of Horatio Alger, Lew Wallace's contemporary.

After the publication of *Ben-Hur: A Tale of the Christ*, serious fandom dogged Wallace for the rest of his life—and beyond. He received thousands of letters from adoring readers, informing him of the book's effect in their lives. For theater impresarios, the tome's power was like that of honey to a bear—irresistible, seductive, golden. Wallace received countless requests for permission to bring his work to the stage. Concerned his majestic story might end up as a bawdy production, he resisted such offers for a decade. Then, he met veteran showmen Abraham Erlanger and Marc Klaw. Through serious lobbying, they convinced Wallace, and his publisher, Harper & Brothers, of their sincere desire to remain faithful to the spirit of the general's *Ben-Hur*.

For instance, they agreed that the role of Jesus would be played by a beam of light, not an actor. A sign of reverence? Maybe. A cagey public relations move? Definitely. Had a faux Jesus indulged in the sins that shadowed many a thespian—excessive alcohol and non-connubial sex—and then been found out, a ribald rumpus in newspapers and gossip would have followed. Klaw and Erlanger won the day, and in 1899, *Ben-Hur* opened on Broadway with Wallace's blessing. It ran for twenty years and was seen by more than twenty million people.

When the general died in 1905, the study on the grounds of his Crawfordsville, Indiana, home was opened to the public. He erected the building in 1895, on the spot where he wrote his magnum opus, as a repository for books, memorabilia, and artifacts he prized during his life.

An 1893 photo of famous author, Lew Wallace, whose novel, *Ben-Hur: A Tale of the Christ*, drew a worldwide readership. This picture was featured in Wallace's 1906 book, *Lew Wallace: An Autobiography*, published by Harper & Brothers.

Above the building's entrance, a wholly imagined limestone visage of Judah Ben-Hur keeps a larger-than-life unblinking eye on visitors to his birthplace. On a study wall there hangs a framed synopsis of the 1911 Supreme Court ruling against Kalem Pictures for copyright infringement of Wallace's novel. Had the author been alive to savor this legal victory, he might have toasted the decision as more evidence of the book's miraculous power to change lives—and fortunes.

Making a film version of *Ben-Hur* was the brainchild of Kalem Pictures' production chief, Sidney Olcott. When he was interviewed in 1925 by *Motion Picture Magazine*, Olcott talked about making the 1907 film. "A pyrotechnic display was given at Sheepshead Bay . . . along with a much-advertised chariot race. 'Here's a beautiful opportunity to make *Ben-Hur* cheap,' we all figured. So I took a cameraman and a couple of actors down to the track and 'shot' the race. A reel of interiors was added to this, and presto, *Ben Hur* was screened." For Olcott and his crew, subject, location, and opportunity merged at the Sheepshead Bay event for the right price—practically nothing.

It's a safe bet that Olcott wasn't the only filmmaker at the time who was dreaming of Wallace's blockbuster flickering on a small screen. What his interview reveals are the circumstances that shaped the chaotic world of early cinema—produce the picture on a shoestring budget, use ready-made content when possible, distribute finished reels far, and often. Money, time, audience. Filmmaking was always a numbers game.

Kalem Pictures, Inc., organized in 1907, came to life in the Wild West days of the moving picture industry. Nickelodeons—early movie theaters, usually converted storefronts, that charged a five-cent admission—spread across the nation like soft butter on warm toast. Demand outstripped supply when it came to getting finished product to film exhibitors. Cheap, fast production was the profit driver. If a film had something approximating production values, it was a happy, unintended consequence.

This was also the era of litigation. Every facet of moviemaking was a legal minefield. Thomas Edison alone, via Edison Manufacturing Company—a soup-to-nuts film enterprise that made the equipment that showed the films produced by the company and distributed through its licensed sales reps—sued every other filmmaking company in America between 1902 and 1905. Much of the squabbling was over technology and process patents, but copyright protections for finished films were also part of the melee.

Making a moving picture based on an existing literary or dramatic creation was standard operating procedure in the 1907 film industry. For example, *The Merry Widow, Dr. Jekyll and Mr. Hyde, William Tell*, and *Monte Cristo* are just a few of the films produced and exhibited that year. *Uncle Tom's Cabin*, another wildly popular novel from the nineteenth century, was made into a movie by Edison Manufacturing Company in 1903. It was the twenty-minute brainchild of Edwin S. Porter. Director, cameraman, content generator, casting agent, and film editor, Porter *was* Edison films from 1899 until his departure in 1909. He produced *Uncle Tom* by turning his camera on a touring troupe hired to perform the melodrama. He not only got the actors, but he also had use of their costumes and sets. "Borrowing" was the lubricant that kept the cameras rolling—and thousands of screens flickering.

Duping was the industry's boldest form of piracy. The practice was simple and inexpensive: lay hands on a finished film, make a duplicate print, sell the copy to exhibitors, pocket the money. American companies, including Edison's, seized on foreign films for duping since producers of those moving pictures usually hadn't filed for copyright protection in the United States. It's no wonder Kalem Pictures believed the lawsuit over *Ben Hur* was rude.

Looking at the film today, it's easy to see why the Kalem crew couldn't imagine a copyright problem lurking behind Olcott's potted plants. Copyright law at the time banned "printing, reprinting, copying, publicly performing, or representing" a copyrighted work without permission. But if it weren't for the words on two of the title cards—"Ben Hur" at the beginning and "Ben Hur Victor" near the film's end—there is little else that looks unique to the novel. Maybe the chariot race? Given there was no dialogue or narrative of any kind lifted from either book or play, Kalem argued their moving picture was nothing more than a series of "photographs," not a public performance of *Ben-Hur*.

Lawyers for the plaintiffs put the emphasis on the pesky word "representing," a broad term that covered, in their estimation, the defendants' actions. What other possible interpretation could there be for a film advertised as *Ben Hur*, with actors pantomiming famous scenes from the book, *Ben-Hur*, then to conclude it was a *representation* of *Ben-Hur*. They had a point.

Judge Lacombe of the US Circuit Court was the first to hear the case. He sided with the plaintiffs. His decision, reported in the May 6, 1908, edition of the *New York Times,* ran under the headline, "Must Pay Royalties on Moving Pictures." Lacombe determined that "moving picture shows come under the copyright law, and that the exhibition of films of scenes of copyrighted plays or books are violations of copyright, in that they are pantomimes, and, therefore, theatrical productions." He granted the injunction. The defendants appealed the decision.

Judge Ward of the US Circuit Court of Appeals was next to weigh in on the case. He handed down his decision the following year. He needed about a hundred words to say that Kalem Pictures "made movies,"

Sydney Olcott was lauded as the cinema's greatest director following release of his 1912 masterpiece, *From the Manger to the Cross*, which made a profit of $1 million dollars for the Kalem Company and influenced the likes of D. W. Griffith and Cecil B. DeMille. While his 1907 *Ben Hur* film was a box office loser, it brought about a seismic shift in the film industry.

exhibited in "theatoriums," a measure of how new the art form still was since neither law *nor* language had kept pace. Judge Ward upheld the decision of the lower court. Kalem Pictures would have none of it. Next step, petition the United States Supreme Court. It worked. The justices, sensitive to the rapidly changing entertainment culture, decided it was time to clear up the muddied legal waters surrounding films and copyrighted material. They accepted the case.

By 1911, when Justice Oliver Wendell Holmes wrote the majority opinion on behalf of the Court, it no longer took a hundred-word explanation as to what "moving-picture film" meant. Holmes made a pointed statement that "the operation and effect" of movies are "too well known to require description." Films had arrived in the mainstream of American culture. He quickly moved to a crucial phrase—"films give the illusion of reality"—and then briefly described the pre-filming process Kalem Pictures had used to develop their version of *Ben-Hur*. A man was hired to "read *Ben-Hur* and to write out such a description or scenario of certain portions that it could be followed in action; these portions giving enough of the story to be identified with ease." Kalem had the scenes reenacted and then "took negatives of moving pictures of the scenes, from which it produced films suitable for exhibition."

Justice Holmes noted that the films were distributed and publicized under the title *Ben Hur*. So far, this is the same information that the lower courts had laid out as justification for their decisions. Then the chief justice moved to the issue considered most important in the case: "whether the public exhibition of these moving pictures infringed any rights under the copyright law." Holmes stated that existing law made plain that "authors have the exclusive right to dramatize any of their works." And so, "if the exhibition was or was founded on a dramatizing of 'Ben-Hur,' this copyright was infringed."

With his next sentences, Holmes sealed the fate of Kalem Pictures and forever altered the landscape of moviemaking in America: "We are of the opinion that 'Ben Hur' was dramatized by what was done . . . drama may be achieved by action as well as by speech. Action can tell a story, display all the most vivid relations between men, and depict every kind of human emotion, without the aid of a word."

The opinion went on to knock down each reason claimed by Kalem as to why the film did not violate copyright law, including the equating of movies with photographs. Holmes countered that argument with a slick twist. He agreed that pictures of scenes from a novel can be created and exhibited without violating the law. And he pointed out that the lower courts had said films "could be copyrighted . . . and could be exhibited as photographs." Then, the learned judge pivoted: This argument didn't matter, because the photos would be of an "unlawful dramatization of the novel . . . as we have tried to show, moving pictures may be used for dramatizing a novel, [so] when the photographs are used in that way, they are used to infringe a right which the statute reserves."

The opinion continued, but the last two words were the most important for the litigants: "Decree affirmed." The lower court rulings were upheld. Kalem Pictures had reached the end of its legal rope. They came to a settlement with Harper & Brothers, Klaw and Erlanger, and the Wallace estate. The damages paid—$25,000—were significant for the time. (An equivalent sum today would be slightly more than $660,000.) Kalem survived the settlement. The company continued to do a decent business until it was sold in 1917 to Vitagraph Pictures.

In the Wallace Library and Museum there's a photo, an image of the chariot-racing firemen from the 1907 film. This was meant to be the only surviving image of the movie. It's not. A restored version of "the Most Superb Moving Picture Spectacle Ever Produced in America, in Sixteen Magnificent Scenes" is posted on YouTube. Olcott's *Ben Hur* plays on, a flickering icon to copyright and literary justice—a nostalgic reminder of early cinema's waning days as a lawless, creative shadowland.

BORROWED

Ferdinand Waldo Demara Jr.

A Pretentious Pettifogger

On January 28, 1952, a lengthy profile piece appeared in the era's classic American magazine, Life. *The subject of the article was one Ferdinand Waldo (Fred) Demara Jr. Fame was not Demara's friend. The reason was simple: Fred was an unrepentant impostor. "Borrowing" identities was his specialty. Joe McCarthy, author of the* Life *profile, "Master Imposter: An Incredible Tale," wrote that Fred's life was "one of the most intriguing impostor stories since the tale of Huckleberry Finn's encounter with the Duke and the Dauphin." The story of Ferdinand Waldo Demara Jr. seems oddly quaint in today's supercharged culture of tech scams and identity fraud. What sets him apart is his skewed altruism, and his restless search to fit in and stand out—simultaneously. Fred claimed, "Rascality, pure rascality," was his motivation. Of course, lying was his strong suit.*

THE CAPER THAT BROUGHT FRED DEMARA JR. INTO THE CULTURAL zeitgeist was his remarkable performance as Surgeon-Lieutenant Dr. Joseph C. Cyr of the Royal Canadian Navy (RCN). In the summer of 1951, Dr. Cyr received a commendation from South Korea for his pro bono medical work on the island of Chinnampo. A month later, Dr. Cyr was removed from his post as medical officer aboard the destroyer *Cayuga*. Two months after that, Dr. Cyr was quietly discharged from the RCN and escorted to the US–Canadian border.

For Fred Demara Jr., the stint in Canada's navy was a boundary marker. His adult life neatly divided into time before Cyr and time after. Arguably, the Cyr deception was the high point of Fred's impersonation career—a sobering thought, since he wasn't even thirty years old in the summer of 1951, the season of his commanding success as a field surgeon and humanitarian.

Before his role as Dr. Cyr, Fred, a high school dropout, posed as Dr. Robert Linton French, a Stanford PhD graduate with a post-doc appointment at Yale, and Dr. Cecil Boyce Hamann, a medical doctor and psychology instructor. Fred, who proved a better student than his high school record revealed, successfully did a year of law school at Northeastern University in Boston and a year of graduate-level theology at DePaul University. He was a soldier in the US Army until he went AWOL, and a sailor in the US Navy until he faked his own suicide.

But the groups he most wanted to join were Catholic societies. He was either a novitiate or member of monastic communities or Catholic-affiliated colleges and hospitals in Rhode Island, Massachusetts, Ontario, Iowa, Kentucky, Arkansas, Illinois, Wisconsin, New Jersey, Pennsylvania, California, Washington, and Maine. Despite his best efforts, Fred's tenure typically lasted from a few days to a few months. His longest stint in the Catholic world was his first one with the Trappist order at Our Lady of the Valley monastery in Rhode Island, and that was only for a year or two.

Fred's post-Cyr career was not nearly as colorful. Widespread publicity, including photos, hobbled his ability to impersonate anyone else without being recognized. He did achieve success in one setting—a Texas prison, where he was elevated to the post of deputy warden. But that fell apart after an inmate spotted Fred's story in *Life* magazine. As he had in other roles, Fred brought a different perspective and spirit to the job of warden, which seemed to have been the highlight of his post-Canada life. The next best position he held after Texas was a teaching position at a small school on a small island off the coast of Maine. It didn't last. He was outed—again.

Without question, Fred Demara Jr. led an unusual, adventurous life. He was often described as genial and funny, a raconteur who could mesmerize a room filled with strangers. But he also drank too much and failed, often. He never married, never had a lasting romance, never had a pet. His intellect seemed undeniable, but it was restless, undisciplined. He was one of those guys who always had potential but never followed through. What's notable is Fred's ego and chutzpah and desire to *live into* whatever life he adopted. His tale raises two timeless and surprisingly ordinary questions when it comes to schemers and scammers of any distinction. How did he do it? And why?

When Fred sold his story to *Life* in the fall of 1951, he told McCarthy his attraction to pranking started when he was about ten or eleven years old. One afternoon, coming home from school, young Fred discovered a pair of mannequin legs in a trash barrel, the kind used in store displays for ladies' stockings. His curiosity flipped into high gear. He looked at the street near his discovered treasure and noticed it was lined with snowbanks. His idea was simple, the type of prank a schoolboy could easily pull off.

Young Fred stuck the disembodied legs, thigh first, into a snow mound near the road. The feet-in-the-air limbs produced a startled reaction from passing drivers that satisfied Fred's curiosity and his mirth. The prank came off splendidly. A spooked motorist, thinking someone was headfirst in the snow, would stop to pull the victim out, only to end up getting back in the car cursing, sputtering, and very confused. In later years, when Fred told the story to journalists or on social occasions, he

Publicity from *Life* magazine story made it difficult to continue as a professional impostor. Still, Fred enjoyed being in front of a camera. His easy smile made him popular.
COURTESY OF ALCHETRON.COM

would gleefully recount how he'd fooled passing drivers over and over until he'd had his fill of fun.

His life as a professional impersonator was a more daring extension of this prankster nature. He never wavered from his claim that his deceptions were motivated by nothing deeper than a desire for some harmless, mischievous fun.

But Robert Crichton's 1959 biography, *The Great Impostor*, suggests the forces that shaped Fred's penchant to disappear into another life were darker, and had appeared on the horizon even earlier. Born in Lawrence, Massachusetts, on December 12, 1921—a cold, cloudy, gloomy day of the sort usual for a New England winter—Fred was a welcomed son. His French-Canadian father Ferdinand Sr. and his Irish-American mother Mary were both devout Catholics. Fred grew up with his older sister Elaine in a large, lavish Victorian house on Jackson Street, considered one of the finest neighborhoods in the city. Home to one hundred thousand residents, Lawrence was a mill town, a city on the banks of the Merrimack River that came into existence during the Civil War for one reason—textiles.

Sprawling brick mills flanked by worker dormitories dominated the town's early landscape. The housing was inadequate from the start, and then it was totally outstripped thanks to mill owners who expanded the factories without adding more worker accommodations. When the lousy conditions got so unbearable that girls from the surrounding farms would no longer work in Lawrence, owners turned to recruiting labor from the poorest slums in Mediterranean Europe. By the 1920s, the town had residents from more than fifty countries and a cacophony of conversations carried on in seventy different languages and dialects.

But while the population was diverse, the employment base was fearfully tied to a single industry. When times were good, they were very, very good. And when they were bad, it was horrid. "You either were a cynic or a hopeless optimist; that was the only way to survive it," Crichton wrote of the Lawrence where Fred grew up. "You took the chance and trusted to your personal fate and luck. . . . The situation was fluid and there were people who drowned in it every day in Lawrence."

The Demara family didn't drown, but they sank up to their chins.

Fred Jr. lived in comfortable surroundings during his early years. Moving pictures were the family's source of wealth. As a young man, his father, a film projectionist, harbored broader professional dreams. His dreams became reality through hard work, penny-pinching, and a partner. In the 1920s, Ferdinand Sr. owned four movie theaters in Lawrence, a lucrative proposition in a working-class town. Fred's mother Mary ran the household and entertained her husband's business associates with the help of servants.

One of Fred Jr.'s most evocative memories stemmed from a celebration on his fourth birthday. Fred Sr., young son at his side, assembled the house staff and formally presented the preschooler as the young "master" who should now be addressed as *Mr.* Demara. Family legend has it that each servant came forward, shook the child's hand, and said, "Happy birthday, Mr. Demara." The attentive child then spied a vase of roses, removed four of the flowers, and solemnly handed one to each servant. The gesture was either uncannily insightful or smoothly manipulative. Unfortunately, this charmed existence lasted only for another few years. Fred Jr., never forgot how it felt to be accorded deference.

Young Fred started his education in public school but never felt like he belonged. He was different from his classmates, mostly very poor children in shabby clothes and shoes that didn't fit right. Ignored by the other kids, Fred later claimed he enjoyed being a loner. And though he joined in when asked, Fred only played with others if the activity was nonviolent and he was the leader. Other boys weren't keen about his demands, but that wasn't all of it. There was another, more troubling behavior that scared Fred's peers: He was seriously physically strong, with a temper that boiled up from his core like hot lava exploding through the earth's crust. In the grip of rage, Fred would hold his breath until he turned purple, and he wasn't beyond smashing objects close at hand. The boy's erratic anger and instinct for self-preservation was exemplified by a recess showdown in fifth grade that brought him up on the wrong side of the school—and the law.

One of Fred's classmates that year broke a school rule and was punished. The perpetrator was sure that Fred had squealed on him. A posse of the boy's incensed friends let Fred know he was dead meat as soon as they could get at him. Fred took the threat seriously. During a morning break, he slipped out of school, ran home, retrieved a dueling pistol, and returned to class. At the midday recess, the vigilante boys found Fred and began taunting him. Slowly, they poked at him, backing him up until he was against the cold metal of the monkey bars. Fred was surrounded with nowhere to go. When the next kid touched him, he reached under his sweater and shirt, pulled out his pistol, and threatened to shoot "their guts out." His tormentors scattered, scared and chagrined.

Later that afternoon, the cops showed up, found the gun in Fred's school bag, and carted him off to the station. Being escorted out of the school by policemen made the schoolboy a hit with his peers. "I remember it felt good to be one of the guys," he said. It was a lesson that Fred perfected as an adult—breaking rules garnered recognition and acceptance. His behavior in grade school, however, stayed on the wrong side of acceptable, and got worse. It wasn't long before his parents, at the urging of school officials, and tired of his repeated antics, enrolled him in Catholic school. In retrospect, Fred's observation about this move is a bit too obvious. "Maybe," he said, "that was the beginning of the pattern. Just when I belonged, I didn't."

When Fred entered high school his family—and the country—were mired in the Great Depression. His father went bust and lost all his movie theaters. The Demaras were broke, forced to move from their Jackson Street residence into a rented carriage house on a ramshackle estate. The adolescent Fred was mortified, unhappy, and losing his Catholic faith in a benevolent God. To counter his son's waning religiosity, Fred Sr. sent him to spend a few weeks with a cousin, Father Desmarais, whose parish was in Woonsocket, Rhode Island. It was the summer of 1936.

The priest and the teenager turned out to be a good match. Fred enjoyed the cleric's comfortable lifestyle complete with a chauffeured car, a housekeeper, and a roomy, well-appointed manse. An avid reader with an acute intellect and phenomenal memory, Fred found himself challenged and inspired by Father Desmarais. The priest took him seriously and listened closely. Slowly, Fred's disgruntlement with God subsided. But the more profound outcome of this visit came in a chance remark from the priest. On a drive one afternoon, Father Desmarais pointed out to Fred Our Lady of the Valley monastery. It was home to a branch of Cistercians—a stricter variant of Benedictine monks—called Trappist. "Of all the places in the world," said the priest, "this is where I would most like to be." His young companion tucked away the comment in his prodigious memory. A year later, Fred would circle back to it.

When he returned to Lawrence at the end of the summer, little had changed. His family's finances were still dire. They still lived in the same dismal residence. He still shared a bedroom, divided by a curtain, with his older sister, Elaine. He still felt like an outsider. But in Crichton's biography, a strange incident is recounted that allegedly occurred not long after Fred's return.

It was the late fall of 1936. Elaine, out shopping one day, slipped on a patch of ice and hit her head. She complained of a headache that lasted for a few days and then—she *died*.

Another blow was handed to Fred's parents in 1937 when Fred Jr. ran away to join the Trappist monks in Rhode Island ostensibly because he could no longer stand the gloom and grief in his household. But here's the weirdness—Elaine didn't die in 1936, according to another author, Chris Barton. Based on a Request for Information, the US Navy sent Barton information on Fred Jr. from their files, which included a letter from Elaine, dated August 14, 1944. She had made an inquiry looking for "information on the whereabouts of her brother, Fred Demara, who had been AWOL." Following up, Barton learned that Elaine Demara had wed on July 5, 1945, at New York City's St. Patrick's Cathedral. He also got a copy of her death certificate. She *had* died young, but in 1948 not 1936 and at age twenty-nine, not age seventeen.

Maybe it had to do with Fred's lifelong disregard for facts, but to fudge his own sister's death just seems cold, not prankish.

When he left in late spring, 1937, Fred simply walked out of the house one morning for school and never came back. He sold his bike, bought a train ticket to Boston, took another train to Providence, and finally, boarded a bus to Valley Falls, Rhode Island. He presented himself at the gate of Our Lady of the Valley. The sixteen-year-old boy, built like a linebacker but determined to be a monk, had started his crusade to belong to the Church. In time, he would travel through a dozen Catholic-affiliated organizations, mostly using assumed names. But this first time, he used his real name.

Considered one of the most demanding of the monastic orders, Trappists require strict adherence to rules they believe are in service to the contemplative life. They don't eat meat, fish, fowl, eggs, or cheese. Milk is a luxury. Challenging physical labor is required. Most difficult of all is the vow of silence and the confession of sins in front of the monastic community. It is a rigorous life filled with deprivations. Beyond everyone's wildest expectations, Fred succeeded in passing through his novitiate training, earning his robes and acquiring a holy name, Brother Mary Jerome. But sometime after his first year, possibly his second, the Abbott and elders of the monastery were kind but firm. Fred had accomplished much, but he was not suitable for the order. He was asked to leave.

On his last night at the abbey, long after all the monks were asleep, he made his way to the stable where two recalcitrant mules he had been assigned to train were housed. He brought the dozing animals into the stable yard and then, with the kind of perversity that revealed his hurt and rage and desire for retribution, he caned the poor beasts. With the animals' braying howls ringing in his ears, Fred made his way down the drive to the main road. The clamoring mules plus Fred's loud whooping more than shattered the coveted silence of Our Lady of the Valley.

Brothers of Charity, a Boston-based religious order that specialized in running schools, homes, mission centers, and the like, was Fred's next stop. He had a decent recommendation from the Rhode Island abbey, so he was welcomed in by the Brothers. Again, he passed the novice training. He was first assigned as a kitchen helper in a home for elderly and suspended priests, on the outskirts of Montreal. Humility, a hallmark of the order, was not Fred's strength. His disdain for how his gifts were being used was no secret. His nonverbal cues were unmistakable. When he was confronted about his attitude by a small group of fellow monks, he listened without comment and later seethed.

That same evening, after the meeting, he packed his bag, stole some money from the office of the Brother Superior, and left. He caught the night train to Boston. When Fred arrived at the Brothers of Charity headquarters, he gave a sob story to the director about why Montreal hadn't worked out. He was redeployed to Boyhaven, a home for boys run by the Brothers, not far from his family in Lawrence. Fred, who hadn't revealed his own lack of formal education, was assigned to teach fourth grade at the Boyhaven school.

An unconventional instructor who believed children learned best while having fun, Fred's unorthodox lessons included impromptu field trips, games, and story times. He was a hit with the children. His placement at the school gave Fred the opportunity to reconnect with his family. His parents, excited by his teaching career, helped him start a donation program, Bundles for Boyhaven, which collected toys, clothing, supplies, and money for Fred's class. But Fred's teaching stint came to a screeching halt one fine June day. Having bought swimsuits for his class with the donations he'd received, Fred took the boys outside, turned on some hoses, and proceeded to hold a sprinkler party. When the laughter and shouting wafted into the school building, other boys watched the fun, sullen and upset at what they were missing.

Boyhaven's Brother Superior was miffed. He came out, pulled Fred aside, and said, "I'll have to ask you to tell your class to take off the swimming suits." His voice was tight with annoyance. Fred demurred and pointed out that the suits had been bought with money collected for his use with his class. The Brother Superior told Fred he'd have him ousted from the order if he didn't comply.

Humility wasn't Fred's only shortcoming. He also possessed very little patience with authority. He went back to his room, packed his bag, and started across the school grounds toward the main house. On the way, Fred noticed the school's station wagon sitting in the drive, keys in the ignition. Without a second thought, or any driving experience, he hopped in the car, turned the engine over, and headed for New Hampshire.

The next morning, he drove through Lawrence on his way to Boston where, that evening, he left the car parked near North Station. After a fine dinner and drinks at the Olde Union Oyster House, Fred was feeling dandy and reckless—so reckless that on a whim, he stopped at a military recruiting booth and enlisted in the United States Army. He used his real name. The year was 1941. Pearl Harbor was still months away.

Not yet twenty years old, Fred knew the first morning he awoke as a fresh recruit that he'd made a mistake. He spent his training time at Keesler Air Force Base in Biloxi, Mississippi, finding ways to get around process, protocol, and deadly chores like peeling potatoes. With the other guys, he was an outsider, too naive in the ways of women and the world. Luckily, he had a tent mate—Keesler was under construction when Fred was there—who became a buddy, Anthony Ignolia. When he eventually deserted, Fred used Anthony as his ticket to a new life.

Ignolia's home was on the outskirts of New Orleans. On one of Anthony's weekend trips home, he brought Fred with him. During the visit, Anthony's mother brought out a wooden box, the keeper of all things important to her son, including "records of his life." Worried Fred would be bored with his mother's show-and-tell, Anthony needled her to put the stuff away. But Fred wasn't bored. He was glued to the story of Anthony's life told through mementos and documents. "'Whattya see in those things?'" Anthony asked him. "'Life; I see a whole life ahead of me,'" was Fred's reply.

Weeks after the visit, Fred put his plan into action. He forged a pass, packed a bag, walked off base, thumbed a ride to Biloxi, then caught a bus to New Orleans, where he landed on the front stoop of the Ignolia home. Anthony's mother invited him in. She was flattered the tall young man was so interested in Anthony, and at Fred's request, once more pulled out the wooden box containing her son's life. That night, she went to bed and left Fred still reviewing the contents of the box.

Next morning, the private was gone. He'd left a sweet thank-you note and returned Anthony's box to its place. Mrs. Ignolia didn't bother to check its contents. Just as well. It would have been a shock. Every bit of documentation that bolstered Fred's takeover of Anthony Ignolia's identity was gone. Wanted under his own name for car theft in Massachusetts, and determined to join another religious community engaged in good works, Fred reasoned that he needed a new name for a fresh start. He believed that his act—stealing another man's papers—was justified, since all he intended to do in the world was good, not evil.

This time, Fred made his way to Louisville, Kentucky, and another Trappist order, the Abbey of Our Lady of Gethsemani. He passed as

Ignolia, and Ignolia passed the cursory background check used by religious orders to verify candidates. Fred's stay was cut short, in any case. At Gethsemani was a monk who'd transferred from Our Lady of the Valley. The brother recognized Fred. Even though Fred told the monk he was mistaken, he knew it was only a matter of time before he was outed.

Within days, Fred, alias, Anthony, left Gethsemani. He headed for Des Moines, Iowa, and another monastery located at New Melleray. He used Ignolia's name again and watched for a letter addressed to the Brother Superior with a New Orleans return address. It arrived. Fred pinched the letter, which was a reply to the monastery's request for a reference from the bishop's office in the candidate's home parish, as well as any other religious communities where the candidate had served. His worst fears were realized. The bishop's letter revealed his real name, his fraud, and his deserter status.

By now, the pattern was set. Fred pocketed the testimonial, packed his bag, and slipped away. Fred used Ignolia's identity one more time with one more monastery, where he stayed just long enough to write home. His parents wrote back and sent money for him to come home. When he got to Lawrence, Fred was exhausted and befuddled. His escape plan, from army private to silent monk, had unraveled. He was stumped. After days of sleeping, eating, and mulling over his options, Fred told his parents he was ready to report back to the army and face his punishment.

He changed his mind somewhere between Lawrence and Boston. Next stop—New York City. Anchors aweigh.

Ferdinand Waldo Demara Jr., technically still in the army, now enlisted in the navy. After basic training, which he abhorred, he was assigned to a destroyer, the USS *Ellis*, which operated in the North Atlantic. Fred was miffed when he was denied the opportunity to get medical training past the corpsman level simply because he lacked a high school diploma. He decided to obtain academic credentials but without going to college. Guys with a string of academic letters after their name might be jerks, but they were admired, and usually, they were officers. Fred applied for a commission.

Using college catalogs, Fred found the names of former faculty members or PhD graduates whose metrics were like his. Once he'd chosen his avatar, he wrote to the institution or office on official stationery, stolen to fit the situation. With his navy application, he used letterhead stolen from a former commanding officer. He always used a return address with a mailbox he could monitor. When the documents arrived, he would pinch the papers, substitute his name in the right places, have the revised documents professionally reprinted, and voila—his dossier of academic credentials, false birth certificate, or any other necessary document was complete.

The navy accepted Fred's materials, but one last box—a background investigation—had to be checked. When Fred was informed, he objected; then he challenged the commission board. When it was clear he couldn't bully his way out of the investigation, he capitulated. And then Fred made the same choice he'd made in the past when thwarted: He split. This time, he faked his own suicide; at least, that's the story he told his biographer, Crichton. But the navy story, as told in *Life* magazine, was different. In that version, Fred said he presented a transcript that didn't have enough math courses, so the navy turned down his application. Then the board got suspicious when he presented another transcript with beefed-up math courses. Fred never mentioned faking his suicide in the *Life* article—only that he'd left.

The navy interlude highlighted four rules Fred followed when it came to deception: First, if questioned, be vague on facts; second, when confronted, always act aggrieved; third, discredit your attacker or the information presented, sowing seeds of doubt; and fourth, once there's a whiff of being exposed, leave the scene as soon as possible.

While on the run this time, Fred borrowed the life of Dr. Robert Linton French and gained entry to several religious orders and teaching positions. All of them ended within days or weeks for one reason or another, until he was finally arrested by Navy authorities for desertion during time of war. At his court-martial, he acted as his own defense counsel. He ended up serving eighteen months in a US Navy disciplinary facility, his sentence considerably shortened from the initial six-year term, for good behavior. When he was discharged—dishonorably—from both the navy and the army, he went home to Lawrence.

Aside from Dr. French's identity, Fred picked up something else during this time that would haunt him for the rest of his days—a taste for alcohol.

Fred's next run, as Dr. Cecil Boyce Hamman, carried him through a year of law school at Northeastern University. He did well but found it boring, so he took Hamman on the road. In this guise, he went to Alfred, Maine, where Dr. Hamman was embraced by the Brothers of Christian Instruction. It was during his novitiate training with the Brothers in New Brunswick, Canada, that he met Dr. Richard C. Cyr, a general practitioner. It was Dr. Cyr's identity that carried Fred to his greatest challenge.

Fred learned that Cyr was anxious to get licensed in Maine so he could treat patients on both sides of the border. Seeing an opportunity, Fred, alias Dr. Hamman, offered to take Cyr's credentials back to Maine when he finished his training. Cyr put together an extensive file with all the papers needed to apply for a medical license and handed it over to

Frank DeMara appeared on the popular quiz show *You Bet Your Life*, hosted by Groucho Marx. The episode aired on November 12, 1959. Ironically, despite his prodigious cognitive abilities, Frank missed the first question: "What is a homonym?"
COURTESY OF ALCHETRON.COM

Fred. Armed with Cyr's documents, Fred returned to Alfred, and when he later left his teaching position at the Brothers' Notre Dame Normal School, a small junior college, he took Cyr's file with him. This identity would open the door to the RCN.

When Fred left the Brothers, he stole a car from the religious order and drove to Boston. He left the car parked in the city and then, having pilfered some cash, took a bus back to New Brunswick, Canada, as Dr. Richard C. Cyr. Dr. Cyr located the offices of the RCN and volunteered to serve. It was 1951, and the Korean conflict was under way. Without hesitation, the RCN scooped up the faux Dr. Cyr and within hours had him on a train to Ottawa, where his paperwork was processed. He was cleared for duty in record time.

Fred's first assignment as a surgeon-lieutenant was at a naval hospital in Halifax. When he arrived, Fred pulled a clever move. He sought out his superior and asked the man to work with him on a simple layman's guide for how to diagnose and treat routine medical events. The doctor was flattered and produced a document that Fred used throughout his entire tour.

But the event that truly impacted his life in Halifax had nothing to do with medicine and everything to do with falling in love.

Women were typically out of bounds for Fred because, he would say later, he couldn't reveal his identity. Anyway, on a warm afternoon in June of 1951, looking trim and immaculate in his officer whites, Fred was strolling through Halifax when he spied Catherine, a navy nurse, "serene and calm and beautiful," seated on a park lawn. It was love at first sight for him. How long it took Catherine to fall in love isn't known, but within days they were talking marriage. Well, *she* was talking marriage. Fred was getting more and more confounded. He couldn't figure out how to tell her who he really was. By the end of June, the romance was on hold. Fred, alias Dr. Cyr, was on his way to Korea. It was an out, and Fred, true to form, took it. It's hazy whether he requested to be shipped out or if it was the navy's idea. Either way, he left Halifax.

At Esquimalt, British Columbia, Surgeon-Lieutenant Dr. Richard C. Cyr was assigned to His Majesty's Canadian Ship, *Cayuga*, a destroyer headed for the waters off Korea with 12 officers and 280 enlisted men on board. As soon as he stepped on deck, he was confronted with a medical emergency. Captain Plomer's mouth was a massive pit of pain, thanks to a rotten tooth. Fred, after quickly reading up on dental procedures and throwing back a hefty slug of rum, firm in his belief that massive doses of Novocaine and antibiotics can work miracles, marched into Plomer's quarters ready for action. He found the right tooth and performed the extraction. Plomer was impressed. Fred was stunned.

Most of Fred's time was taken up with the standard medical fare—colds and infections, a few minor surgeries, cuts, burns, and sprains. But in late September of 1951, Fred was put to the test. The story he told went like this:

A Korean sailing ship pulled alongside the *Cayuga*, which that day was patrolling near the island of Chinnampo. On the floor of the open vessel were three wounded Korean nationals. (By the time Fred told this story in 1959, the number of wounded South Korean soldiers piled into this boat had risen to nineteen.) One fact remained constant: The South Koreans were desperate for medical attention. As Dr. Cyr, Fred agreed to attend to the soldiers. One of the men had a bullet (or a piece of shrapnel) lodged near his heart. It was a risky operation, but if it wasn't removed, death seemed inevitable. Relying on his prodigious memory, Fred later said that he quickly perused his medical texts, gathered his instruments, fortified himself with rum, and prepared to operate. His makeshift surgery suite was the captain's quarters.

"I couldn't have been nervous even if I felt like it," he said. "Practically everybody on the bloody ship was standing there, watching me." Armed with plenty of antibiotics and enough Gelfoam—a coagulant agent—to dose an elephant, Fred got to work. He was quick, sure, and successful. The fragment of lead, just a fraction of an inch from the heart, was removed and the wound clotted almost immediately. Fred closed the incision, bandaged the guy, and gave him a whopping huge dose of penicillin. Dr. Cyr was a hero.

In Crichton's *The Great Impostor*, Fred's South Korean story continued, with the heroic doctor making regular visits to Chinnampo every time the *Cayuga* was in nearby waters. He claimed that he started a small clinic on the island to treat the locals, and, working alone, performed amputations and once, a lung resection. How many of Fred's treatment tales are true is hazy at best. But he aroused enough admiration from his shipmates that the *Cayuga's* information officer, Jenkins, wrote a radio press release about Dr. Cyr, the humanitarian medical officer whose care of South Korean soldiers and civilians prompted a South Korean military commander, Captain Kim, to walk seventeen miles to personally thank the doctor. (Fred later transformed this appreciation from Kim into an award from the South Korean government.)

A good publicist, Jenkins interviewed Fred, who really couldn't stop himself from talking. Loaded with dramatic details, the release was picked up by Canadian news media. The real Dr. Richard Cyr, happily practicing in New Brunswick, started getting calls, including one from his mother. Cyr, when he saw a photo of Fred, connected the dots. It wasn't long before Captain Plomer received a telegram from RCN headquarters. The ship's medical officer was immediately suspended. Plomer, according to Fred, was devastated, as were the other members of the crew. Dr. Fred was congenial and strangely competent. He never lost a patient. In the *Life* article, Captain Plomer said, "He was a remarkable personality. He had a warm, sympathetic regard for all the officers and men on the ship and a high perception of human character . . . to my knowledge, he performed his duty with considerable skill . . . the whole affair is one of the greatest individual tragedies I've ever encountered."

The words were prophetic. A tribunal was convened in Canada and serious charges were drawn up, but the RCN decided to pursue a quiet course. No more adverse publicity, thank you very much. After Fred agreed to leave the country and not return, he was escorted to the border.

Fred never saw Catherine again and he never married. Not long after his dispatch from the RCN, Fred's interview appeared in *Life*, which made it much more difficult to use a false identity. Though still a young man, Fred never saw himself as a candidate for the conventional life. He spent a few years drifting and drinking, and pulled off a couple more noteworthy deceptions, especially his tenure with the Texas prison system. And despite his capers, he never lost the kind support of his parents.

"I love the boy, but I don't know him," his father said in the *Life* interview. "He's good and he's kind, and he has a really brilliant mind.

But I've never been able to understand him. I don't think anybody else understands him either."

After the release of Crichton's book, *The Great Impostor*, in 1959, Fred was offered a small role as a surgeon in a 1960 horror pic, *The Hypnotic Eye*. It was a box-office disaster. A proficient actor off-screen, Fred bombed on-screen. It ended his movie career.

In 1961, the movie *The Great Impostor*, based on Fred's biography, was released. It was a mild box-office success, a casually cheerful film starring Tony Curtis as Fred. But the resulting fame soon subsided, and Fred ended his working days as a hospital orderly in Anaheim, California. Always a large guy, as he got older, Fred's girth expanded. His obesity led to diabetes, which eventually led to amputation of both legs. He died of heart failure in 1982 at the age of sixty, according to a short piece in

Actor Tony Curtis played Fred in the 1961 screen adaptation of Robert Crichton's book *The Great Impostor*. The movie earned Robert Mulligan an academy nomination for Best Director. It was a modest hit when released and turned a profit at the box office.

the *National Catholic Reporter*. Having never made any money from his adventures, Fred's final days were spent at the home of a doctor friend.

In his 2010 book, *Introduction to Criminology*, Frank E. Hagan holds Fred up as a fine example of an *innovator*, "a person who accepts the goal of success but rejects the traditional paths of education and training to achieve it." He wrote, "Demara was disappointed that people had to spend so much of their lives preparing usually for only one occupation." Had he read this description of himself, it's likely Fred would have appreciated the title of innovator. He would have been pleased that his fame lasted far longer than his career as an impostor.

Then again, Fred might have read Hagan's explanation of his behavior only to shake his head, laugh, and mutter under his breath, "Wrong. It was all rascality, pure rascality."

Paul Jordan-Smith

The Art World's Talented Trickster

In his autobiography, Paul Jordan-Smith offered a reason for perpetrating a remarkable prank—he wanted to school some folks. "There's one moral in this tale," he wrote, "which may become apparent.... Too many critics of this century seem to lack all cultural standards and to be ignorant of cultural history and tradition out of which all of our arts and sciences have been born.... They have forgotten that one of the primary tasks of education is to teach people to discriminate between the sound and the shoddy, and to seek always for the first-rate."

For three years, Jordan-Smith, an ordained minister, writer, and literary scholar, led a secret life as a Disumbrationist. He adopted this pose for a reason familiar to biblical texts, Shakespearean plays, and novels—retaliation. His motivation for revenge was not centered in money or unrequited love or a grievous injustice. Instead, he wanted to take a poke at the pretentious art mavens who believed themselves the standard-bearers of quality and discriminating taste.

PAUL JORDAN SMITH—WHO WOULD HYPHENATE HIS NAME YEARS later—was born on April 19, 1885, in Wytheville, Virginia to John Wesley Smith, a frustrated Southern Methodist pastor, and his wife, Lucy née Jordan.

Growing up, Paul had never had an easy time with his father, a stiff-necked gentleman with little tolerance for behavior or ideas from his son that struck him as frivolous or sinful. But the serious rift between Paul and John started over Paul's college education. He first enrolled at Emory & Henry College, a small, historic liberal arts school in southwest Virginia affiliated then and now with the Methodist Church. How he felt about the education at Emory & Henry was eclipsed by meeting the young woman who became his first wife and the mother of his three children—before the scandal.

Ethel Sloan Park was twenty years old in September of 1904 when she secretly married nineteen-year-old Paul. Eleven months later, Paul and Ethel's first child, Isabel, was born. In a letter dated October 12, 1904, the new bride, living with her parents, wrote to her student husband with plenty of homey details about canning preserves and sewing a new waist—a tailored shirt worn as part of a traveling outfit—in anticipation of her upcoming visit with Paul. She talked about being separated from him, and sprinkled among the domestic news several reminders of her devotion and his new status as a married man. Ethel's anxiety over her husband can be seen in her first sentence, which starts with "your wife," and ends with an assurance she didn't want to bother her "beloved" with her unhappiness. By the middle of the page, her utter sadness is revealed in a single line that stands alone. She asked Paul two questions: "Are you being good in school?" followed by, "Do you think you'll get E in deportment?" If Ethel was interested in his studies, it took a backseat to her fear over his unchaperoned behavior. Her concerns were prescient. Less than a decade later, Paul's deportment would make headlines.

Paul received his first undergraduate degree from U. S. Grant University—now Tennessee Wesleyan University—near Chattanooga, in 1906. He transferred out of Emory & Henry mostly to frustrate his father, who was only willing to support his education if Paul prepared for the Methodist ministry or became a chemist. Vexed with Reverend Smith's constant nagging about his behavior and reading choices, Paul elected to finish his last two years of school on his own terms, and with his own dollars. By the time he graduated from Grant, Paul had two children: one-year-old daughter Isabel and infant son Wilbur. The young family left Chattanooga for Galesburg, Illinois, where Paul enrolled in divinity studies at Lombard College's Ryder School of Divinity, a Universalist seminary—a faith tradition far removed from the Southern Methodism of his father. In 1908, Paul received a degree in divinity studies and welcomed another son, Ralph, into the family.

The newly ordained Pastor Paul served two different congregations in two years, but by 1910, the family was in Chicago, where Paul was a part-time graduate student at the University of Chicago. It was in this environment that he developed friendships with radical thinkers like Emma Goldman and writers such as John Cowper Powys and Floyd Dell. His interests expanded to art and architecture, literature, the modern school movement, and modern political theory. He made money working in a settlement house and as pastor at the Chicago Lawn Con gregational Church.

While Paul's intellectual horizons were expanding, his marriage was collapsing. In September of 1913, Ethel Smith petitioned for divorce with blistering allegations of being beaten and neglected by Paul. She also charged that he "brutally abused his children, claimed they ought to be ruled with a club like savages, and finally abandoned and refused to support them." Paul didn't bother to show up at the divorce hearing, preferring to let his lawyer take the heat. His no-show prompted the irritated judge to make a very public, very scathing remark on his absence. Ethel was awarded alimony and full custody of the children.

The Smiths' divorce attracted press attention. The story that ran in the *Chicago Examiner* on the day of the hearing, noted that the couple's marital woes had buzzed around Paul's congregation since August 1912, when Ethel had Paul arrested. A quote attributed to the beleaguered mother of three offered a glimpse of the Reverend Paul's burgeoning arrogance. "I worked hard . . . and helped him get through university, and then he turned against me and said I was not intellectual—I was domestic!" If it's true, Paul sneered at Ethel's intellectual abilities too soon. A year after the divorce, Ethel married Dr. James Perkins Richardson, who admired her industry and intellect. He encouraged her to continue her education in pursuits that interested her. She became a recognized expert in folk music, published a collection of songs from the Ozarks, hosted her own radio program in the 1930s on WOR "The Voice of New York," and won the grand prize of $100,000 on an early television quiz show, *The Big Surprise*, answering questions on "hillbilly music."

Overall, the year 1913 was not a stellar time for Paul Smith. Divorced and disgraced, he sank further into gloom with the death of his mother. But his fortunes looked cheerier by the summer of 1914. With letters of introduction in his pocket, he landed in California, accepted a temporary preaching assignment in Eureka, and enrolled as a part-time doctoral student and teaching fellow in the English Department at UC Berkeley. While happily toiling away at the university, he wasted no time in sabotaging both his academic career and his pastoral credentials.

Arthur Maxson Smith led the congregation at Berkeley's First Unitarian Church. Married in 1896 to the writer and heiress, Sarah Hathaway Bixby, he was the father of four children and an unrepentant philanderer. Sarah, whose California roots were deep and impressive, had sponsored Arthur's graduate education at the University of Chicago and Harvard. He repaid her by having trysts with multiple students and even his children's nanny. Dear Sarah finally hired a private detective to get the goods on Arthur, which he did. Early in 1915, she filed for divorce, and Arthur left his church position under foul circumstances. Into the pulpit void of First Unitarian stepped the Reverend Paul Jordan Smith, PhD candidate, divorced, and Sarah's junior by fourteen years.

Drawn to each other, Sarah and Paul started an affair in the midst of Sarah's divorce proceedings, and collaborated on a writing project, *The Soul of Woman: On Interpretation of the Philosophy of Feminism*. It was published in 1916, under Paul's name, by Paul Elder and Company. The manifesto reads like a dissertation—"In the highest sense, woman asks her freedom that, removing economic fetters and political imbecilities, and ethical perversions, her spiritual nature may expand; and this not alone for her sake, but for the salvation of the human race." Reading the treatise affects the brain in the same way a car is hampered by driving through thick mud—it's a slow-going, wheel-spinning slog.

But Sarah was a match for Paul in every way. They were intellectual and romantic partners, each other's equal on the intensity index, and attracted to the same literary, social, and political persuasions. Nonetheless, entanglement with a still-married woman was risky, and they both knew it. An unverified bit of gossip suggested the pastor hyphenated his last name to Jordan-Smith when the liaison rumors became public, believing it would somehow confuse the Berkeley faculty. With or without the hyphen, the English department got wind of the affair and revoked Paul's funding. His doctoral studies were over, and whatever hopes he had for a brilliant career at an impressive academy were finished.

Sarah's divorce was finalized in 1916, and she married Paul on March 31 of that year. Hampered by the rumors—and truths—of their scandalous affair, it was time for the Jordan-Smiths to leave Berkeley and return to Claremont, where Sarah's fourteen-room home was located. Leased to a private boys' school until 1917, once the contract ended, Sarah and Paul had the house and grounds restored to their pre-schoolboy elegance. They renamed the property "Erewhon," a literary reference honoring Samuel Butler, a writer Paul admired. Butler, a British novelist, had published a work entitled *Erewhon*, which ridiculed Victorian-inspired English manners. Butler constructed the clever name, Erewhon—for a fictitious land—by spelling "nowhere" backwards and switching the placement of the "w" and "h." The Smiths' Erewhon was also a land populated by nonconformists, mostly from the Los Angeles literati community. It didn't take long for the Claremont home to become a gathering place for writers, artists, academics, and activists, eager to converse, drink, eat, pontificate, despair, and argue over the hot topic of the moment—America's entry into World War I.

Paul and Sarah moved in a world populated by people like Edward Weston, Eugene Debs, John Cowper Powys, Upton Sinclair, Emma Goldman, Floyd Dell, Clara Packard, and Kate Crane Gartz. The Smiths were ensconced with people dedicated to upending the norms. This excerpt from various letters written in 1921 by Pauline Schindler—writer, activist, editor, and critic—offers a taste of the militant freedom espoused in LA's nonconformist circles: "The Walt Whitman School [Paul and Sarah were significant participants in the formation of this alternative school] . . . gives each child such complete freedom, that one walks about the buildings and gardens wondering where the school is, for there are no formal classes! No assigned lessons, no rewards, no punishments, no authority, and no discipline! The parents, of course, are radicals . . . and are giving the children at home something of the feeling that is needed for the revolution."

Between 1917 and 1924, when his secret life started, Paul was free to indulge his scholarly passions. Sarah's money supported him, and his pursuits. He was a Latin scholar and collector of rare books, and the foremost authority of the time on Robert Burton, a seventeenth-century British scholar. Burton's opus magnum, *The Anatomy of Melancholy*, was and is a foundational literary work—a monstrous compendium "of all the books that existed in a seventeenth-century library . . . compiled in order to explain . . . all human emotion and thought." A sought-after lecturer, Paul was often invited to speak at the Friday Morning Club and Ebell Club—prestigious women's organizations that were the lifeblood of intellectual discourse, debate, and social action for middle-class and wealthy women. He taught classes at the University of California's extension center in Los Angeles, served as the director of education for the experimental Walt Whitman School, and organized chapters of the People's Councils for Peace and Democracy, a World War I pacifist organization intent on keeping America out of the conflict.

But Paul's work was upended after the country's entrance into the war. Government agents visited him and threatened imprisonment based on the hastily passed Espionage Act of 1917. Paul agreed to stop his activities, took an oath of allegiance, and swore he didn't know any Germans. Despite this capitulation to government pressure, Paul continued his friendships and affections for the edgy and controversial individuals who were part of America's progressive, politically radical intelligentsia.

By the beginning of 1924, Paul had published one novel, *Cables of Cobwebs*, and was finishing his second, *Nomad*. Two other projects were also in the works—a guide on how to make sense of James Joyce's stupefying work, *Ulysses*, and a massive editorial undertaking with Floyd Dell, journalist, poet, novelist, and editor, to produce a new edition of Robert Burton's *Anatomy of Melancholy*. In the postwar years, Paul remained engaged with radical social and political thinkers but there was one sphere where he checked his iconoclastic instincts—modern art. His disdain for the genre moved into high gear after an incident piqued his anger.

Paul Jordan-Smith entered his Disumbrationist period midway through America's Roaring Twenties. He wrote about the genesis of his Pavel Jerdanowitch persona in his 1960 autobiography, *The Road I Came*. He said the trigger for creating his alter ego was a heated discussion with his close friend, photographer Edward Weston, and Edward Kaminsky, an art professor at Pomona College, over the merits and aesthetics of the new modernists. His distaste for the genre was sparked by a 1913 exhibit at the Art Institute of Chicago. The International Exhibition of Modern Art, or Armory Show—it was first staged at the 69th Regiment Armory building in New York City—was a *massive* display of works from three hundred of the era's leading avant-garde painters and sculptors. Even if not an art connoisseur, the roster featured names so familiar today, it's hard to imagine these creatives were once controversial. The show featured pieces by Marcel Duchamp, Henri Matisse, Paul Cezanne, Paul Gauguin, Henri Rousseau, Auguste Rodin, Marguerite Zorach, Kate Cory, and Pablo Picasso.

But in 1913, the exhibition drew a significant amount of indignation and outrage. A few lines from a review in the *San Francisco Chronicle*, dated March 23, 1913, made the "degenerate" case this way: "The art exhibit just closed revealed in showing the human form in its most grotesque caricatures, malformations, hideous of form, color, suggestion, revolting from every phase from which anything may be judged. Perhaps that which was most sadly lacking was logic." Though the review was not written by Paul, it could have been. He found nothing worthwhile in the exhibition, despite the artists' bold break from old forms and rules and ideas of beauty. Modern art was the radical ethos in visible form. It didn't matter. Paul Jordan-Smith didn't care for it. He made a bet with Weston that he, Paul, could attract critical attention if he daubed paint on a canvas and signed the work with a funny-sounding name.

Not long after that disagreeable conversation, Professor Kaminsky, who chaired the annual Pomona Valley Art Exhibition, encouraged Paul's wife, Sarah, to enter the show. An amateur artist, she enjoyed painting representational landscapes and portraits. Kaminsky suggested she modernize her style for the show. When Sarah reported the conversation to Paul, the Disumbrationist School's most famous student, Pavel Jerdanowitch, went into action. Borrowing paints and old brushes from his wife, Paul "slapped out a picture of a savage woman with her arm lifted on high . . . placed a skull in the background, high on a pole to give a touch of cannibalism . . . [to] help along the modernity of the creation . . . drew the woman a hut which appeared to be toppling over on one side . . . [and] made her eyes a ghastly Gauguinesque white," according to his autobiography. He called his creation *Yes, We Have No Bananas*. Aside from amusing his family, little more came of the venture other than to use the painting as a fireplace screen.

Llewellyn Bixby Smith, Sarah's oldest son, got the idea of bringing around a friend, a budding art critic who had attended Pomona College, to assess the family's new acquisition. The fellow was captivated by the "bananas" painting. That did it. Remembering his argument with Weston and Kaminsky about snooty critics too cowardly to stand up to their peers in the art world, Paul saw an opportunity to prove his point. As Pavel Jerdanowitch, he applied to submit his work, renamed *Exaltation* and given a hefty price tag, to the Ninth Annual Exhibition of the Society of Independent Artists in the "No Jury" category. The show was scheduled for the spring of 1925 at New York's Waldorf Astoria Hotel.

Exaltation was a critical sensation, as Paul had predicted. Comte Chabrier, a French critic, was particularly captivated. He wanted to feature the work in his article for the French journal, *Revue du Vrai et du Beau* (Review of the True and the Beautiful). Chabrier requested a bio and picture from the artist. Pavel happily agreed. For his publicity photo,

Paul Jordan Smith side-by-side with the publicity photo of his alter ego, the critically acclaimed artist of the Disumbrationist School, Pavel Jerdanowitch.

Paul went heavy with the dark face paint around his eyes and eyebrows, and created deep lines in his forehead. The picture is noticeably blurry. Had he added a scraggly beard, he could have stepped out of a Dostoevsky novel. Jerdanowitch claimed he was born in Russia but had been brought to Chicago by his parents. He had attended Chicago's Art Institute until tuberculosis forced him to give up his studies. Support from friends allowed him to go on a health cruise to the South Sea Islands, where he got acquainted with the natives. He returned to the States and his current address was the California desert. Oh, and a true disciple of the Disumbrationist School painted without shadows.

Chabrier's piece appeared in the September 10, 1925, issue of the journal. He wrote, in part, "Pavel Jerdanowitch is not satisfied to follow the beaten paths of art. He prefers to discover new lands, explore the heights, and peer into the abysses. His spirit delights in intoxication, and he is prey to aesthetic agonies which are not experienced without suffering." The reception of his work was beyond Pavel's wildest dreams. Paul's next Jerdanowitch creation was titled *Aspiration*, which he submitted to a 1926 No Jury exhibition at the Marshall Field's Gallery in Chicago. The art critic for the *Chicago Evening Post* called *Aspiration* "a delightful jumble of Gauguin, Pop Hart [popular name for George Overbury, an early twentieth–century American artist] and Negro minstrelsy with a lot of Jerdanowitch individuality." Paul/Pavel kept going.

Jerdanowitch's total verified works number seven—*Exaltation, Aspiration, Adoration, Illumination, Gination, Capitulation, and Collation.* He called his collection the Seven Deadly Sins. At the Waldorf Exhibition in 1927, Pavel Jerdanowitch exhibited two works, *Adoration* and *Illumination.* A description of the paintings in the *Los Angeles Times* stated, "The first depicted a woman kneeling before a totem pole, with a background of snow mountains. The second was sprinkled with eyes and slashed across with zig-zag streaks of lightning." Again, Pavel was singled out for special mention. *La Revue Moderne* of June 30, 1927, commented: "The post-impressionists are among the spiritual masters of our painters. Notably Gauguin, who, like Jerdanowitch, got most of his impressions from the islands." Once you've been compared to Gauguin, what else is left? Well, nothing. Paul got tired of the game. He'd made his point and he had other things to do.

On August 14, 1927, Paul announced to the world the death of Pavel Jerdanowitch. He came clean to *Los Angeles Times* journalist Alma Whitaker. First, he wanted to be clear to everyone that he knew nothing about painting. Nothing. As Whitaker wrote, "He says that he has demonstrated that it is unnecessary to know anything about it to win the plaudits of at least a particular class of 'modernists' in the world of art. The worse the pictures, he contends, the louder the praise." Paul explained his motivation for the prank to Whitaker a bit differently than he did in his autobiography. His newspaper confession revealed that Sarah, a portrait painter, had entered a picture in a Claremont exhibition only to be dismissed by "futuristic critics as 'being distinctly of the old school.'" He found the comment arrogant, and decided to teach the experts a lesson. Thirty years later, Paul wrote, "Many of the critics in America contended that since I was already a writer and knew something about organization, I had artistic ability, but was either too ignorant or too stubborn to see it and acknowledge it. Even my old friend, Havelock Ellis, wrote a letter reproving me for making light of my talent."

One final exhibition was arranged by Paul with the Vose Gallery in Boston. It took place in 1928. The marketing material included an explanation of the Disumbrationist School and short interpretations of each work. *Exaltation* represented "breaking the shackles of womanhood. The lady has just killed a missionary, represented by a skull. She is hungry. Women are forbidden to eat bananas on that Island. She has just taken a luscious bite and is waving the banana skin in triumph." For *Aspiration*, he claimed, "The entire painting affords a marvelous illustration of the law of dynamic symmetry; everything directs the eye of the beholder towards the central symbol so that at first we are like the washer woman (who stares at the cosmic rooster: this is why the painting is called *Aspiration*) and fail to notice the hand of greed reaching for her purse." You get the idea—and of course, it's all fiction, fiction, and more fiction.

It wasn't lost on Paul that he'd gained more fame and notoriety for his paintings than for all his other accomplishments. Pavel Jerdanowitch became the creation that he's still best known for today. He played a delicious prank on the critics, but as a legacy, it was thin. Less than a decade after Pavel was buried, Paul went to work for the *Los Angeles Times* as literary editor and critic, joining the ranks of the taste-setters, a role he'd once mocked. His nonconformist days were behind him. After twenty years with the *Times,* Paul Jordan-Smith was a card-carrying member of the literary establishment.

When he moved on from his near-revolutionary period, Paul also moved on from his marriage. He and Sarah divorced after Paul announced he was in love with his cousin Dorothy. Not long after the marriage ended, in 1935, Sarah died from trichinosis. Though Paul was never sanguine over the lasting notoriety Pavel Jerdanowitch had brought him, he was generally amused by the story for the rest of his life. He died in 1971 at the age of eighty-six, still holding to the sentiments penned by G. K. Chesterton: "Modern art has to be what is called 'intense.' It is not easy to define being intense; but, roughly speaking, it means saying only one thing at a time, and saying it wrong."

Thomas Paine

A Patriot Pulled from the Grave

A nineteenth-century legend was recorded by the scholar Moncure Daniel Conway, Thomas Paine's biographer. It seems this story was passed along by ministers and clerics to keep would-be Christian doubters in line. Wrongly considered an atheist when he died, and rightly considered a political radical who didn't care a whit for monarchies, Mr. Paine was portrayed as a man "so wicked that he could not be buried. The earth would not hold him. His bones were placed in a box and carried about from one place to another until, at last, they came into the hands of a button-maker, and now his bones are traveling about the world in the form of buttons."

As legends go, this is a familiar one. Sinners of all stripes—think, jealous brother-killer, Cain, the disobedient Israelites in the desert, or the current crop of pop culture zombies, vampires, and spirits—have been condemned to wandering the earth without rest. And while the roving of the undead has taken on a quasi-sexy, magical ambience, for most of human history, perpetual rest was considered a reward for enduring this earthly life so far removed from the paradise hosted by the Almighty.

The once-popular idea that Thomas Paine's bones were reduced to keeping waistcoats and breeches pulled together is odd, but there are slivers of truth to the tale. His bones did travel. His reputation was in tatters. His skeleton did suffer being disassembled. The American patriot's afterlife was drama-filled and packed with politics, powerful men, and financial distress; in short, the redoubtable Mr. Paine's posthumous existence mirrored his earthly one.

THERE ARE THREE KEY FIGURES IN THIS STORY OF WANDERING BONES— William Cobbett, Moncure Conway, and the prize himself, Thomas

Paine. This tale is like a cursed treasure hunt filled with false clues, wrong directions, and rumors.

Thomas Paine died at the age of seventy-two in New York City on June 8, 1809. In the three and a half decades between his arrival in Philadelphia in the fall of 1775 and his death, he wrote—continuously—essays, pamphlets, articles, constitutions, treatises, and reams of letters. And for all that he wrote about his ideas and sentiments, his passions and his criticisms, much more has been written *about* him, dissecting and deconstructing his words.

Many Americans are familiar, at least a bit, with Paine's full-throated support of the American Revolution outlined in his best-selling pamphlet, *Common Sense*. Yet Paine left the United States in 1787 and wrote some of his most rousing prose in defense of liberty to support democratic movements in England and a revolution in France. Possibly his best-known work, *Rights of Man*—essays that offer a thoughtful, pointed rebuttal to English critics of the French Revolution—earned Paine not only a kind of political and philosophical immortality, but also a trial, in absentia, in England. He was charged with sedition. In France, it earned him a seat in the nation's democratic governing body and a request for help in drafting a French constitution.

Unfortunately, in the orgy of excessive, bloody beheadings and tortures ushered in during France's Reign of Terror, 300,000 souls were imprisoned without trial. An estimated 27,000 victims died in this purge—17,000 by execution, with another 10,000 perishing in prison. The Terror, which lasted a year, shredded much of the goodwill for the revolutionaries felt in other countries. It also cast a shadow on the reputation of men such as Paine who stuck by the French cause—even though he openly deplored the way royalists were rounded up and murdered.

Two additional events during Paine's sojourns in England and France put his reputation into a death spiral in America. One was the release of his three-part extended reflection, *Age of Reason*, which examined the deleterious effects of theology on the progress of mankind. Though he took care to spell out his deist principles and his regard for Jesus of Nazareth as a good man, Paine's belief in a Supreme Being got lost. "Of all the systems of religion that ever were invented," he argued, "there is none more derogatory to the Almighty, more unedifying to man, more repugnant to reason, and more contradictory to itself than this thing called Christianity."

His view that Christian adherents had bought into little more than myths and superstitions was thought to be heresy at best and Satanic at worst. He was decried in many American newspapers as an atheist. This quote from the *New England Palladium*, after learning of Jefferson's invitation to Paine to return to America in 1802, illustrates the depth of disdain for the man and his views: "What! invite to the United States that lying, drunken, brutal infidel, who rejoices in the opportunity of basking and wallowing in the confusion, devastation, bloodshed, rapine and murder, in which his soul delights?" Harsh.

If the *Age of Reason* was enough to bar Paine from America's shores, he deepened public acrimony in 1796 by publishing a petulant, caustic letter addressed to his former friend, George Washington. Why? Because in 1794, Paine was rotting in a Luxembourg prison after a falling-out with the leaders of France's revolutionary radicals. He exercised his privilege as an American citizen to claim protection through the American emissary to France, but his petition wasn't answered. He blamed President Washington for failing to come to his aid and charged him with selling out France and liberty by supporting the Jay Treaty—an agreement with England to reestablish relations, especially on trade, between the two nations.

Never one for subtlety, Paine's letter to Washington stated: "Monopolies of every kind marked your administration almost in the moment of its commencement. The lands obtained by the Revolution were lavished upon partisans; the interest of the disbanded soldier was sold to the speculator. . . . In what fraudulent light must Mr. Washington's character appear in the world, when his declarations and his conduct are compared together!" He not only leveled a charge against a hero, but he also leveled a false accusation. It was Gouverneur Morris, another American patriot, who let Tom sit in a crummy prison cell. Morris, America's minister to France, never passed along Paine's petition, verifying his citizenship, to President Washington whose signature was required on the document.

Fortunately, President Washington replaced Morris in 1794. His successor, James Monroe, quickly arranged for Paine's release, and a good thing that was. Distinguished historian Eric Foner wrote this about Paine's imprisonment: "He expected every day would be his last on earth, and it is probable that he was once saved from the guillotine by the mistake of a guard in marking his door. He nearly died because of an ulcer in his side and was more dead than alive when rescued from prison by James Monroe. . . . Even ten months after his release Monroe, who nursed Paine at his own home, did not believe he would live long." Though Paine had good reason to be miffed about his treatment at the hands of President Washington's emissary, publicly blasting a man considered a near-saint by his fellow Americans was not the ticket for winning friends and influencing enemies in the United States.

Despite his frustration with American politics in the aftermath of the Revolution, Paine took up Jefferson's invitation and left France for the States in 1802. Unfortunately, when he died seven years later, Paine's reputation with most of his American countrymen had hardly improved. He was targeted and smeared by reactionary clergy and Federalist-leaning detractors of Jeffersonian democracy. A line from an obituary that appeared in several newspapers, including the *New York Citizen*, offered a concise evaluation of how the stalwart, curmudgeonly patriot, who believed in the promise of American democracy, was viewed: "He had lived long, did some good and much harm." Rough words for the writer whose own words had fueled the struggle for a nation where "abridging the freedom . . . of the press" was considered a constitutional offense.

It would take a hundred years before this trashing of Thomas Paine was soundly refuted. And during that century, another remarkable chapter of Paine's saga unfolded.

Denied a cemetery plot by the Quakers because of his views on Christianity, Thomas, unmarried and childless, was buried on his New Rochelle farm, a gift from the State of New York for his Revolutionary War service. A simple headstone marked the lonely, slightly unkempt grave. His burial spot remained undisturbed, though it was the occasional target of stoning from passersby—likely devout Christians—who wished to show their scorn for the heathen. But this relative quietude was short-lived—eternally speaking. The fate of Thomas Paine's corpse took a macabre turn thanks to one of his British countrymen, William Cobbett.

Like Paine, William Cobbett was an author, philosopher, and political journalist, committed, as he wrote, to the "digging and rooting up of all corruptions," especially in government. In his book, *Cobbett*, G. K. Chesterton described the eloquent, erratic William as a man whose "whole life was a resistance to the degradation of the poor; to their degradation in the literal sense in the loss of a step, of a standing, of a status."

Born in Farnham, England, in 1763, Cobbett's first published work was produced in 1794 during a sojourn in America. Having gotten into difficulties while in the British army, he had to leave England—quickly. He packed up his wife and sailed for France. The Cobbetts stayed long enough for William to master French grammar and then they left for another haven of liberty and equality, the United States. In the new democracy, Cobbett came to public attention for commentary on America's support of France, despite that nation's horrendous "Reign of Terror." Though a champion of reform, Cobbett found the mindless bloodletting by Robespierre a travesty. His pamphlet, printed and distributed in England as well as the States, launched Cobbett as a political pundit.

For the next six years, Cobbett focused his pen and punditry on American politics. By 1800, his sarcastic wit and penchant for making up snarky nicknames for his subjects, once popular with his readers, had alienated much of his audience, including a judge who presided over a defamation case brought against Cobbett. The suit did not go in the writer's favor, and a substantial award was granted to the plaintiff. Cobbett quickly decided his best option was not to pay the award but instead pay for his passage back to England.

Once more in Britain, Cobbett continued his provocative discourse by producing the *Weekly Political Register*. Begun in 1802, Cobbett's paper was almost continuously in print for over three decades, and his journalism was later credited with advancing British political reform during the nineteenth century. Cobbett's unwavering conviction that the pen was mightier than the politician often brought him up on the wrong side of powerful men. He was bound to end up in a tight spot.

That shoe dropped in 1810 when he was convicted on a charge of seditious libel and sentenced to two years in London's Newgate Prison. Not only was he imprisoned, but he also received a hefty fine that effectively ruined him financially for the rest of his life. Though he continued to write from prison and was feted by hundreds of admirers on his release in 1812, the painful experience left him soured and hardened. In May of 1817, Cobbett relocated again to America with two of his sons. He fled England when the House of Lords—a skittish body after the French Revolution had targeted royals for execution—suspended the Habeas Corpus Act and decided to arrest writers whose works were deemed treacherous.

On this return trip to America, Cobbett, believing Thomas Paine was a kindred political spirit, concocted a plan to rescue the man from his "little hole under the grass and weeds of an obscure farm in America." He wrote that Paine's "fame is the property of England; and if no other people will show that they value that fame, the people of England will." Unfortunately, the English people were not as keen on their prodigal son as Cobbett. The reading of popular opinion was not one of the pamphleteer's strengths. And so, based on a Rumpelstiltskin notion that he could spin old Paine into a British golden boy, Cobbett, aided and abetted by his eldest son, embarked on the journey to liberate liberty's bony avatar.

"Our expedition," Cobbett wrote, "set out from New York in the middle of the night; got to the place [twenty-two miles off] at peak of day; took up the coffin entire; and just as we found it, goes to England. Let it be considered the act of the Reformers of England, Scotland and Ireland. In their name we opened the grave, and in their name will the tomb be raised." Picturing Cobbett digging out a corpse takes a strong imagination, as he was a corpulent fifty-six-year-old when he embarked on this caper.

Cobbett and his son raced to New Rochelle's wharves on the Hudson River—their bounty transferred from its mahogany casket to a plain box—just ahead of the authorities, who had been alerted by a tavern keeper that mischief was afoot. They got out of New Rochelle and returned to the family farm on Long Island. The following week, the two men, along with their peculiar package, boarded the sailing ship *Hercules*, bound for England. When they arrived at Liverpool on November 21, 1819, Cobbett wrote about the customs inspection of the bag holding Paine: "The customs officer took out a coffin plate, inscribed 'Thomas Paine, aged 74, died 8th June 1809,' and having lifted up several of the bones, replaced the whole and passed them." Cobbett said that he announced, "There, gentlemen, are the mortal remains of the immortal Thomas Paine," to the small crowd that had gathered to stare at the human bones being displayed. Although Thomas Paine was declared an outlaw in 1792 and forbidden to enter England, what was left of him managed to slip in through Liverpool.

Cobbett had also stolen Paine's headstone during the gravesite raid but apparently had gotten rid of the weighty item before departing for Britain. In a letter to a New York publication, *The Truth Seeker*, dated August 9, 1909, one James Dow reported: "Since October 1819, the [Paine] gravestone has been in the quiet and continuous custody of the Rushton family in this city. It has never been publicly exhibited, and is regarded as an heirloom. . . . The gravestone was presented by William Cobbett to Edward Rushton between the 31st Oct 1819 and the 28th Nov."

To continue with this bizarre tale, we must turn to Moncure Daniel Conway, Paine's biographer. Conway was yet another extraordinary player in Thomas Paine's post-life odyssey. Born nearly a century after Paine, in March of 1832, he was welcomed into a Stafford County, Virginia, family as near to American aristocracy as any family can claim in a country without royalty. His father was a prominent, slaveholding plantation owner, magistrate, and representative to the Virginia legislature. His mother traced her lineage to the earliest days of the Commonwealth. Two of his brothers would fight for the Confederacy during America's Civil War. Yet, Conway would become an outspoken abolitionist and expat who spent most of his adult life in England and France.

Like Paine and Cobbett, Conway's existence was a life of the mind, his passion, beyond his wife, was the trifecta of scholarly pursuits—reading, writing, and philosophical study. The similarities don't end there, for Conway, too, was once a pariah in his homeland for actions long on justice and short on political acumen.

Sent to England on a lecture tour in 1863, at the behest of New England abolitionists, Conway's job was to convince the British *not* to support the Confederacy cause. One of the few abolitionists to act on his convictions, he had led a party of his father's former slaves to freedom in 1862.

Conway was intense and impatient when it came to emancipation. His emotions, however, outstripped his reason, and while in England, he tried to strike a deal with James Murray Mason, the Confederate emissary to Britain. Claiming he represented all of the American abolitionist movement, Conway proposed that the Confederate states free all slaves in their territory, and in exchange, they could secede peacefully. It was nuts—a suggestion that received a derisive response from Mason, a wrathful rebuke from Henry Seward, Lincoln's secretary of state, and a moral reproach from the abolitionists that had sponsored his trip.

Soon after this event, when he was drafted into the Union Army, Conway, on the road to becoming an avowed pacifist, paid another to take his place. Disowned by his father, unwelcome in the South, and ridiculed in the North, Moncure Conway never again had a permanent home in America. But sometime after 1895, he wrote about his efforts to trace the American patriot and fellow freethinker, Thomas Paine. Conway's meticulous search for information on what happened to Paine's bones is the source that's most complete and closest in time to when Cobbett unearthed the skeleton. Based on Conway's narrative, here's what happened.

It wasn't long before the raid on Thomas Paine's grave became a news item. The *Northern Whig* of Hudson, New York, ran the following editorial comment on October 19, 1819: "Tom Paine has of late become literally a 'bone of contention.' Mr. Cobbett, it was reported, had formed a determination to ship off the rotting carcass of his fellow countryman, that it might finish the process of putrefication in the land where it germinated. Upon this, a very respectable writer observes, 'It is as it should be, let England be the sepulcher of her own blasphemy.' The *Democratic Press*, and the *National Advocate*, take offence at such sentiments; and aver that Mr. Cobbett, if he has done the foul and 'sacrilegious' deed, ought to be sent to the state prison."

But it was too late. Cobbett and his pirated treasure were already on the high seas. One of Cobbett's grave-digging henchmen, William Benbow, explained to Americans in a letter to the *National Advocate* newspaper that "In answer to numerous questions relative to the removal of the bones of the greatest man of the age . . . I have to say we mean to raise a colossal statue in his memory, which will prove to you, in the first place, the value we as Englishmen set upon the merits of Mr. Paine. . . . Mr. Paine's remains are gone to the land where they will be honored; and, being instrumental in the removal, forms one of the happiest periods of my life." As it happened, this letter marked the end of Benbow's association with Mr. Paine.

Cobbett's plan to hold an "interment and ceremony . . . on sacred ground at St. Paul's Church" was received "with mingled wrath and ridicule." He ran into political headwinds almost immediately. Earl Grosvenor observed: "I beg leave to mention the way in which a posthumous production, the bones of Thomas Paine, has been treated in this country. . . . Was there ever any subject treated with more laughter, contempt, and derision than the introduction of these miserable bones[?]"

Whatever plans Will Cobbett had held for Thomas Paine's bones, they were on the fast track to nowhere. The reason for this, Conway explained, was that in 1820, widespread attention had turned to "the sufferings of Queen Caroline and the affairs of George IV," who became the British monarchs that year on January 29, Paine's birthdate, after King George III died. Death of the king sucked up all the public's oxygen. No one was interested in giving money for a grand burial of a man who had left England nearly fifty years earlier.

So the burial scheme was forgotten and the bones were tucked away.

On June 18, 1835, the remarkable Mr. William Cobbett died. He left his son, James Paul Cobbett, Normandy Farm, his debts, and the bones. Years later, Conway learned about this from an 1889 letter in the *Surrey Times* from a D. M. Stevens. Mr. Stevens wrote that Cobbett's farm and its contents were sold by an auctioneer named Thomas Piggott in the fall of 1835. But the principled Mr. Piggott had refused to auction human remains.

In an 1845 publication, *The Beacon*, Mr. Gilbert Vale claimed that when the bones couldn't be auctioned, they "fell into the hands of an elderly female, a nurse in Cobbett's family." The unnamed nurse either gave or sold the bones to the gardener of a Lord King, whose estate was near Normandy Farm. But wait! There's more from Gilbert Vale, who authored an 1841 biography of Thomas Paine. Moncure Conway claimed he had in his possession a letter signed by Vale in which he wrote: "Cobbett did take the bones of Paine to London: they are in the hands of the friends of Paine, who will one day put a monument up to him. I saw some of the parties in charge of them in 1848, and I have a pamphlet on the subject which I suppose I brought from England in that year." With the pamphlet, another name finds its way into Conway's narrative—James Watson.

The 1847 pamphlet Gilbert Vale referenced was written by James Watson, an English political activist, labor organizer, and radical publisher. Like Cobbett and Conway, Watson was active in freethinker circles. Conway was sure Watson had secured his information for the document, *A Brief History of the Remains of the late Thomas Paine, from the time of their disinterment in 1819 by the late William Cobbett M.P., down to the year 1846*, directly from Benjamin Tilley, who was, "a tailor, a factotum of Cobbett in London." Using information from Mr. Vale, who relied on information from Mr. Watson, who got his report from Mr. Tilley, who worked for Mr. Cobbett, Conway pieced together a more exact account of what happened to Paine's bones once they arrived in England:

William Cobbett first deposited the remains with a friend in Hampshire. Shortly thereafter, he brought them to London, where they remained in Cobbett's house, Bolt Court, until January 1833. Benjamin Tilly, employed by Cobbett, sent the bones to Normandy Farm, where they stayed until Cobbett's death. James Paul Cobbett, William's son, at some moment during these years, scratched his own name on Thomas Paine's skull. Whether he did this to prove ownership or friendship or as decoration is a mystery.

One Jesse Oldfield then sued James Cobbett for money he was owed by William Cobbett. James couldn't pay his father's debt. The lawsuit resulted in the court appointing a receiver, George West, for the Normandy Farm estate. Cobbett's worldly goods were indeed auctioned in January of 1836, but the auctioneer refused to sell Paine's bones. And so, as of January 1836, George West had the remains. West asked the court what he should do with this last remnant of Cobbett's goods. The court didn't recognize the bones as part of the estate and refused to issue an order as to their disposal.

Although West's receivership duties ended in 1839, he kept the bones until 1844. In March of that year, West returned the bones to Benjamin Tilly in London. Watson said that West said that Tilly said he wanted to fulfill Cobbett's wishes regarding the bones. Based on this assertion, Watson concluded that Tilly would hold on to the bones "in all probability . . . until a public funeral of them can be arranged." Hope springs eternal.

Mr. Conway's lengthy report on the bones—which are with William Cobbett from 1819 to 1835, then passed to James Paul Cobbett until 1836, then moved to George West, the receiver, from 1836 to 1844, and finally, passed to Benjamin Tilly, the tailor—digresses into information from two tangential anecdotes. He related that in January of 1868, a publication, *Notes & Queries*, offered a statement from "A Native of Guilford [*sic*]." This Guildford writer claimed that in the summer of 1849 he "saw Paine's bones in a box in the house of John Chennell, corn merchant in Guildford, who told him that they had been purchased at the Cobbett sale . . . by someone ignorant of the contents of the chest." Conway discounts this intel because the sale was at Normandy Farm, and it didn't line up with an 1889 letter to the *Surrey Times*. This letter writer claimed "the same merchant, Chennell," had a porcelain jar with a cover that read, "The Great Paine's Bones." Just a few bones were in the container. The editor of the Surrey paper added that an American correspondent was assured that in 1849 the bones were in the cellar of Mr. Chennell's house. What's the story? Were the bones with Mr. Chennell in 1849, or were they in Mr. Tilley's possession? Here's how Conway worked it out: He believed the bones were in both places. The skeleton had been separated.

Mr. West, the receiver, likely had Mr. Chennell, a local merchant he knew, keep the bones for him. Then, in 1844, Mr. West took the bones—well, most of them—to Mr. Tilly in London and left some bones with Mr. Chennell. Confused? Hold on; the tangled tale gets messier.

Conway wrote that Benjamin Tilly died in 1860 while staying at the home of a Mr. Ginn, who was a wood dealer. Mr. Tilly left to Mr. Ginn objects that had belonged to Mr. Cobbett—some manuscripts, and a few pieces of Paine memorabilia. Mr. Conway then was told by a Mr. George Reynolds that in 1879, when he was in the pulpit of the Baptist Church, Mr. Ginn's daughter told him about the Paine relics. Mr. Reynolds bought the box of relics and discovered, tucked among the Cobbett manuscripts, "some of the brain and hair of Paine." Reynolds told Moncure Conway he still had the Paine pieces. He went on to say that when he learned

Tilly had the skeleton—or most of it—he inquired of Mrs. Ginn where the rest of the bones might be. Mrs. Ginn, wife of Mr. Ginn, who owned the house where Tilly died, told Mr. Reynolds she sold the bones to a rag-and-bone picker because she didn't know they were human. Conway decided this detail about selling the skeleton was a lie.

Here's where we are: Most of the skeleton went from Chennell to Tilly in 1844, who took them to Ginn's house where Tilly died in 1860. Ginn held on to the Paine relics that Tilly left to him. After Mr. Ginn died, his daughter sold two locks of hair and a piece of brain to Mr. Reynolds, the Baptist minister, in 1879. What Mr. Conway also put together was that the skull and right hand of Paine had been removed before Tilly died and "gone on a career of their own."

Conway's narrative then turned to the hand and head. He got a story from a Joseph Cowen, but it's not clear what year he got it. It seems James Watson, the pamphlet writer, consulted Cowen in 1853 or '54 about holding a public burial for Thomas Paine. Watson told Cowen the bones were with a tailor who kept them in a box at his shop. Cowen and Watson went to Tilly-the-tailor's London shop, in the "neighborhood of Red Lion Square," a couple of times, but never found him there. On their last visit, Tilly was gone, presumably to stay with the Ginn family. Cowen let the matter go, but told Conway that he'd once asked James Cobbett about the bones, and James had claimed he had no idea what had happened to them. Cowen thought he was evasive but never pressed it. Another dead end in Moncure Conway's attempt to track down as complete a skeleton as possible.

In 1874 and 1875, after putting some inquiries into newspapers, Conway hears from a few people, but still no bones. Then, in 1876, after he gave a lecture in London on Thomas Paine, the bone trail heated up again. A man named Edward Truelove, another publisher, wrote Conway a letter dated December 2, 1876. Truelove said that in 1853 or '54, a clergyman named Robert Ainslie visited him at his place of business. When Ainslie saw that Truelove had published Paine's writings, he "volunteered the very startling information that he . . . had in his possession the skull and right hand of Thomas Paine." Truelove tried to get Ainslie to spill the beans on how he'd come by these bones, but Ainslie stayed mum. Ainslie visited Truelove once more but still refused to say how he got the bones. Oddly, Reverend Ainslie was a fierce, public opponent of the freethought movement, or deism, so his possession of Thomas Paine's hand and skull is doubly weird.

Conway wrote to the Reverend Ainslie in 1877. It turned out Ainslie was dead, but his daughter, Margaretta Reynolds, answered the inquiry. She stated, "Mr. Thomas Paine's bones were in our possession. I remember them as a child, but I believe they were lost in the various movings which my father had some years ago. I can find no trace of them." Another lead gone cold. But at least Conway now knew that Ainslie had had the skull and hand *before* the skeleton was taken from Chennell by Mr. West in 1844, and delivered to Mr. Tilley. Margaretta Reynolds died in 1880. However, there is still one more tantalizing piece to this puzzle that Conway picked up.

Remember several thousand words ago, the factoid about a nurse who worked for Cobbett and passed along bones to the gardener at the Lord King estate? It seems there was another employee of that estate, a veterinarian surgeon named Ainslie, who was the brother of Reverend Robert Ainslie. The minister heard about Paine's bones from his horse-doctor brother. Oliver Ainslie, son of Robert Ainslie, told Mr. Conway that his father had purchased the skull and hand from an auctioneer named Richards. Conway deduced that when George West brought the bones to Benjamin Tilly, Tilly didn't have a permanent address. He either took the box of bones to Richards for safekeeping, and Richards sold the skull and hand, or, the skull and hand were sold by West to Chennell and then by Chennell to Richards before Tilly got the bones.

And so, Moncure Conway had, at last, all the clues he would ever get regarding Thomas Paine's bones. Moncure ended the record of his hunt like this: "[A]mid all the tangle of conjectures the certainties are that Tilly [the tailor] had the skeleton without the skull and right hand, a portion of the brain and several pieces of hair, and that Ainslie [the Baptist minister] possessed the cranium and right hand. . . . Some little time after his father's death, the skull and hand were brought from where the Rev. Robert Ainslie had resided, to Mr. Oliver Ainslie's house . . . whence they were taken away by a Mr. Penny [perhaps a ragpicker]. . . . Mr. Oliver Ainslie became interested in the remains only when too late to save them, and has not been able to find Mr. Penny, nor does he know his full name. He fears that Penny may have disposed of the skull to one of the wastepaper dealers nearby. But this appears to me improbable . . . it is probable that Paine's skull is now in some doctor's office or craniological collection."

Sadly, this story isn't quite over.

Moncure Conway wrote his saga sometime at the very end of the nineteenth or near the start of the twentieth century. At that moment, the only *sure pieces* of Thomas Paine that were known consisted of a brain remnant and two locks of hair. Mr. Conway, who was an early president of the Thomas Paine National Historical Association (TPNHA), headquartered in New Rochelle, New York, acquired those relics and presented them to the Association somewhere near 1900. The current secretary of the TPNHA, Gary Berton, said: "Our collection is now held by Iona College in New Rochelle, New York, and it contains the hair samples. They came over with the brain stem at the turn of the last century. The brain stem was buried beneath the Paine Monument in New Rochelle around 1905 when the monument was moved a few yards . . . to make room for widening the road. . . . At that time, the monument was turned over to the City, along with that artifact. It remains there, and was never part of our Collection since."

And so, the journey of Thomas Paine's mortal remains came full circle. To date, the only *documented* fragments of Mr. Paine were returned to America. A statue in his honor was erected in his hometown of Thetford, England. Another monument stands in Paris, France. The nation that had shown little interest in honoring Thomas Paine when he died, erected a monument to the patriot at New Rochelle in November of 1839. The project was spearheaded by Gilbert Vale and two women who hosted Paine as a boarder, Mrs. Badeau and Mrs. Bayeaux. Sculptor and architect John Frazee created the marble design free of charge. Apparently, Mr. Cobbett gave up too soon on Americans' gratitude for Mr. Paine.

There are rumors that a skull in Australia—purchased in England by a man claiming to be Paine's descendant through an illegitimate son— might belong to the patriot, based on descriptions of the relic.

It's a long shot.

Maybe.

Walt Whitman

The Case of the Nabbed Notebooks

Human beings—we are compelled by an inner force to gather, organize, and display the objects and art that hold meaning in our lives. These are the elements we use to represent the influences and ideas, colors and forms, emotions and beliefs that have shaped our moment on the planet. We are the makers, collectors, and worshippers of stuff, and nowhere is our affection for it more evident than in our public museums.

But the business of acquiring the art and artifacts of human existence—with its cadre of academic experts, polished professionals, and moneyed patrons—is not the genteel endeavor it appears to be. In fact, it's a competitive enterprise shadowed by stolen goods and shady money. It's a secretive world riddled with criminal activity. The Federal Bureau of Investigation (FBI) estimates that worldwide, between $6 billion and $8 billion in art and cultural property is stolen every year.

Near the end of World War II, staff at the Library of Congress were startled to discover that a cache of journals and one very special photo prop had been stolen from the library's Walt Whitman collection. Ironically, the theft occurred sometime between 1941 and 1944 when the materials had been placed in storage facilities—due to the war—for safekeeping.

THE LIBRARY OF CONGRESS (LOC) IS AMERICA'S OLDEST CULTURAL institution. It was authorized in 1800 by Congress in the same legislation that moved the nation's capital from Philadelphia to Washington, DC. It was designated as an exclusive resource for members of Congress, a repository of information to assist lawmakers with the research necessary to formulate legislation and cast informed votes. That remains the primary mandate of the LOC, though today congressional requests are handled by a staff of six hundred analysts—lawyers, scientists, librarians, economists—who are members of the Congressional Research Service, a department within the LOC.

As the world's most extensive library, boasting an inventory of 164 *million* items, the LOC holds Gershwin's piano and a Gutenberg Bible, Rosa Parks's recipe for peanut butter pancakes and a draft of the Declaration of Independence, Disney's Dumbo and Walt Whitman's cardboard butterfly—a small, inexpensive bauble now worth a small fortune because of the finger it once adorned. For fifty years, this faux Lepidoptera, along with several Whitman notebooks held by the LOC, were missing in action and believed to have vanished.

After the Japanese bombing of Pearl Harbor on December 7, 1941, Americans were grimly aware that the nation was vulnerable to an air attack on either coast. Worried about what might happen to the LOC's extensive collections, staff filled five thousand crates with carefully selected books, papers, and ephemera, including the institution's trove of material from their Walt Whitman collections. Once packed, the containers were shipped to different inland locations. The Declaration of Independence went to Fort Knox, Kentucky, but the primary storehouses were located at Denison University in Granville, Ohio; the Virginia Military Institute and Washington and Lee University in Lexington, Virginia; and the University of Virginia in Charlottesville.

In 1944, when the Library's inventory—enough to fill twenty-six freight cars—was returned to Washington, the small crate containing the Whitman notebooks was light, although it was still sealed. When, where, and how the notebooks and butterfly were lifted has never been solved despite all the investigative effort that's been put into the case. And it's still a mystery today, although there is information in the FBI and the LOC files that's been deemed off-limits on the chance that all the missing material might someday be located. Here's what has been *publicly* shared.

Alice L. Birney, the American literature specialist in the LOC's Manuscript Division, got a call at the end of January 1995 from Mr. Selby Kiffer, a vice president and head of Sotheby's Books and Manuscripts Department. Kiffer said he was on the hunt for information about a

Whitman notebook that contained material published in Emory Holloway's 1921 *Uncollected Poetry and Prose of Whitman*. The question Kiffer posed to Birney was whether the notebook Holloway cited in his publication as "made available by Harned" (one of Whitman's three literary executors) meant the notebook was a permanent gift to the LOC. When Birney looked up the Holloway citation, she realized Kiffer had asked about the journal considered the "earliest known, most important" of Whitman's notebooks, as described in a 1954 pamphlet produced by the LOC, "Ten Notebooks and a Cardboard Butterfly Missing from the Walt Whitman Papers."

For a decade following the discovery of the missing journals, the LOC staff combed through their inventory, looking for the lost items. But neither clues nor the stolen material turned up until the call came from Sotheby's in January 1995. "We never knew for sure that they [the notebooks] got out of the Library," Birney wrote in an essay for the spring 1995 issue of the *Walt Whitman Quarterly Review*, "this is the big break [Kiffer's call] I never dreamed would happen." Birney got back in touch with Selby Kiffer to stake a claim on the notebook when she learned that he wanted the LOC information for a Sotheby's client.

Birney's simmering excitement that a notebook had surfaced comes through in her description of the conversation with Kiffer: "I said that the notebook should be returned to the LOC as it was clearly government property. He requested a copy of the 1954 publication, which I said had been prepared on the advice of the Federal Bureau of Investigation, and asked me to repeat its whole title. Little did I know that my mention of the 'cardboard butterfly' named in our publication was critical to their [Sotheby's] decision that government property had been offered to Sotheby's. I promised to mail the booklet, as it was not suited for fax transmission."

The next message Birney got from Kiffer was a request for five more copies of the pamphlet. David Redden, senior vice president of Sotheby's, made a call to Birney after the auction house staff had reviewed the pamphlet. He said that Sotheby's actually had four notebooks and the butterfly in their possession. The items were received from a lawyer who had found the material while settling his father's estate. Redden reported that

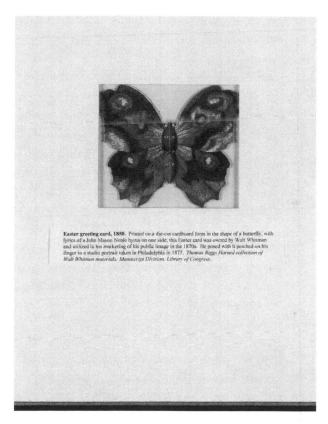

Easter greeting card, 1850. Printed on a die-cut cardboard form in the shape of a butterfly, with lyrics of a John Mason Neale hymn on one side, this Easter card was owned by Walt Whitman and utilized in his marketing of his public image in the 1870s. He posed with it perched on his finger in a studio portrait taken in Philadelphia in 1877. *Thomas Biggs Harned collection of Walt Whitman materials. Manuscript Division. Library of Congress.*

Photo of the missing faux butterfly used by Walt Whitman as a prop in a studio portrait of the poet that graced the frontispiece of *Leaves of Grass*, the 1899 birthday edition.

when he called the LOC, Dr. James H. Billington, about the find, Billington exclaimed: "This is an event of national importance." But the national event turned out to be an exercise in protocol and process.

The guy with the four notebooks, whose name has never been publicly disclosed, was blindsided by the revelation he was in possession of missing government property. If he relinquished the materials from his father's estate, he knew the family heirs would demand to know why. Like any decent lawyer, he decided to do his own due diligence to support the LOC's claim to the items as well as proof the notebooks had not been deaccessioned from the LOC's inventory. He also insisted that Sotheby's *not* disclose his identity. Birney spent a week putting together a dossier of materials substantiating the government's demand.

What happened next is bureaucracy at its finest. First, Birney's file needed to be approved by LOC's legal department before it was forwarded to Sotheby's. Once their client saw the information, he agreed to relinquish the Whitman material with the stipulation that he remain anonymous. Legal then reported the situation to the LOC's protective services department. A detective from that office was dispatched to interview Birney. After the interview, the detective got in touch with the FBI, which had been asked to investigate the disappearance of the ten notebooks forty years earlier. It was on FBI advice that the Library had produced the 1954 pamphlet in the first place. The LOC detective wanted to know if the case was still open with the FBI. Since there were still six notebooks missing, he questioned if the case of the missing journals should be aired on the television program, *Unsolved Mysteries*. The FBI quickly scuttled that idea.

The handoff was scheduled for February 25, 1995, at Sotheby's Manhattan offices. It was a marathon event that included Alice Birney, three FBI agents, and two LOC conservators. In her essay, Birney said she was met at the auction house by "Special Agent of the FBI Pat Gibbons, who controls the case from the DC office; two New York [FBI] agents; and Terry Wallis, Library of Congress, rare book conservator."

Sotheby's representation was handled by an unnamed staff member who showed everyone to "the elegant Founder's room, furnished with two library tables . . . where we had to work rapidly." It seems the auction house management was *not* pleased at losing a prize, and precious, consignment. Birney verified the four notebooks, assigned them the proper LOC identifiers, counted the pages or leaves in every journal, and, for good measure, made a notation of each notebook's number based on information found in the 1954 pamphlet.

But that's not the end of it. Birney wrote, "As I certified each item, an agent photographed it, and the conservator created custom-made travel housings with foam backings and then locked the notebooks into a hard suitcase." The government contingent only had the room for an hour because a luncheon sponsored by Sotheby's was scheduled for the space. The government interlopers weren't invited. When the luncheon guests showed up, Agent Gibbons grabbed the suitcase and the notebook rescue team left. The Washington contingent was delivered to New York's Penn Station by the FBI agents "in a mysteriously ragged car" that sped away after dropping them off—shades of *The French Connection*. On the four-hour train ride from Manhattan to Washington, the prized suitcase never left the sight or hand of an LOC staffer.

The worst nightmare of any conservator or bibliophile is to see a historical document in damaged condition, and that's what confronted the LOC staff when they had a chance to really examine the returned materials. Some of the notebooks had "torn leaves and badly faded pages." Another journal had loose pages that had been hastily reassembled in their cover but not in the correct order. On the upside, Special Agent Gibbons and Alice Birney developed a close, collegial friendship on this caper. And Gibbons, a Whitman enthusiast, got interested in tracking down the remaining six notebooks.

Retrieval day was at last over after Agent Gibbons spent a half-hour filling out the proper forms to "officially" return the suitcase of materials to the custody of the Library. Alice Birney signed as the LOC's official representative. If the small group popped the cork on a bottle of champagne to celebrate the prodigal notebooks' homecoming, it wasn't recorded. Birney drove Agent Gibbons back to FBI headquarters, "in the rather sinister area of Buzzard's Point," and then went home. Ms. Birney deemed it the "most remarkable day" in her twenty-two years with the LOC.

Like a beleaguered father hearing that his kidnapped child had been found unharmed, David Wigdor, assistant chief of the Library's Manuscript Division, was ecstatic. He said the notebooks were "definitely the most important literary material we could have hoped to recover of anything known in American literature." Wigdor went on to proclaim the journals simply "transcendent" in their usefulness to scholars. Wow. What made those notebooks so special? After all, by 1995, the LOC housed almost *98,000* items related to Whitman.

Alice Birney estimated that Whitman probably created more than one hundred notebooks over the course of his lifetime. The pages were filled with bits and pieces of himself, revealing the evolution of his poems, and the recounting of his days. Some journals were small enough for a pocket, the nineteenth-century equivalent of a Twitter feed. But one reason these retrieved notebooks created such a sensation is that they contained some of the earliest materials generated by the writer and received by the LOC. They were among the twenty-four notebooks donated by Thomas Harned, one of Walt Whitman's three literary executors. Altogether, the items deposited by Harned—three thousand total—included poetry and prose manuscripts, letters, notes, ledgers, the journals, and the butterfly.

Scholars had studied the Thomas Biggs Harned Collection of Walt Whitman Papers for about twenty years before the materials were carted away for safekeeping, always leaving out content that didn't interest them or wasn't germane to the focus of their study. One of the four returned notebooks contained names and addresses of wounded Civil War soldiers tended by Whitman when he was a volunteer nurse at a Washington, DC, hospital. This information was not available from any other source. It provides invaluable clues for contacts a researcher might tap to locate additional Whitman information—just in case there's some tidbit about the bard not yet revealed in the ocean of resources at the LOC.

Another of the repatriated notebooks, considered the oldest, "contains 47 small leaves densely written in pencil with aphorisms, observations, and extensively revised poetry, including early drafts of 'Song of Myself,' [. . .] with prose breaking into poetry." This pocket-sized jotter, packed with penciled ideas, snatches of verse, and notes about daily routines—his record of visits with the soldiers, maimed and dying, are especially poignant —are a window into the heart and mind of Whitman prior to the 1855 publication of his groundbreaking poetry collection, *Leaves of Grass*.

And the butterfly. . . . What does that say about the man?

Published in 1899, the birthday edition of *Leaves of Grass* had a frontispiece image of the seventy-year-old Whitman seated in profile, peering intently at his finger. He's wearing a soft-crowned, broad-brimmed hat over shaggy gray hair that falls past his shirt collar. The lower half of his face is covered by an unruly gray beard and mustache that converge and tumble over a dark cardigan, buttoned up in a manner familiar to viewers of *Mister Rogers' Neighborhood.* And there it is—the object of Whitman's contemplation—a butterfly, posed as if it had just alighted on his outstretched finger. Despite the poet's claim to his biographer Horace Taubel that it was "an actual moth . . . the picture is substantially literal: we were good friends," twelve scholars concluded the cardboard butterfly—retrieved from Sotheby's—was "the moth." The old poet had wired it into place for his photo shoot. "Ever the self-promoter," wrote Birney, "Whitman liked to convey an image of himself as one with nature."

But there's another possibility for the prop. Printed on the backside of the colorful, winged insect are the words of an Easter hymn by John Mason Neale. It's an ode to Christ's resurrection and the immortality that is conveyed to all "the Saints" who, "like Him shall die." If there's a patron bug of transformation, it's the butterfly. Perhaps the elderly Walt Whitman was recalling the dying young soldiers he visited in the hospital, those fragile saints who only wished for "some fig, an orange, some licorice, a book." Perhaps the esteemed writer was letting everyone know he was one with eternity rather than nature; that his immortality was assured. The aged Whitman surely knew he would live forever through his words. "The proof of a poet," he wrote, "is that his country absorbs him as affectionately as he has absorbed it." He would be pleased to know his country holds him so dear, it never stops looking for him.

John Scott Harrison

A Case of Body Snatching Most Foul

Augustus Devin was a very young man of twenty-three when he departed this life on May 18, 1878. He died of tuberculosis, leaving behind his widowed mother and at least one brother, Bernard Devin. Like all victims of consumption, Augustus wasted away to a shadow before his body finally succumbed to the illness. Following his funeral at the Cleves Presbyterian Church in North Bend, Ohio, he was buried in the Congress Green Cemetery on the outskirts of Cincinnati. As deaths go, Augustus's demise was sad, but not unusual—until his mortal remains took an unexpected journey that led to a gruesome discovery.

TODAY, IT'S DIFFICULT TO TRACE THE PRECISE CONNECTION BETWEEN the Devin family and the president-producing Harrisons. They were certainly neighbors and long-standing friends, and perhaps distantly related by blood or marriage. But in this tale, it's death and science that united the Devin and Harrison clans.

Their interrelated saga began a week after Devin's death, when seventy-three-year-old John Scott Harrison unexpectedly dropped dead sometime in the overnight hours between Saturday, May 25, 1878, and Sunday morning, May 26. John, the father of thirteen children with eight still living when he died, was the reigning patriarch of a family with deep roots in American politics. (His grandfather, Benjamin Harrison V, was a cosigner to the Declaration of Independence. William Henry Harrison, who served a nanosecond—just thirty-one days—as the ninth president of the United States, before pneumonia killed him, was John Scott's father. And Benjamin Harrison, the one-term twenty-third president of the country, elected in 1888, was John's son.)

William Henry Harrison served for thirty-one days as the ninth US president before dying of typhoid. He was the first president to die in office, the shortest-term president in US history, and the only president whose grandson, Benjamin Harrison, was also elected president. William Henry Harrison was the father of John Scott Harrison.

Prior to his death, John retained the fine patrician looks of his youth—deep-set eyes, a high, wide forehead that expanded as his hairline receded, a long aquiline nose, prominent cheekbones, and a pronounced jawline that tapered to a firm cleft chin. As an older man, he added a biblical gravitas to his appearance with a very white, very long, very full beard and longish, equally bright white hair that grazed the top of his high-collared shirts. In some photos, he bears an eerie resemblance to the Sistine Chapel's ceiling-bound Jehovah. Whether it was a heart attack or stroke that took out John isn't clear. On his last evening alive, he dined with his son Carter and Carter's family at the spacious Harrison homestead, Point Farm, in North Bend, Ohio. Before retiring, John reviewed his notes for a talk he was scheduled to deliver the following day.

Sunday morning, a grandson was sent to fetch the senior Harrison for breakfast, and discovered his grandfather partially dressed, unconscious and crumpled on the floor. Within hours, Carter Harrison notified his siblings their father was dead. Benjamin Harrison received the message at his Indianapolis home when he returned from church. With his wife, Caroline, Benjamin left that afternoon for North Bend. They arrived at Point Farm to a press of friends, family members, and neighbors. A steady parade of mourners came through the house over the next two days bringing food, prayers, and condolences. The funeral was scheduled for Wednesday, October 29, at the Presbyterian church in Cleves, the same location that hosted the young Augustus Devin's service. Fondly referred to by residents of North Bend as the "little church on the hill," Cleves Presbyterian was built by the late president, William Henry Harrison. On the day of John's funeral, the church pews were filled, and a standing crowd spilled beyond the sanctuary doors.

After leaving the church, the funeral procession wound through the Congress Green Cemetery to the Harrison family plot. An ominous sign filled the grieving family with dread as they followed John Scott's casket. The dirt over the grave of Augustus Devin had been disturbed. Was it body snatchers or rooting pigs? Mourners' opinions were split on the matter, but the pigs' scenario was preferable. Whether the grave had been assaulted by porcine or human marauders, everyone agreed that the widowed mother of Augustus must not be alerted to the situation. It was feared she might be overcome by distress at the idea of her son's body having been snatched. Resurrectionists—the popular nineteenth-century name for grave robbers, as if they were God's handymen—was the era's most feared graveyard scourge. This terror took root three hundred years earlier in Europe when the practice of medicine was no longer confined to monks and nuns.

Despite the hint of divine approval implied by the name, resurrectionists were people who walked in darkness. Dissecting a cadaver was a desecration, a heinous defilement in the eyes of the European populace who fervently believed they were going to enjoy a corporeal reuniting with friends, family, and God. But by the late sixteenth and early seventeenth centuries, there was grudging acknowledgment that physicians needed to be familiar with human anatomy. As the demand for bodies grew in the medical field, it became standard procedure to turn over to academia the remains of executed criminals and the unclaimed bodies of paupers. It's notable that poverty and criminal activity were interchangeable when it came to pariah status. This practice, prevalent in England, came across the pond to America with British colonial rule.

Grave robbing came into its own as a market opportunity—with organized systems of corpse retrieval and delivery—to fill the gap between legally released, usable remains and the clamor for them. Though rare, it wasn't unusual to read newspaper accounts of bodies packed in barrels and crates, awaiting shipment to medical schools, being left on a wharf only to be discovered after the stench of rotting flesh made the containers impossible to ignore.

Another contributing factor that made body snatching an appealing moneymaker was the lack of meaningful punishment if caught. It seems the act was only considered a crime if something of material value—a piece of clothing or a burial shroud—was also taken while pinching the corpse, or if there was damage to the headstone or coffin. Legal action was based on injury—which implied ownership or victimization—to one's property, person, or pocketbook. Since a corpse belonged to no one nor could it suffer, there was no harm, no foul in stealing it. If caught meddling in a grave, the act drew a small fine and perhaps some jail time, but only if the right individuals, from nightwatchmen to judges, hadn't been properly paid off by cither the resurrectionists or the medical school.

Across the Atlantic, in the early 1800s, more than one thousand medical students in London alone were vying for access to approximately two hundred legally released corpses. With that discrepancy, it's no mystery as to how and why the resurrectionists' trade thrived, and in some high-profile cases, turned from the retrieval of recently buried persons to the generation of corpses through murder. One of the more lurid of these operations was carried on by the Irish criminal duo of William Burke and William Hare in the city of Edinburgh. It's a creepy story, but a fine illustration of unintended consequences.

Hare, in 1828, owned a flophouse that catered to the innumerable paupers, beggars, prostitutes, and tramps that crowded into the slums of Edinburgh looking for ways to survive. Burke, an intermittent cobbler, was one of Hare's tenants. Their dodgy partnership in crime started when another tenant who owed Hare back rent died at the rooming house. Hare decided to retrieve his lost rent by selling the poor man's body to a private medical school run by Robert Knox. Hare turned to Burke for help with the delivery. The cadaver commanded a good price from Knox and netted a tidy little profit for Hare.

The next moneymaking opportunity for Hare and Burke arose when another tenant became ill. This time, the two men weighed in on the life-or-death outcome for their victim by smothering the man with a pillow. Such a fresh body commanded an even higher price from Knox. The die was cast. Hare and Burke were hooked on this relatively simple means of achieving financial stability.

Their method of relocating a person from this world to the next was speedy and easily accomplished with minimal up-front investment. After plying a victim with enough cheap alcohol to induce a semicomatose state, a pillow was placed over the poor chap or lady's face; while one man performed the suffocation, the other sat on the soon-to-be cadaver's legs to prevent a struggle. Their method left little in the way of injury or marks, driving up the cadaver's market value without raising suspicions. As Hare and Burke were in all other respects quite conventional, they drew no attention to themselves.

Contemporaneous accounts call out Hare as the more-brutal member of the team, in part because of his appearance. "He was described as 'an evil man of evil looks, the black eyes of a snake set at different levels, hollow cheeks creasing into deep gullies when he went into bouts of unamused laughter, a vicious and dangerous man.'" Although this may have been true, Hare escaped the gallows.

Before they were arrested, Burke and Hare managed to murder sixteen individuals and sell their corpses. What finally brought the partners to the attention of police was the 1827 Halloween murder of one Mrs. Docherty. It seems a cosmic prank that Halloween marked the unraveling of the duo's wicked pursuits. As it happened, Burke accosted the victim at a pub and invited her to his rooms, insisting they were distantly related. She obliged, but instead of falling into a stupor after a few drinks, she brightened and insisted on visiting a Mrs. Connoway who lived nearby. Burke and his lady were off, taking the bottle with them.

Now, on this occasion, Burke had borrowed the home of a family he knew, the Grays, as the location for carrying out his evil deed. He had sent the Gray family to spend the night at Hare's boardinghouse, but Mrs.

Gray returned to the house, seeking to retrieve some forgotten item, and walked in on the carousing Hare and Mrs. Docherty. The next morning when the Gray family, the Connoways, and the Hares all showed up for breakfast, Mrs. Docherty was nowhere to be seen. "Burke lost his head, afraid someone would smell the corpse. He threw whiskey over the straw and shouted at Mrs. Gray for lighting a match near the pile. This aroused her curiosity, and later that day she and her husband returned, discovered the body, and denounced Burke and Hare to the police."

Hare was granted immunity from prosecution in exchange for ratting out his accomplice. Burke was executed, having made a full confession after Hare turned on him. As a convicted murderer, his body wound up on the dissecting table to illustrate a public lecture on anatomy. Hare, while freed, didn't escape punishment. He signed on as a laborer, but his workmates found it hard to accommodate an ex-murderer in their midst. Rumor had it they dumped him into a lime trough, which left him blind. He spent the next forty years as a street beggar. He did, however, leave a legacy. "Burking" is a term used to this day when a murder is committed with intent to sell the corpse.

Most of the grave robbing in America was performed by medical students and porters working at medical colleges. Public ire was usually directed at the schools and the medical profession, though there were notable exceptions. Some resurrectionists became so well-known and feared for their audacity, cunning, and success at plucking bodies from seemingly impenetrable gravesites that families would often go to great lengths to protect the final resting place of their loved ones.

When members of John Scott Harrison's funeral cortege had the opportunity to examine Devin's burial site, it was thought the young man's body had indeed been stolen. Seeing the disturbance of that grave prompted quick, preventive measures by the Harrisons. John Scott's children, rightly alarmed, immediately arranged to increase the security precautions at his burial site, a business overseen by Benjamin Harrison and his younger brother, also named John.

The Harrison brothers had decided that the pit holding John Scott's coffin would be eight feet long and eight feet wide. This roomy trough allowed for a brick, vault-like structure with thick stone walls and floor

An 1896 studio portrait of Benjamin Harrison, twenty-third US president; son of John Scott Harrison and grandson of William Henry Harrison, ninth US president

to rest within the pit. This vault became the receptacle for John Scott's metallic coffin. Once the casket was placed, three large stones at least eight inches thick were lowered onto the coffin's lid where they were cemented into place. A guard was posted at the site and the grave was left open for many hours to ensure proper drying of the cement. Finally, dirt, dirt, and more dirt was shoveled into the deep hole, creating another barrier between the senior Harrison's body and would-be resurrectionists—at least, that was the plan.

A last precaution, taken by Benjamin, was to hire a watchman to keep an eye on the site for thirty nights. He was to be paid a total of thirty dollars for this job. Even desperate medical colleges did not use a corpse that had been in the ground for a month. And so, with the casket secured in its underground fortress, the younger Harrisons left the cemetery, satisfied that their beloved father was safely ensconced for eternity.

On the evening of the funeral, General and Mrs. Benjamin Harrison departed by train for their home in Indianapolis. Friends and family accompanied them to the station in Cincinnati. That night, younger brother John Harrison remained in the city. He was on a mission to track down the missing corpse of Augustus Devin. The next morning, with his cousin George Eaton in tow, John got a search warrant from the magistrate, Squire Wright, corralled a constable named Lacey, a detective named Snelbaker, and an unnamed police officer. The five men, based on a very thin tip, started their search for the body at the Ohio Medical College.

The morning edition of the *Cincinnati Enquirer* reported that a buggy pulled into an alley that ran next to the school. "Something white was taken out and disappeared" before the carriage "left rapidly. The general impression," stated the *Enquirer*, "was that a 'stiff' was being smuggled into the Ohio Medical College." John Harrison was doubtful the body was that of Augustus. He assumed, given when the young man died, that the corpse had been taken and sold several days earlier. But the police insisted the college building be searched.

The five men, armed with their search warrant, compelled the college's janitor, A. Q. Marshall, to let them search the building. The story goes that during the search, the men encountered some boxes of body parts, the body of an infant, and a med student "chipping away" at the "head and breast of a black woman." Marshall insisted there were no fresh bodies to be found—and he almost pulled off the deception.

The search party, after a thorough if futile ransacking of the building, including a chute that opened in the alleyway and ran into the school's basement, were about to depart. Before they left, the janitor insisted he needed to inform the faculty. Detective Snelbaker let him go but had the policeman follow him. Marshall unwittingly led the officer to a dissecting room at the very top of the building. The officer, in turn, returned to the search party and led them back to the dissecting room, where no corpse was found.

As the group was about to exit, however, Constable Lacey and Detective Snelbaker noticed something odd: a taut rope hitched to a windlass, disappearing beneath a trapdoor. Several hard turns of the windlass brought up a stout, entirely naked body suspended either by the neck or shoulders. The face and head of the poor, dangling man were completely covered by a cloth. John Harrison protested that he needn't see the face, as this was clearly *not* Augustus Devin. His conclusion made sense. Augustus had been emaciated when he died, a result of the tuberculosis, while the body on the rope was corpulent. Also, what little hair was visible was white, that of an elderly rather than a young man.

Nonetheless, Snelbaker and Lacey insisted the body be placed on the floor and the face covering removed. Harrison couldn't bring himself to lift the cloth, so Constable Lacey, using a stick, did the deed. Poor John Harrison went white and began trembling. His "eyes bulged from their sockets," and his body struggled between retching and fainting. "My God," he rasped, "that's my father."

While John was making the ghastly identification of his father in Cincinnati, a few miles distant, in North Bend, family members had gone to visit John Scott's grave only to discover that the body had been taken.

The ghoulish accomplishment was quite a feat. First, it required the stones at the foot of the coffin to be upended. Once that was completed, holes were drilled into the outer casket and the lid at the foot end pried up. Breaking the inner glass seal, the culprits then tied a rope around

John Scott Harrison, son of one American president and father to another, served in the US House of Representatives from 1853 to 1857. He was elected in 1852 as a Whig Party candidate and was reelected as an antislavery Oppositionist Party candidate in 1854.
COURTESY OF WIKIMEDIA COMMONS

the feet and pulled John Scott's body, feet first, from the casket. As this was not the standard removal practice, the family suspected that one or more of the thieves must have been present at the burial ceremony. What the hired watchman might have known or seen, or whether he colluded with the grave robbers, was never revealed, as he had disappeared from the area.

Carter Harrison, along with his cousin, Archie Eaton, the brother of George Eaton, immediately took off for Cincinnati to inform their respective siblings of the horrible news from the graveyard. When Carter and John Harrison met, the conversation reportedly opened with Carter declaring their father's body had been snatched, while John exclaimed he'd found their father's body at the Ohio Medical College. Despite trying to keep the news of the lost—and found—body a private matter, reporters got wind of the situation. The story was snapped up by newspapers around the country.

Benjamin Harrison was apprised of what had happened by telegram. He immediately left Indianapolis for Cincinnati. When he arrived, his brothers told him the tale. Fortunately, the elder Mr. Harrison was once more in the hands of an undertaker while arrangements for a reinterment were made. Marshall, the janitor, was arrested for knowingly accepting a purloined body. He was jailed but soon released on $5,000 bail, posted by the faculty of the medical school.

The public was outraged. Newspapers savaged the medical school, which is understandable. The faculty, through the dean of the college, Dr. Roberts Bartholow, released a self-serving statement to the *Cincinnati Times*. Yes, yes, they were sorry that such a notable person as John Scott Harrison had found his way into their cadaver pit. It was an unfortunate mistake, as the dissection tables were usually reserved for paupers. But it wasn't the fault of the school, and the faculty neither knew about nor were responsible for the theft that had been committed by "an anonymous resurrectionist taking 'this means to replenish his exchequer.'" Besides, the training of competent doctors required courses in anatomy, which meant human bodies had to be procured for dissection. A glorious example of a non-apology apology.

Benjamin Harrison was infuriated when he read the school's mea culpa. Without hesitation, he wrote a scathing open letter addressed to the "People of Cincinnati" that was filled with pathos. It read, in part:

Your janitor denied that [the body] laid upon your tables, but the clean incision into the carotid artery, the thread with which it was ligatured, the injected veins, prove him a liar. Who made that incision and injected that body, gentlemen of the Faculty? The surgeons who examined his work say that he was no bungler. While he lay upon your table, the long white beard, which the hands of infant grandchildren had often stroked in love, was rudely shorn from his face. Have you so little care of your college that an unseen and an unknown man may do all this? Who took him from that table and hung him by the neck in the pit?

Despite the desire of Benjamin Harrison and his brothers to see the faculty of the Ohio Medical College brought to justice, they determined that a criminal action would be impossible. However, testimony before a grand jury and repeated badgering of the faculty by reporters did produce one piece of useful information: The Ohio school, like many others, did indeed contract with certain "providers" to ensure a supply of cadavers to keep dissection tables filled throughout the school year. It was also revealed that Cincinnati was home to an Amazon-style distribution center for "dead traffic" to schools in smaller locations, such as Ann Arbor and Fort Wayne. Chilling reports in the newspapers detailed how "these cadaver-producing contracts obliged the resurrectionist to prepare the bodies for immediate use—'a simple process, easily taught, and one in which all professional body-snatchers were proficient.' In all cases, it was understood, so the doctors testified, that private graves were not to be disturbed. The only fair territory for this ghoulish profession was the public burying ground for paupers."

As deliberations by the grand jury continued and the Harrison horror remained in the public eye, the search for Augustus Devin was quietly pursued. Detective Snelbaker led the investigation team, which included

Carter and John Harrison; their cousins, George and Archie Eaton; and Augustus's brother, Bernard Devin.

A break came when the janitor at the Miami (of Ohio) Medical College confessed to the school's professor of surgical anatomy, Dr. Clendenin, that he had accepted a bribe from the dreaded resurrection man, "Charles Morton, alias Gabriel, alias Dr. Christian, alias Dr. Gordon," to allow the school's facilities to be used as Morton's prep site for the human bodies he snatched, all destined for the dissection table. In fact, even though there was no direct evidence that tied him to the actual taking of John Scott Harrison's body from the grave, Morton was indicted by the grand jury and ended up arrested. It's unclear what happened to him.

Terrified, the Miami Medical College janitor also confessed that many of the bodies prepared by Morton were shipped to the medical college in Ann Arbor, packed in containers marked Quimby and Co. This preparation and shipping activity took place at Miami Medical College in the first month of summer recess, when faculty members were only on the premises

Designed in the eighteenth century, this heavy iron cage is called a mortsafe. It was placed over a grave site to prevent body snatchers from removing the corpse.
COURTESY OF WIKIMEDIA COMMONS

a couple of hours each day. After Clendenin consulted with the rest of the faculty, the decision was made to get in front of the information.

A full disclosure of the alarming facts was given to Detective Snelbaker —the break he was looking for, as nearly a month had passed since Augustus Devin's body had been stolen. After some additional detective work, Snelbaker concluded that the cadaver had shipped from Cincinnati on May 24 and arrived at the Ann Arbor college on May 25. The determined detective went to Ann Arbor armed with legal documents, grabbed the local sheriff, and together the two men went to the "gloomy stone structure where the cadavers were kept. Negler, a four-foot-ten-inch, squat German watchman-janitor, who had spent twenty-four years in ghoul-guarding, refused admittance to the two searchers."

The short, fierce Negler couldn't keep Snelbaker out for long. Eventually, the wily detective got inside the building and found a barrel filled with brine and a body that he suspected was Augustus. He sent for Bernard Devin to help make the identification, a tough task given that decomposition was well under way. Bernard, along with George Eaton, went to Ann Arbor, and at the charnel house, confirmed the body was that of Augustus. According to an account in the *Commercial*, a local newspaper:

> *In a room whose walls were stacked high with coffins, trunks, and barrels, the latter crammed with mouldy human bones, the sickening process took place . . . Young Devin . . . after a long, intent look, took a steel probe . . . and after running it up the nose of the corpse, exclaimed, "This is Gus. Here is a little hole he had in the wall of his nose, and here are the decayed teeth; here the moustache, and here the scar on the leg. It's Gus and I'll take my oath on it."*

And with that, the Devin/Harrison saga ended. John Scott and Augustus were placed once more in their respective graves, family and friends looking on.

Both the Harrisons and Devins filed civil suits against the respective medical colleges involved in the body-snatching incidents. Dean Bartholow's notorious statement denying that the faculty had any knowledge of the Harrison horror was nonetheless an admission that medical schools paid for the services of resurrectionists. Ten thousand dollars was the demand for damages due to pain and suffering. In a letter dated October 11, 1878, Benjamin Harrison wrote, "I expect I will have to go to Cin[cinnati] sometime this month to try that case for the stealing of my father's body. You know how I dread to go over the details of that horror again." The trail is cold as to the outcome of the litigation, which likely went on for years. Nothing was reported in the papers, and court records were destroyed by fire in 1884.

Despite no criminal action, the plundering of John Scott Harrison's grave did have an impact. Less than two years after the event, Ohio passed legislation that helped push the grave-robbing trade into extinction. The law, which revised an 1877 statute, significantly increased the penalties for body snatching and for receiving stolen bodies. It also provided a wider circle of legitimate sources for cadavers that could be accessed by medical schools.

Charles O. Morton, the infamous resurrectionist whose real name was Henri Le Caron, was a physician who started his body-snatching career while a student at the Detroit Medical College. He began his business by selling cadavers to the University of Michigan. He later formed a partnership with his brother, Henry, and a friend, Thomas Beverly. The three men contracted to provide bodies for dissection to an Ann Arbor–based firm called A. H. Jones and Company. When he was indicted in the Harrison case, Charles O. Morton had shipped to A. H. Jones sixty bodies on a seventy-count order. Arrested in Toledo, Ohio, Morton was jailed but escaped before he was brought to trial. Morton's life after his career as a resurrectionist remains a mystery.

STOLEN

Frank Norfleet

From Chump to Chastiser

Midway on the north–south route, between the West Texas cities of Amarillo and Lubbock, sits the incorporated town of Hale Center. Named for its location in the geographic center of Hale County, the 1.1-square-mile municipality—population 2,253 persons in the 2010 census—boasts the semiarid climate of the high plains. Summers are hot. Winters are cold. Vistas are wide. Dust is prevalent. So is mud.

On the grounds of Hale Center's town hall stands a marker, a plaque in honor of J. Frank Norfleet, a man who epitomized the American West's mythologized cowboy-turned-lawman in every way but one: appearance. Frank was not tall or lanky. He wasn't even close, in looks, to the Gary Cooper sheriff in High Noon, *though he did share that lawman's values when it came to personal integrity and decency and loathing for corruption. The final paragraph of the Hale Center marker summarized the situation that catapulted J. Frank to fame. It reads:*

> *In 1919, while in Dallas, Norfleet was swindled out of $45,000 by a bunco game. Enraged at losing his savings, he spent almost five years searching the United States, Mexico, Canada, and Havana, Cuba, for the five thieves. His determination won him the nickname of "Little Tiger." After the capture, which reportedly netted about seventy-five other confidence ring members, he wrote* Norfleet, *a book about his adventures.*

Ironically, it was Norfleet's stature, and his virtues, which cemented his status as a mark for the con men who made his reputation.

John Franklin Norfleet as a young man. Though his height was a modest five-foot-five, his spirit was large and his actions were bold.

BY HIS OWN PROUD ADMISSION, J. FRANK WAS AS UPRIGHT AS A WELL-placed fence post. "I don't drink, chew tobacco, smoke, cuss, or tell lies. The last is the most important. I never tell a damn lie."Those self-imposed virtues—applauded by his church friends and fellow ranchers—were also prized by fraudsters hunting for a patsy. Norfleet was a man whose hand-shake on a land purchase or livestock sale was as good as the signature on his marriage license. As 1919 unfolded, J. Frank was a comfortable man—from finances to family—respected in his community and trusted in his business dealings. He had confidence in himself, in his common sense, and his business acumen. His firm self-assurance made J. Frank the kind of chump beloved by scammers. He was a man of integrity and high ideals who believed he had a sixth sense when it came to the integ-rity of others. Bunco operators could spot a mark like J. Frank a mile off, the way a high-flying, cruising eagle spots a tasty rabbit skittering over the ground.

Standing a full five-foot-five with his boots on, the mustachioed Norfleet looked unassuming. His bowed legs signaled long years in the saddle while the pant cuffs tucked into his boots screamed rube. In the polite environs of Dallas, J. Frank was the walking embodiment of a rus-tic, unsophisticated visitor. On the day his fleecing began, he arrived at the St. George Hotel with a bundle of cash from a recent sale of mules that had reaped a tidy profit. J. Frank was in the city with a chunk of money to offer as a down payment for ten thousand acres of choice land owned by a nearby cattle baron, Captain Dick Slaughter. The remainder of the land's sale price would come when Norfleet sold a two-thousand-acre parcel of his own farmland.

The rancher from Hale Center arrived in the city primed to do busi-ness. What he didn't know that November day when he walked into that hotel lobby is that two men—Reno Hamlin and W. B. Spencer—were tracking his every move. They, too, had come to Dallas to do business. While Norfleet may have looked a bit rustic, he wasn't a bumpkin stand-out. Reno Hamlin had preselected the rancher by doing reconnaissance work earlier. He trolled the train station and hotels listening to conversa-tions and peeking at lobby registers and receipts. His victim had to be a visitor from a smaller city or town, in Dallas on business. Of course, it would have to be a man, since men typically made all pocketbook decisions without consultation. Women rarely controlled the purse strings or made big-purchase decisions on their own. The victim must also be prosperous, able to procure tens of thousands of dollars within a couple of days without going through a bevy of bankers, accountants, and lawyers. A self-made man who was confident he had an eye for opportunity was best. Also, he should be unfamiliar with the intricacies of the stock market.

Norfleet had risen to the top of Hamlin's potential hit list. The man from Hale Center was tagged before he ever stepped into the St. George.

Reno Hamlin introduced himself to Norfleet in the lobby using a false name. A beefy-necked, thickset man with a square head, Hamlin was dressed similarly to J. Frank. Slightly overwhelmed by his surroundings, Norfleet saw in Hamlin a kindred spirit, and they fell into easy conversation. It wasn't long before Hamlin played the opening gambit of the con. He told Norfleet he was interested in purchasing a carload of mules. Norfleet, who raised mules, jumped on the comment, and without missing a beat, the two men agreed on a deal: "Hamlin would buy a shipment of them, as well as two freight cars of kafir corn and maize." It was the start of a beautiful friendship—at least that's what J. Frank believed.

A jubilant Norfleet, now eager to disclose his business chops, gave Hamlin the rundown on the land deals that had brought him to the city. This detail allowed Hamlin to move the con forward. Enter bunco man number two, W. B. Spencer. On a cue from Hamline, Spencer, who was waiting outside the St. George, walked into the lobby. Hamlin hailed his partner and presented him to Norfleet as his friend. Using a fake name, Spencer introduced himself as a purchasing agent for the Minneapolis-based Green Immigration Land Company. This was Hamlin's cue to promote Norfleet's farm acreage. He suggested Spencer ought to acquire the land for his company.

Attired like a city slicker in a suit that accentuated his "finely etched features, his curly hair swept back off his brow as if he were facing the wind of the future," Spencer played it cool. After listening to Hamlin's spiel, he offered a courteous "maybe," but appeared disinterested. It was the old hard-to-get ploy, used in both love and business, which invited pursuit. It worked like a charm.

J. Frank Norfleet didn't blink and didn't excuse himself. He wanted to know more about this newcomer. The men agreed to meet the following day.

Norfleet was on the hook. Phase two of the operation was in the offing.

The next morning, Spencer told Norfleet he had changed his mind about purchasing the land, as another deal had evaporated. He used this lost land approach for a couple of reasons—it would tamp down any suspicions as to why he changed his mind and it reinforced Spencer's image as a businessman familiar with the ups and downs of dealmaking. Spencer then made a show of sending a telegram to Green Immigration with details on Norfleet's acreage. The possibility of a land sale was music to Norfleet's ears. Next, Spencer invited the rancher to share a double room with him at the Jefferson Hotel. He pointed out that the move would save money. The flattered and frugal Norfleet accepted. He liked Spencer.

So far, the con was moving along without a hitch. It was time for the next play—a telegram to Spencer from his nonexistent boss, Garrett Thompson. The faux communication instructed Spencer to bring Norfleet to the Adolphus Hotel in Dallas the next day to meet Thompson.

The day after Norfleet moved into the Jefferson with Spencer, Hamlin left. His job done, he was out of the game, the mule-buying caper forgotten like yesterday's news. The bunco men had deftly turned Norfleet's attention to his potential land sale. Spencer was now Norfleet's companion. As directed, the two men went to the Adolphus Hotel, where they were to meet Spencer's elusive boss. The game continued. Spencer left Norfleet seated in the lobby while he sallied over to the front desk to inquire about Garrett Thompson.

A few minutes later, Spencer returned to where Norfleet was seated, distracted him, then slipped a wallet under his chair cushion. When Norfleet felt something pressed against his thigh, he discovered the billfold stuffed with cash, a bond note, and a cipher code card. Papers in the wallet identified the owner as Mr. J. B. Stetson.

Joe Furey—considered the cleverest bunco artist in the nation—played the part of J. B. Stetson. After checking at the front desk, Spencer and Norfleet went to Furey's room and returned the missing wallet. Pretending relief, Furey offered each man a reward of $100. The upstanding rancher gave an angry refusal, exactly as Furey had expected. It was the opening he needed to draw Norfleet deeper into the con.

In his Stetson role, Furey posed as a stockbroker in town to place orders for his company on the Dallas exchange. He told Norfleet he would invest the rebuffed $100 reward and see what came of it. Spencer handed over his reward money as well. Furey hurried off to the exchange leaving the men in his lavish room. He returned in less than an hour. As Furey strode into the suite, he declared, "This is what your $100 made for you," and waved $800 in Norfleet's direction before offering him the money.

If Norfleet took the cash, it was a sure tell that he believed Furey was on the level. It also meant Norfleet rationalized gambling on stock trades like gambling in a poker game. This was important because if J. Frank believed a shady deal had gone down, the con would fold. Norfleet took the money. He and Spencer, as they left the hotel room, agreed to meet Furey the next afternoon.

The following day, before meeting with Furey, J. Frank unwittingly took a step that tied him tighter to the con. Buoyed by his $800 windfall, he paid a visit to Captain Dick Slaughter's representative and put a $5,000 cash deposit on the Slaughter land. He signed a promissory note for the outstanding balance of $90,000 to be paid in ninety days. This meant Norfleet had to quickly sell his other property to pay the note.

Later in the day, when he and Spencer met with Furey, the fake stockbroker took the next step in his bunco playbook. He invited the men to take a tour with him of the Dallas Cotton Exchange. J. Frank was impressed with the operation, never realizing that *cotton* was the only commodity traded at the exchange. Furey banked on this ignorance.

On the tour, con man number four, E. J. Ward, entered the drama. He was introduced to Norfleet and Spencer as the secretary of the exchange. As part of the con, Ward politely told the two men that since they weren't members, they couldn't stay. Mission accomplished, Furey left with Norfleet and Spencer in tow, and the three men returned to Furey's room at the Adolphus.

Furey's next move cemented Norfleet's fate. Using an unctuous tone, he asked Norfleet and Spencer if he could place orders on the exchange using their names. He explained that it would look suspicious if he, a broker for another organization, made trades for himself. Like a nagging conscience, Norfleet asked if it was an aboveboard proposition. Furey, no surprise, said it was. Norfleet and Spencer agreed to the deal, and with that, Furey did the paperwork, went to the exchange, and placed the orders. When he returned, he brought with him what appeared to be $68,000 in cash, neatly rolled and banded. This was the payoff, Furey implied, from the savvy stock bets he had made—bets he had made in the names of Norfleet and Spencer.

Norfleet took his cut, a cool $28,000, without counting it. Had he looked, he likely would have found that a few hundred-dollar bills were coiled around wads of newsprint. But he went on faith, and along with Spencer, rolled his loot in a newspaper. The two men were about to leave Furey's hotel room when the door was thrown open and a scowling E. J. Ward stepped across the threshold.

Ward, as secretary of the exchange, explained that the orders Furey had placed were improper, as neither Norfleet nor Spencer were exchange members. Ward then confiscated their money. He told the men he would hold the cash in his safe at the exchange. To get their money out of hock, they must show up in Ward's office with a cool $70,000 to demonstrate they were creditworthy and *could* have covered trading losses had they occurred.

Ward left. Furey apologized. Norfleet was dumbfounded but fell for the "creditworthy" line. Having bet no money of his own up to this point, Norfleet could have walked away without any real loss. What the bunco men counted on is that he wouldn't turn his back on a windfall, just as he hadn't walked away from the $800.

Furey suggested the men pool their resources to come up with the $70,000 Ward was demanding. Norfleet said he could find $20,000. Furey and Spencer agreed they could find the other $50,000. The men planned to meet in three days with cash in hand, and on that stipulation, Furey left.

To secure his share, Norfleet returned to Hale Center, a trip Spencer insisted on taking with him. Spencer used the excuse the trip would allow him to appraise the land J. Frank wanted to sell to the Green Immigration Land Company. This was bogus, of course. Spencer had to go with

Norfleet to keep an eye on him and make sure he didn't drop out of the scheme.

On his first day at Norfleet's ranch, Spencer made a show of scrutinizing the land and sending a favorable report to his company. On day two in Hale Center, Spencer told Norfleet he had approval from the company to offer slightly more than $100,000 for the acreage.

Elated with the *promised* offer, Norfleet got a bank loan for $20,000. Money in hand, the men returned to Dallas on day three to meet Furey, but he wasn't there. Instead, there was a telegram from him that directed the Spencer and Norfleet to meet him in Fort Worth. "The next morning," Norfleet wrote in his autobiography, "we went to the Terminal Hotel to see Stetson [Joe Furey]. He was deciphering what looked like coded messages. This was part of his stockbroker charade. "He [Furey] would often give stock quotations," Norfleet wrote, "before they were printed in the daily papers . . . he always quoted them right . . . convincing me that he had advance information."

What happened next was predictable: The men combined their cash. Norfleet now had a chunk of his own money in the game.

The finale moved quickly. After making a show of decoding instructions from his home office, Furey claimed he had a sure stock bet. He wrote out the directions and sent Spencer with the $68,000 that was supposed to ransom the Dallas money, so they could place the order before the Fort Worth stock market closed. Spencer returned with the receipt. Furey feigned despair and cried, "Spencer, you have ruined us. You have lost every dollar that we have, and that we had coming to us. I could knock your head off." Spencer supposedly had *bought* rather than *sold* the selected stock as Furey directed. Spencer sobbed. Furey relented and said he would try to rescue the situation. It was all a sham.

Hurrying from the hotel room, Furey soon returned with a haul of $160,000. He said he had hedged the deal Spencer had made. Norfleet's supposed cut of $28,000 from the Dallas deal had now swelled to $45,000.

But wait! Con man number five was about to enter the action.

That evening, Charles Gerber, another player in the swindle, showed up at Furey's hotel room. He posed as the secretary of the Fort Worth exchange. He went through the spiel of Norfleet and Spencer being nonmembers. Gerber confiscated their earnings. He said he wouldn't give it back until the men had come to his office with $80,000, the amount they *would have* needed if the order had turned sour. Gerber left. Spencer, Furey, and Norfleet put their heads together. They would pool their money. Déjà vu.

Norfleet went home to raise more cash. He borrowed $25,000 from his brother-in-law and then returned to Fort Worth, this time with a revolver. His trust was frayed—finally. The three men gathered once more in Furey's room, this time at Fort Worth's Westbrook Hotel. They had $70,000, a mere $10,000 shy of the $80,000 they needed. Spencer offered to go to Austin the next day, sell some Liberty bonds, and wire the money to Norfleet.

Meanwhile, Furey would go to Dallas with the cash in hand to ransom their $68,000 from the Dallas exchange. When Spencer's $10,000 reached him, he'd have enough to rescue their money from the Fort Worth exchange. It sounded like a plan. But that evening, something—a gesture, a word, a look—convinced Spencer and Furey to search Norfleet's belongings while he was out running an errand. They found the revolver concealed in his overcoat and removed both coat and gun from the room. The bunco boys were now wise to Norfleet's suspicions.

The next morning, Furey and Spencer played the con very, very carefully. When Norfleet announced his overcoat was gone, they said nothing. When Norfleet stated he needed to run another quick errand, neither went with him. When Norfleet returned from his errand, the swindlers were wary.

The dénouement began in Furey's room. Norfleet wanted a change of plan. Furey held his breath as the man continued. J. Frank no longer wanted to hand all the cash to Furey. Instead, he wanted to wait until all the money was in hand. The men would visit the Dallas and Fort Worth exchanges *together*. Furey brushed off what he thought was merely a suggestion, wrapped the money in a newspaper, and said they would go forward with the original plan. Norfleet got angry. Furey held his ground and left the room. At the elevator, Norfleet caught up to Furey, shoved a gun in his side, and said, "You are going back to the room to settle this matter or this will be as good a place as any to settle it." Furey pleaded, "Don't do anything rash, for God's sake. I will go back to the room."

Norfleet shared two versions of the next bit of melodrama. In the first, Furey and Norfleet return to the room. Furey throws down the money, tells Norfleet to "go to blazes," and dares him to take the cash. After a quick mental calculation, the hapless Norfleet realized that even with all the money, he would still be $20,000 short on the Slaughter debt, and he would be unable to bail out his money in Dallas and Fort Worth. He backes off.

In his memoir, Norfleet described a more dramatic scene: The two men go back to the room, where Norfleet waves his gun, acquired that morning, threatening destruction if Furey and Spencer don't admit they were in cahoots. Furey throws the money *and himself* down on the bed. Spencer moves to stand behind a chair. Norfleet turns the gun on Spencer. The young man drops to his knees, grabs a Bible, and swears on his mother's head that he's not a crook. "I never did nor never will prove false to you and that I never did see this man before I met you," sobs Spencer. Furey hops off the bed and, wrote Norfleet, "[gives] me the grand hailing sign of distress of a Master Mason." Based on that bit of theatrical display, Norfleet pockets his revolver. He doesn't wish to harm a brother Mason. Crisis over.

Norfleet believed Furey had lied about the money but not about being a Mason. Curious.

The game continued. Tempers cooled.

Furey devised another plan. Spencer and Norfleet would go to the local express office—think Western Union—where a $30,000 installment from the Green Immigration Land Company awaited. It was the company's first payment on Norfleet's land. The money would have to be held in a safe deposit box until the attorney for the land company verified the title, but that could happen the next day. Spencer would then go to Austin to sell his bonds. Norfleet and Furey would meet at the Cadillac Hotel in Dallas the next day. Together they would go to the exchange with the $70,000 and ransom as much of their stock earnings as possible.

For some unfathomable reason, this altered plan satisfied the desperate Mr. Norfleet. He left the hotel room for the local telegram office with Spencer in tow. Before the two men parted they stashed the $30,000—supposedly from the land company but really sent by one of Furey's accomplices—in a safe deposit box. The sting operation was complete. Furey got the first train he could out of Texas. Spencer wasn't far behind.

Poor Norfleet didn't fully comprehend the game until the next morning when he arrived at the Cadillac and learned there was no Mr. Stetson, aka Furey, registered. It was the beginning of a long day. No Furey. No Spencer. No cash in a safe deposit box. No E. J. Ward, secretary of the Dallas exchange. No Charles Gerber, secretary of the Fort Worth exchange. "Sickening fear choked me. . . ." Norfleet wrote. "Forty-five thousand dollars gone! Ninety thousand dollars in debt! Fifty-four years old. The knowledge paralyzed me then shook me like an earthquake, crumbling my castles into ashes about my feet." He'd lost the equivalent of more than $2 million in today's dollars.

If the story stopped here, this would be just another cautionary tale, a reminder that when an honorable but naive man betrays his values, it can lead to severe consequences. But this con had a much longer shelf life. Norfleet was not your standard-issue patsy. The experience of being played left him short on money but long on reprisal.

When he got back to Hale Center, J. Frank was determined to get justice. He told his wife, Eliza, "I want to go after those crooks myself. I want to go get them with my own wits and gun." Her reply revealed that she knew her husband well. "Of course you do. I'll take care of the ranch. You just go and get those good-for-nothing crooks. And remember, Frank, bring them in alive. Any fool can kill a man." Norfleet, a crack shot, left his ranch with his revolvers in December 1919. But his wife's caution turned his thoughts away from a Western melodrama. He was hell-bent on catching the five con men with his wits, not violence.

When you read the next act in J. Frank's saga, it's easy to imagine him telling his tale with a wink and a nod. Or maybe not. What's difficult to reconcile is how serendipity suddenly shifted in Norfleet's favor. It took five years, and a boatload of lucky coincidences, before Joe Furey and his four conspirators were all behind bars.

The outrageous luck started almost immediately.

Soon after he returned home from Dallas, Norfleet confessed his foolishness to the press. He had a hunch that a newspaper story might bring him leads, and maybe spare another businessman from a costly embarrassment. His next step was to plan where and how to track the culprits. In a conversation with his wife, she mentioned that when Spencer had visited to appraise their land, he had talked about his travels across the country. One state she said he never mentioned was California. Eliza speculated that meant the gang's hideout was in the Golden State. But why?

If the Eliza incident was true, J. Frank never explained the logic she used to reach her conclusion. Still, he got on it like a bear going after honey. Within hours, he boarded the train to California. His approach was simple: He would search for his prey by working his way north from his first stop in the state, San Bernardino. On Christmas morning, 1919, J. Frank went to the sheriff's office in that town. There, he met with Walter Shay and poured out his story. The sheriff handed him a gift. It just so happened he had Charles Gerber and E. J. Ward locked up in adjoining cells. It seems that a Texan named Cathey was in San Bernardino on business when he read about the Norfleet swindle. Cathey immediately knew the business venture that had brought him to California was a scam run by the same men who had stripped Norfleet of his money. Cathey located the nearest police officer, told his story, and brought him back to the hotel where he was staying. Alas, Cathey had been spotted by the swindlers talking to the cop. They made a run for it. Furey and Spencer got away, but Sheriff Shay arrested Gerber and Ward at the train station. Two down, three to go.

Norfleet's next target was Joe Furey, but first, he returned by rail to Fort Worth to appear in front of a grand jury for indictments on Ward and Gerber, ensuring their extradition to Texas. More luck! On the train ride from California to Texas, he fell into conversation with a lovely lady who was on her way to Florida. After hearing about Norfleet's woes, she promised to keep an eye out for the three swindlers who were still at large. And wouldn't you know it, she was a retired detective.

There's more. After Norfleet got off in Texas, the ex-detective sent him a message. She had spotted a man on the train that fit Furey's description. Through a little casual eavesdropping, she learned he was on his way to Miami, with a layover in Jacksonville, to "play the game." Norfleet was ecstatic. He convinced the Texas authorities to deputize him and issue an arrest warrant for Furey. Once he accomplished those tasks, he headed to

Florida taking his guns, disguises, court order, and newly minted deputy sheriff credentials with him. He was sure his quarry was in Jacksonville.

Unfortunately, the lucky clue didn't pan out. Furey was not in Jacksonville. He wasn't in Tampa, St. Augustine, or St. Petersburg. Norfleet got a tip Furey might be in Key West. When he arrived on the island, Norfleet told the local cops why he was in town and who he was tracking. But he spoke to the wrong officers. They were on the take and tipped off Furey. He got away.

Norfleet thought Furey's next stop might be Cuba, so he rented a boat and made his way to Havana, stopping at every island on the route. Nothing. After the Cuba goose chase, Norfleet got word he needed to return to his ranch, which was being kept afloat, barely, by his wife. He ended 1919 in Texas.

In the spring of 1920, Norfleet got another slim clue as to Furey's whereabouts. It started with a snatched seal fur coat in San Antonio, which led to the arrest of a pretty female shoplifter who then spilled the beans about the guy who had given her the jacket. When Norfleet read about this caper in the newspaper, he went to San Antonio and interviewed

This photo of Hale County Deputy Sheriff J. Frank Norfleet, on the left, was taken sometime between the years 1921 and 1924. He's standing next to W. H. Mercer, secretary to Senator Earle Bradford Mayfield, who served in both the Texas State and US Senates.
COURTESY OF THE LIBRARY OF CONGRESS PRINTS AND PHOTOGRAPHS DIVISION

the woman. She described a man who sounded like Furey. She said she met him around Christmas of 1919. He was shopping for gifts in San Antonio. Norfleet had a hunch Furey might have sent those presents to his wife. From this conjecture, he checked local shipping offices and discovered a manifest with the right date for a package sent to California. Norfleet took down the address and boarded a train for the West Coast. He visited Los Angeles, where he found Furey's wife, and San Francisco, where he found the con man's mistress. What are the odds this would be the outcome of a chance arrest in another state?

Anyway, armed with warrants and papers attesting to his temporary deputy status, Norfleet checked in with local police. This time, as had happened in Florida, he revealed himself and his business to a couple of corrupt Los Angeles detectives on Furey's payroll. They double-crossed Norfleet. (He got the last laugh a few years later when the LA Police Department decided to clean house, and Furey's crooked cops landed in prison.) Furey escaped Norfleet once again.

J. Frank left California for Texas empty-handed. Back in Hale Center, he resumed his ranching duties. The trail had gone cold, but luck didn't abandon him for long. Close to Christmas 1920, J. Frank got a tip that Furey was back in Florida, this time in Jacksonville. Norfleet purchased train tickets for himself and his son, Pete. When they arrived at their destination, the two men prowled the city. Luck, luck, luck. They spotted Joe Furey in a café near the hotel where he was staying. After a brawl that saw tables and patrons flying in all directions, and Furey sinking his teeth into Norfleet's hand, the local cops arrived. They arrested Furey, J. Frank, *and* Pete. At the police station, Norfleet produced his warrants and identification. The jig was up. The cops handed Furey over to Norfleet and his son, who promptly handcuffed the fugitive. With their con man in tow, J. Frank and Pete headed to the train station.

Getting the bunco gang leader to Fort Worth was another adventure. At one point, Furey dove through a train compartment window to escape his fate, but Norfleet nabbed him again. It wasn't hard. Furey had injured himself and couldn't run. On January 24, 1921, J. Frank, Pete, and a severely impaired Furey arrived in Texas. Wanted on warrants from two other states, the criminal Furey was remanded to the Tarrant County Jail.

Three of the swindlers were now behind bars. Only two were left, and one of those two, mule buyer Reno Hamlin—the guy who set the sting in motion—was soon apprehended by Norfleet and hauled to Fort Worth as well.

Four down. Now, it was E. B. Spencer's turn to be in Norfleet's crosshairs.

Between testifying at trials, talking to the press, and giving interviews to magazines, Norfleet, from clues, intuition, and dumb luck, tracked Spencer through Utah and Montana, then to Spencer's hometown of Kingston, Ontario. Spencer managed to stay a step ahead of his stalker. From Canada, Norfleet traced his prey back to the States. While in Canada, he contacted the authorities in Montreal and learned that Spencer had been arrested and booked but then released. But, they had an updated photo of the man, which they sent to Norfleet, who made copies. He handed out the pictures like Halloween candy every place he stopped as he trailed Spencer. The stubborn old Texan finally chased his quarry back to Texas but Spencer eluded him.

Leader of a notorious bunco gang, Joe Furey met his match in Norfleet. Furey was a master at staying out of jail, mostly by paying off cops to give him protection and information. But the one lawman he couldn't corrupt was the upright Deputy Sheriff Norfleet.
COURTESY OF BLONGERBROS.COM

While looking for Spencer in Texas, Norfleet got a tip from an identity expert in the Salt Lake City Police Department. A guy sat in the
Salt Lake City jail booked under another name, but George Chase, the
ID specialist, was confident the detainee was Spencer. He based his conclusion on the photo Norfleet had sent to police stations all around the
country. In October of 1923, Chase contacted Norfleet, who immediately
made his way to Salt Lake. And there he was—W. B. Spencer, booked on
narcotics charges as A. P. Harris. When Norfleet confronted him, Spencer broke down and admitted his guilt. Spencer's wife, who was visiting
her husband, sobbed. In Norfleet's account, Spencer comforted her by
declaring that he'd "rather die and go to hell tonight than live as I have
since I met Norfleet. Every knock on the door, every telephone bell, every
stranger in the night has raised hell with my nerves."

It was over. Five for five. J. Frank Norfleet had more than lived up
to his press nickname, Boomerang Sucker. In the four years and 30,000
miles that elapsed from the moment he swore to apprehend his swindlers, Norfleet had spent a total of $18,000. It paled against the estimated
$80,000 the bunco boys had spent trying to dodge him.

Once J. Frank returned to Hale Center for good, he confronted a
farm and livestock operation in disarray, saddled with a mortgage that
had ballooned, and an income that had plummeted. But, the rancher was
a changed man. He was no longer a Texas cowboy. He was a Texas celebrity. His book, *Norfleet: The Actual Experiences of a Texas Rancher's 30,000-
Mile Transcontinental Chase After Five Confidence Men*, was published in
1924. It got rave reviews; that is, Norfleet, the man, got rave reviews. As
the *Dallas Morning News* put it, "Norfleet himself stands out to readers of
the book in a vital and memorable clearness . . . he contains the germ of
a legendary hero that may someday develop to the proportions of a Jesse
James or even a Robin Hood."

For the next forty years of his life, J. Frank never passed up an opportunity to secure his status as a legend—in print, on the vaudeville stage,
through lecture tours, and yes, by continuing to nab criminals. He even
produced and starred in a film based on his exploits, but it never made it
to the silent, silver screen.

In 1922, Joe Furey, a model inmate who organized the largest Sunday school class seen to that point in the Huntsville Penitentiary, died in the prison's insanity ward either from cancer or at the hands of another inmate. For years, rumors circulated that his death was a hoax. The warden at Huntsville, to silence the stories, had the body disinterred. Official reports corroborated that poor old Joe Furey was in the coffin. Rumors continued anyway.

E. J. Ward, convicted and sentenced in May 1920, committed suicide in a Washington, DC, jail in November 1920. Texas had released him on a $25,000 bond, pending an appeal, but Ward wasn't free long enough to turn around before extradition sent him to the nation's capital, where he was tried and convicted on separate charges of fraud. Following his suicide, Ward's Texas appeals hearing, scheduled for February 1921, was struck from the court docket.

W. B. Spencer was granted a pardon in 1927 by Texas governor Miriam "Ma" Ferguson. He was one of 3,700 convicted felons pardoned by the erstwhile governor during her two years in office, "reportedly in exchange for bribes priced in accordance with the severity of the crime."

J. Frank Norfleet died peacefully in his bed on October 15, 1967. At 102 years of age, he had survived one helluva long and rollicking rodeo.

Klaus Fuchs

Explosive Secrets

Seventy years after the United States blew up the Japanese cities of Hiroshima and Nagasaki with nuclear bombs, poet David Krieger published a collection of poems in March of 2015 entitled Wake Up! *President of the Nuclear Age Peace Foundation, Krieger's poem "Archeology of War" describes the years of war numbing people and grinding them down. Such was the state of the world when Klaus Fuchs was arrested for espionage.*

Fuchs's saga has been told and retold, deconstructed and reconstructed hundreds of times. His arrest revealed the sharp rifts between the British and American intelligence communities when it came to matters of espionage. While the United States was the world's biggest superpower in 1949, Americans remained anxious, indignant that other nations seemed unmoved by this dominance, "unwilling," as British observer Godfrey Hodgson put it, "to be molded by it."

IN THE LATE 1940S, THE IDEA OF US GOVERNMENT AGENCIES BEING infiltrated by cagey, subversive communists was an old trope, one regularly used to smear Franklin D. Roosevelt's New Deal policies and programs. It wasn't surprising, then, that Harry Truman and Joseph McCarthy invoked the old bogeyman again when they scrambled for explanations about growing communist influence in the postwar world and Russian weaponry achievements. When Fuchs was arrested in February 1950 for passing atomic secrets to the Soviets, he'd been in the espionage business for nearly a decade. The saga of how he was finally nabbed started with a decision based on uncertainty.

Russia, though a necessary partner of Britain and the United States in World War II, was never trusted. In early 1943, Colonel Carter W.

Clarke, Chief of Special Branch, Military Intelligence, ordered the initiation of a small, special project code-named "Venona." Clarke didn't trust Joseph Stalin. He worried the Soviet Union would sign a separate peace agreement with Hitler. If that happened, Germany would be free to concentrate all of its firepower on Britain and the United States. The Venona Project was Clarke's answer for keeping an eye on the dodgy Russians, although the war would be quite thoroughly over before the project showed solid results.

American mathematician and cryptanalyst, Gene Grabeel of the US Army's Signal Intelligence Service, headed Venona, which was officially implemented on February 1, 1943. The goal was simple and daunting—crack the code used by the Soviets for sending encrypted messages. A small cadre of crackerjack code hackers went through piles of intercepted cipher messages transmitted between New York and Moscow. The cache included sensitive as well as mundane messages.

Unfortunately, the resources allocated to Venona were limited. It took until 1947 before the Russian code was sufficiently understood to allow for messages to be deciphered with a high degree of certainty. Every document from the war years that was decipherable was broken down. Sensitive information related to the Anglo-American nuclear weapons program was revealed in forty-nine of the decoded messages. Klaus Fuchs's name was in the mix of scientists associated with clandestine activities. A German-born, naturalized British citizen, Fuchs's talent as a theoretical physicist took him to A-bomb Central: Los Alamos, New Mexico—heart of the Manhattan Project.

A British police photo of Klaus, taken in 1940 when he was detained as a German refugee, shows a young man, clean-shaven, wearing round-framed, horn-rimmed spectacles and dressed in a suit jacket, shirt, and tie. He looked a decade younger than his twenty-nine years. But what's startling is how much he looks like what he was—a science nerd. Maybe it's the high forehead, which his combed-back hair emphasized, or his slightly pursed lips that leave the impression of a sensitive, inquisitive man whose brain rarely engaged with life's daily minutiae. Fuchs's appearance of gentle bewilderment elicited a nurturing response from women, especially the wives of his colleagues. He simply does *not look* like a spy.

British police photo of Klaus
Fuchs taken in 1940 when
the young German physi-
cist was sent to a detention
center in Quebec, Canada.
He was labeled as an enemy
alien.
COURTESY OF WIKIMEDIA
COMMONS

This contrast between the man and his actions was not lost on Sir
Percy Sillitoe, former director-general of Britain's domestic counterintelligence service, MI5. "[W]atching that unassuming, unimpressive figure
[Fuchs] in court, I was shocked and appalled. This single foolish individual had, by a curious trick of fate, found himself in a position to alter
the whole balance of world power." Sir Percy engaged in hyperbole when
it came to Fuchs and a complete makeover of the world's power politics
since the scientific community believed it was " within Russia's capabili-
ties and natural resources . . . to produce the atomic bomb without any
information whatever from . . . the West." But Fuchs had shared information that was important. Learning that a theory had been successfully
operationalized was valuable intel when it came to weapons technology. And the same scientists that agreed Russia would have developed
a nuclear bomb with or without Fuchs's information also said that his
espionage likely hastened this development by one, possibly two years.

He may have been an "unimpressive figure," but he evoked a strong
response. A 1952 article about Fuchs's case that appeared in the *Saturday*

Evening Post, a mildly deceptive account authorized by MI5, harshly tagged him as "the world's worst traitor in nearly 2,000 years." Jesus had Judas. Democracy had Klaus—and like Judas, he was a zealot.

Klaus Emil Julius Fuchs was born in Germany, in the duchy of Hesse, on December 29, 1911. He was the third child of Emil Fuchs, a Lutheran pastor and theology instructor, and Else Wagner. His mother committed suicide, as her own mother had, when Klaus was twenty years old. It's telling that in his written confession for MI5 operative, William Skardon, while Klaus mentions his father and a happy childhood, there's no hint of Else anywhere in his narrative.

Emil was away at the University of Kiel when his mother died. He had transferred to that school after completing his first year at the University of Leipzig, where his political activism began. He joined the campus branch of the Social Democrat Party, the party of his Lutheran-pastor-turned-Quaker father. Then he went an extra step and joined the paramilitary arm of the organization that was meant to protect the Democrats. By 1932, convinced the Social Democrats weren't muscular enough to confront the rising Nazi Party, he joined the German Communist Party. He spilled blood for the cause in January of 1933 when he took part in street fighting against the Brown Shirts in Kiel. Fuchs was trounced and thrown into the river. Hitler's continued consolidation of power after being elected chancellor in 1932—coupled with the 1933 Reichstag fire in Berlin—convinced Klaus that being a communist in Nazi Germany was a death sentence. Hitler blamed the fire on anti-Nazi groups, with a special twist of venom for the German Community Party. The blaze became an excuse to round up and imprison thousands of real and suspected communists.

Fuchs somehow managed to escape, leaving Germany for Britain in 1933, where a Quaker family had agreed to help him get established. His first internship on the road toward becoming a star physicist was with Neville Mott, a physics professor at the University of Bristol. By 1937, Fuchs had earned his own PhD in physics. Next, he moved to the University of Edinburgh and worked under the tutelage of the revered Max Born. Klaus Fuchs received his doctor of science degree from Edinburgh in 1939. He was twenty-eight years old, and a doctor of physics twice over.

Granted a residence permit in 1938, without expiration, Klaus applied for British citizenship in 1939. The timing was rotten. By September of that year, Britain and Germany were at war. Klaus, like other German nationals residing in Great Britain, was labeled an enemy alien. He was detained first on the Isle of Wight, then deported to Quebec, Canada. A committed workaholic, regardless of space or place, Klaus managed to publish four scientific papers in collaboration with Max Born during his brief Canadian internment.

The British government, forced to hurriedly marshal the scientific talent needed for war, paid attention when Fuchs's academic colleagues pushed for his release from detention. Deciding his brainpower outweighed his enemy alien status, the authorities released Klaus on Christmas Day, 1940. In short order, he boarded a ship headed for England. On his return, the young scientist was reunited with his former mentor, Professor Born, at the University of Edinburgh. Five months later, Sir Rudolf Peierls, another German-born physicist displaced by the Nazis, tagged Klaus to join his team of brainiacs working on secret government projects. Not yet a citizen, and having been recently detained, Klaus was limited to assignments that didn't require a top-secret clearance, but that didn't stop his colleagues from consulting with him.

Klaus's membership in the German Communist Party was no secret. This information had been forwarded to British authorities by the German Gestapo, not a highly regarded source, years earlier when he had first entered the UK. Klaus also made no secret of his communist sympathies once in Great Britain. In a 2002 article for the journal, *Intelligence and National Security*, Professor Sabine Lee pointed out, "the Communists were suspected of sabotaging the war effort . . . and the British Communist Party, following the Soviet line, argued for a peace with Germany. This in itself was a significant obstacle to his [Fuchs's] employment in a war-related field."

But this obstacle disappeared in time. At first, Dr. Peierls was given approval to hire Klaus, provided "he told nothing of the nature of the work to be undertaken." When Peierls pointed out to the Ministry of Defence "that such a procedure was impractical in research work, the conditions were dropped." Necessity, in this case, was the mother of accommodation.

British authorities pushed through Klaus's security clearance, despite wartime restrictions, and granted the scientist citizenship in 1942. He signed off on the Official Secrets Act and voila, Citizen Fuchs was soon immersed in work on the highly secret Tube Alloys Project, Britain's program to build a nuclear bomb. Before long, Klaus had initiated another secret project—this one all on his own.

Jürgen Kuczynski, German-born and Jewish, was a renowned economist and dedicated communist who had fled Germany in 1936. Well-known in his field and in German political circles, with close ties to Russia, Kuczynski's fate, in Hitler's Germany, was never in doubt. He and his wife fled to England, the country where his parents and four of his sisters had relocated in 1933. He continued his work in economics and left-wing politics, a prominent personality in British Communist circles. Kuczynski and Fuchs crossed paths with each other, and soon after Fuchs was granted citizenship and a security clearance, Kuczynski put him in touch with Simon Kremer at the Soviet Embassy. Kremer was Russia's man in charge of informants. Klaus would know him only as Alexander. On their first meeting, he gave Kremer a copy of his computations on nuclear fission and uranium diffusion.

Klaus was hugely concerned about the fate of Russia. Germany had launched Operation Barbarossa, a full-scale assault with the objective of crushing Russian military capability and bringing the Soviet Union's racially "inferior" Slavic populations under Nazi leadership. In Hitler's world, the Soviet Union was regarded as the natural enemy of Nazi Germany, and a key strategic objective. By the fall of 1942, Kuczynski's sister, Ursula, code-named "Sonya," replaced Kremer as Fuchs's contact. Sonya, a member of the Soviet intelligence service, became Fuchs's handler and superior in the spy hierarchy. Sonya was later considered "one of the most successful GRU [Soviet Military Intelligence Service] spies in Britain." For the next eighteen months, Klaus passed information to Sonya. While the written material he forwarded was all his own work, he wasn't shy about discussing the different projects related to nuclear weaponry, British and American. He truly was an information gold mine when it came to Russian espionage efforts. Klaus was considered so integral to the Allies' nuclear agenda that in 1943, he was sent with a team of

British scientists to work in the United States on the top secret Manhattan Project.

American military and civilian decision-makers were convinced, early in the war, that the Germans were close to achieving the A-bomb. Once the United States officially entered the war, Allied focus on developing nuclear capability shifted from England to the States. Fuchs worked for a year in New York City as an analyst, dissecting theoretical studies. Meanwhile, Soviet intelligence had kept tabs on Dr. Fuchs's whereabouts, and between December 1943 and August 1944, a Russian operative in the states named Harry Gold became Fuchs's contact and intel courier. Gold's name would later surface in other high-profile US spy cases.

Though some of the info Fuchs passed along while working in New York was valuable, it was at his next posting that he committed what *he believed* was his worst espionage sin. From the summer of 1944 until his return to Britain in 1946, Los Alamos, New Mexico—ground zero in the A-bomb program—was Fuchs's home. It was here that he got the complete picture of how development of a nuclear bomb was actually progressing. The total depth and breadth of the intel Klaus whispered to the Russians is still hazy, but it's a good bet that everything he learned of importance in Los Alamos, he relayed to Soviet intelligence.

Reports described the diffident Dr. Fuchs as fitting in with his Manhattan Project colleagues. After his arrest, Dr. Peierls and his wife Genia recalled Klaus as "an easy person to live with: tidy, uncomplicated, quiet and helpful." Having stayed with the Peierls family for a time when he first went to work with Sir Rudolf, the couple knew Klaus as well as anyone. Dr. Edward Teller, with Klaus at Los Alamos, described the physicist as a spare talker. "In talking his spontaneous emission is very low," said Teller, "but his induced emission is quite satisfactory." Genia called Klaus a "penny in the slot person," meaning anyone who cared to talk with him had to get the conversational ball rolling. Klaus prided himself on being uber self-possessed and composed—an exemplar of controlled comportment. He ate sparingly, had no regular hobbies, and didn't care much for games or cards or regular exercise. But he was a good dancer, and a competent skier and mountaineer.

Friends depicted him as unfazed and in command even after prodigious amounts of alcohol. One anecdote that surfaced after his arrest
placed him at a party where, following "a gargantuan draught of spirits, he led the guests on a conga round the house. When it was over, he
summoned up the control again and there he was, Dr. Fuchs." Another
glimpse of the man's personality comes through in an anecdote concerning a violin. He went to the trouble of purchasing the instrument, spent
hours teaching himself to play, then put the violin away and never touched
it again. That was the end of it. He'd mastered the instrument to his satisfaction and moved on. Still, other habits reflected a nervous anxiety that
pushed past his carefully curated will. For instance, he was a chain smoker,
and when seated, would cross his legs at the knees and keep his dangling
foot in constant motion.

Fuchs returned to Britain in 1946, the Manhattan Project having
been successfully concluded—from the Allied perspective—with the
bombing of Nagasaki and Hiroshima, Japan. It wasn't until the summer of
1949 that cryptanalysts with the Federal Bureau of Investigation's Venona
Project deciphered messages labeled the "Fuchs Report." Though spying
activities from within the Manhattan Project had been suspected, this
was the first hard evidence that Soviet intelligence had penetrated the
top-secret operation.

In the deciphered communication, there was no clue as to how the
report had gotten into Russian hands. Had Klaus passed it along himself,
or was it someone else at Los Alamos who'd forwarded the information?
The FBI counterintelligence investigator assigned to follow up on the
Venona information was Robert Lamphere. Since there was no evidence
as to who had passed along Fuchs's top-secret report, Lamphere decided
to take the matter up with Kim Philby. Philby was the Washington liaison
from the British counterintelligence unit, MI6. Philby, later revealed as a
Soviet double agent, always took great interest in the code breakers' work.
He listened carefully to Lamphere's concerns on the Fuchs Report—even
though the man in question had returned to England years earlier.

Once back on British soil, Fuchs was offered and accepted a position with the newly funded Harwell Atomic Energy Research Establishment. He was an early hire. Not only did he participate in the design of

the Harwell laboratory facilities, he was also appointed head of its theoretical physics division. A research scientist to the core of his being—and a tireless worker—Fuchs was most content at Harwell. Acquaintances commented that he seemed a changed man, more thoughtful of others, and more social, a friend who readily extended himself if others needed a favor. His happiest moments were in his lab, in a facility he helped to create. The only exception to this more-relaxed persona was Klaus's near-fanatical concern for security. Colleagues noted that "he was forever going to the security officer to give him his keys for safekeeping, and he was meticulous in [the matter of locking up] documents." In fact, the opening to confront Fuchs about his suspected espionage came through Harwell security.

In October of 1949, Klaus's father, who'd survived the war and was living in Germany, was offered a teaching position at Leipzig University, located in the Soviet-controlled eastern zone. Knowing this might present an issue, given his position, Klaus reported the offer to the British security office at the Harwell complex. What he didn't know, nor did Lamphere, is that Russian intelligence was aware Klaus was being quietly investigated by the Americans. They warned Klaus's US courier that he might need to make a fast getaway. Dr. Fuchs, on the other hand, got no such heads-up.

American and British investigators continued to look for definitive proof that Fuchs was a spy, unaware that the Soviets were on to their suspicions. A break came when another decoded message referenced "a British atomic spy whose sister was then attending an American university." Investigators knew that Fuchs's younger sister, Kristel, was a Swarthmore student during the time that message was sent. It was one more damning clue pointing toward Fuchs as the traitor.

The task of confronting Klaus fell to a celebrated British intelligence investigator, James Skardon. Convinced of Klaus's guilt, but without any solid evidence pointing to him as the direct source of secrets, Skardon's goal was to beguile the scientist into a full admission of his spying activities. Using the pending move of Fuchs's father to Leipzig as the excuse for his visit, Skardon paid a call at Harwell on December 21, 1949. Once the interview with Klaus was under way, the seasoned spy-catcher realized the scientist had two vulnerabilities—a guilty conscience, and abundant affection for Harwell.

Disappointed by the Soviet Union's ham-fisted policies and practices in Eastern Europe, Fuchs had made sporadic efforts to break off his relationship with Russian intelligence. In his later conversations with Skardon, he admitted being convinced the offer to his father was a ploy to get the elderly man under Soviet control and then to force Klaus's continued cooperation. Another possibility for why Fuchs talked might have been anticipation of a nuclear arms race between Russia and the United States after the Soviets successfully tested a nuclear bomb in August of 1949.

Whatever it was that pricked his conscience, Dr. Fuchs, man of few words, talked a lot in that first meeting. Skardon thought he "seemed relieved to talk about his past, including his youthful membership in the Party." The investigator asked Fuchs if he would like to comment, perhaps, "on the existence of 'precise information' that showed he had been in contact with a Soviet agent while working as a Manhattan Project scientist in New York." But the answer to that loaded question didn't come in the first interview. In subsequent conversations, Skardon became convinced the brilliant physicist really had no clue as to the seriousness of his crimes.

Fuchs seemed to think that by being straightforward about his past spying activity, he could retain his position at Harwell—truly, "a naive overestimation of his own importance to British science." But it wasn't all that naive. Fuchs was extremely well-regarded; his contributions to Britain's nuclear program while at Harwell were substantive.

The breakthrough to a full confession came on January 24, 1950, when Fuchs began to talk—and talk. After his verbal recitation of a spy career—that spanned the years from his time on the Tube Alloys Project to early 1949—Fuchs followed up with a written statement dictated to Skardon over the course of several interviews. Throughout this process, from first to last meeting with Skardon, Fuchs, still a free man, never tried to leave the country. An escape likely would have failed anyway, since Russian intelligence had made the decision to abandon him to his fate.

In his comprehensive confession, Fuchs stated that he mostly passed on information about his own work. But while at Los Alamos, he committed what he believed was his worst transgression—he passed along detailed *technical* information about the design of the plutonium bomb. Before he was finished talking, Dr. Klaus Fuchs named names and gave plenty of specifics. On February 2, 1950, he was formally arrested. His trial was held March 1, 1950, his conviction, a foregone conclusion. The proceedings were completed in less than two hours. One witness was called: James Skardon. Convicted on four counts of espionage—which never mentioned anything specific to his Los Alamos appointment—Klaus was sentenced to a fourteen-year prison term, the maximum penalty. He got lucky, it wasn't a death sentence. British law distinguished between handing over secrets to wartime enemies and passing information to friendly countries. Though hard to remember, Russia once was a British ally—at least through most of Klaus's spy career.

Though America's intel community provided the damning bits of information that put Fuchs under British surveillance, officials were keen to keep the United States away from direct contact with the scientist. They weren't interested in giving the Americans another reason to be scornful about the protocols Britain used when vetting individuals for top security clearances. J. Edgar Hoover, certain communists were particularly scurrilous, was unabashedly contemptuous of Britain's intelligence services. He pushed the United States to forward to the UK an extradition demand for Fuchs on charges of espionage. The British denied the request. Failing to approve the extradition was seen by Hoover as one more black mark against the Brits. There was legitimate concern in American intelligence that a public trial of Fuchs would reveal the existence of the Venona Project, which in turn might jeopardize the apprehension of other Soviet spies still on American soil. Hoover, at the very least, wanted a US representative at Fuchs's trial to report back on the proceedings and listen for any testimony that might implicate Venona. Sir Percy Sillitoe's initial refusal of this request sent the FBI director into a tailspin. A flurry of calls and terse communications finally produced an agreement, and FBI Special Agent Lish Whitson attended the trial.

Klaus Fuchs's arrest caused genuine consternation and real pain for many of his colleagues at Harwell. It was a very personal sorrow to Klaus's early supporters and mentors like Dr. Peierls and Max Born. His arrest also cast a pall generally on science and academia, communities often understood by the public as breeding grounds for radical politics and sub-terfuge perpetrated by foreigners. Completely stunned, those who knew Klaus decided that he was a consummate actor. Hans Bethe, his imme-diate supervisor in the war years, said in an interview with the *Wash-ington Star* newspaper that "We were very friendly together, but I didn't know anything of his real opinions. . . . If he was a spy, he played his role perfectly." The explanation Fuchs had for his behavior was "controlled schizophrenia," which allowed him to "divide his conscience into separate compartments." This self-analysis was a balm seized on by many in the security services on both sides of the pond. It let them off the hook for their ten-year failure to uncover Fuchs's activities.

Dr. Max Born, German-born physicist and mathemati-cian received the 1954 Nobel Prize in Physics for his pioneering work in quantum mechanics.
COURTESY OF WIKIMEDIA COMMONS

Dr. Klaus Emil Julius Fuchs served nine years of his fourteen-year sentence. Released in June 1959, he renounced his British citizenship and relocated to East Germany (GDR). There, he was granted both citizenship and a position as deputy director of the Central Institute for Nuclear Research at the Helmholtz-Zentrum Dresden-Rossendorf laboratory. He became an esteemed member of the East German Academy of Sciences and participated in international scientific gatherings where he surely crossed paths with many of his former British and American colleagues. Dr. Fuchs retired in 1979, the same year he received the Karl Marx Medal of Honor, the GDR's highest decoration. It was awarded to individuals who had made outstanding contributions to the Republic's ideology, economy, culture, or science. He died at the age of seventy-six on January 28, 1988. The GDR died two years later when the former East and West German states were unified. Fuchs had the courage of his convictions and acted on them. Whether he was a traitor or a hero depends on who's conferring the label.

In 1944, Allied troops fighting their way to Berlin uncovered a cache of documents that revealed Nazi Germany had never seriously pursued a focused nuclear research program. The regime had no plans to develop an atomic bomb.

The Manhattan Project, at its height, employed 125,000 people at more than 30 locations. The cost for developing the A-bomb was at least $2 billion—more than $34 billion in current dollars. To date, only two of these bombs have been used in warfare—both by the United States of America.

Henry Wallace and Harry Truman

Dubious Dealings

Alistair Cooke, the erudite British-born American journalist, broadcaster, and avuncular host of Masterpiece Theatre, told this revealing story of his encounter with Harry Truman. They crossed paths at the Democratic National Convention on Friday afternoon, July 20, 1944. Cooke was getting something to eat at the concession stand beneath the main-floor auditorium. Next to him was a man holding a paper cup of Coca-Cola, about to take a bite of his hot dog. Cooke described Truman as having "very shiny glasses, a very pink face, almost an electric blue polka-dot bow tie, and a sky-blue double-breasted suit." An announcement from the convention podium, one floor up, cut through the buzz of the lunch stand. "Will the next vice president of the United States come to the rostrum? Will the next vice president come to the rostrum? Will Senator Truman come?" Quietly flustered, the shiny-glasses, pink-faced man muttered, "By golly, that's me!" and rushed off.

The announcement over the public address system was the mundane finish to a legendary contest that had been underway since the nation was founded. Defined by different terms in different eras, in 1944, the struggle was pitched as progressives versus conservatives—or, sometimes, socialists versus capitalists, depending on the level of drama required for the audience. Truman was squarely in the conservative camp. He would be Roosevelt's third, last, and arguably most crucial vice presidential pick. None of the Party's leaders, presidential advisors, cabinet members, or his wife expected the president to last another four years. Except for voters, political insiders knew—and savvy journalists suspected—the convention of '44 wasn't nominating one presidential candidate. It was nominating two.

Roosevelt waltzed into that convention with one partner, Henry A. Wallace, and waltzed out with another, Harry S. Truman. Combine Shakespeare's

Julius Caesar with Adrian Lyne's 1987 film, Fatal Attraction, *and you have the playbook for how the sitting vice president of the United States was dumped in 1944 by his boss. It's a tale of lust, loyalty, betrayal, hubris, and lousy timing. Politics and one-night stands have this in common: Strange bedfellows are to be expected.*

AT THE 1940 DEMOCRATIC NATIONAL CONVENTION, ROOSEVELT HAD insisted Henry A. Wallace replace John Nance "Cactus Jack" Garner as his running mate. A conservative Southern Democrat from Texas, Garner had been useful to Roosevelt in the 1932 and 1936 general elections. But Garner was hard-pressed to embrace Roosevelt's positions on organized labor and broke with him altogether over the president's attempt in 1937 to enlarge the Supreme Court and pack it with his own justices. Garner also had his own presidential ambitions. He ran against Roosevelt for the 1940 Democratic nomination and lost. When Party bosses balked at Wallace in the number-two position, Roosevelt bluntly stated that the Party would either take them both, or he would walk. What follows is a condensed answer to this question: How, in four short years, did Wallace go from being the object of Roosevelt's desire to the focus of his disgruntlement?

Henry Adair Wallace was born in 1888 into a prosperous family of farmer-businessmen. His grandfather and father produced the popular farm journal, *Wallace's Farmer,* where Henry went to work as a writer and editor after his 1910 graduation from Iowa State University. An avid researcher in hybridization, Henry founded, with the help of his wife's money—he married the wealthy Ilo Browne in 1914—the ag-related, immensely successful business, Hi-Bred Corn Company, and Hy-Line Poultry Farms. Naturally curious, Wallace didn't confine his exploration of the wider world to agricultural subjects. He was particularly interested in religious and spiritual movements, including theosophy, a controversial blend of religious philosophies and mystical beliefs with a decided occult flavor. It was a curious path for a man born and raised in the heart of conservative Middle America.

By 1933, Wallace was tapped to be the secretary of agriculture in the Roosevelt administration. It was a significant, high-profile Cabinet position in the New Deal era, and Wallace was an immensely popular figure with farmers. He was a respected member of the rural brotherhood without the taint of electoral politics. He understood farmers' struggles, and in the Great Depression, was moved to act boldly by the nation's desperate need for a cohesive approach to the agriculture industry. He manipulated prices, paid farmers to keep fields fallow, bought up surplus products to stabilize prices, and issued an order to slaughter piglets to keep pork prices from cratering. His tactics paid off. Wallace was credited with proposing and implementing policies that brought order out of chaos in the farm business.

Widely respected, even by critics, for his deft leadership of the Department of Agriculture throughout the 1930s—about 45 percent of the US population still lived in rural areas—Wallace was not well liked by many of the political bosses in the Democratic Party. For one thing, he was strictly a teetotaler; he also tried various fad diets—including a milk-and-popcorn regimen. He walked all over Washington, DC, and threw himself into sports and liberal causes, like ending hunger, with equal enthusiasm. Wallace was brainy, disciplined, unorthodox. "With an oblong face, a thick shock of gray hair, and a starchy voice, Wallace resembled a pillar of Washington rectitude from a Hollywood drama," wrote Alex Ross in a 2013 *New Yorker* article. He was Jimmy Stewart's 1939 movie character, Jefferson Smith, in the flesh. But Wallace had drawbacks that made him vulnerable to political attack. Socially awkward, he appeared obtuse. Painfully shy and inept at small talk, Wallace was handicapped in a town where gossip and vapid conversations were guzzled like champagne on New Year's Eve.

Though he eventually moved away from theosophy, his intense flirtation with the subject attracted scorn from political opponents. One unfortunate incident involved a self-styled theosophy guru named Nicholas Roerich, an artist who, with his wife, Helena, developed a doctrine called Agni Yoga. In 1934, Wallace, quite smitten with Roerich's teachings, appointed him to lead a Department of Agriculture expedition to the Gobi Desert. Alas, the guru had little interest in drought-resistant grasses and more interest in adventures with "a band of rifle-bearing Cossacks." Aside from ignoring his mission, Roerich's choice of swashbuckling

A 1934 photo of a smiling, relaxed Henry A. Wallace, US secretary of agriculture in the Roosevelt administration.
COURTESY OF WIKIMEDIA COMMONS

friends didn't sit well with the diplomatic or bureaucratic establishments. Much later, Wallace pointed to Roosevelt as the culprit behind Roerich's appointment. To his credit, Wallace recalled the expedition, and when he suspected his chosen mentor might be shady rather than inspired, he forwarded Roerich's name to the Internal Revenue Service as a possible audit subject. Hell hath no fury like a righteous man scorned.

By the late 1930s, enthusiasm for the New Deal was fading, yet Wallace remained an outspoken champion of Roosevelt's progressive policies. He offered a keen observation in 1936 that foreshadowed today's current global, environmental crisis. Capitalism, he noted, can too easily tip into an "emphasis on unfettered individualism [that] results in exploitation of natural resources," and leads to the savaging of the very essentials required for national survival. Wallace's zeal for progressive social policies, his substantial popularity with organized labor, farmers, and Black Americans, coupled with his lack of desire for the president's job, made him attractive to Roosevelt in 1940. Even when word spread through political circles of letters from Wallace to Roerich that contained some zany-sounding passages like, "Now I must live in the outer world . . . and make over my mind and body to serve as fit instruments for the Lord of Justice. . . . Yes, the Chalice is filling," Roosevelt was unconcerned. He, too, had dabbled in the mystical. He held firm on Wallace, and let it be known that if his Republican opponent, Wendell Willkie, published the Roerich letters, Roosevelt would expose Willkie's "affair with Irita Van Doren, literary editor of the *Herald Tribune*."

An unofficial truce took hold, and the boys, Franklin and Wendell, stayed in their respective corners. The 1940 ticket of Roosevelt and Wallace won the popular vote in thirty-eight states. Willkie and running mate Charles McNary prevailed in the other ten. One concern that Roosevelt, the consummate political animal, had voiced about his vice president was Wallace's lack of experience in electoral politics, and his reluctance to schmooze and compromise. Of course, Roosevelt, ever the crafty statesman, exploited that deficit when it suited his purposes, and it suited him in 1944.

Perhaps Roosevelt's disaffection for Wallace began in 1942 after Wallace gave a remarkable speech entitled "The Price of Free World Victory." Americans were in the throes of wartime angst and debate over the nation's role in shaping the future of global geopolitics. Wallace's speech was a weird mix of liberal vision—a world free of corporate greed and nationalist imperialism—laced with religious references. "The people's revolution is on the march," he said, "and the devil and all his angels cannot prevail against it." He voiced support for Roosevelt's aspirations of a world guided by the four freedoms—"freedom of religion, freedom of speech, freedom from want, and freedom from fear"—but took a swipe at Henry Luce's conceit of the "American Century." Wallace declared that it was time for "the century of the common man." The country "had an obligation to contribute to the war and to the post-war settlement." In the minds of conservatives, the reference to "common man" had a suspicious ring to it.

Wallace's lack of political acumen came to the fore when he got into a protracted struggle with Jesse Jones, secretary of commerce, in 1943. Wallace accused Jones of being a drag on the war effort with his conservative leadership on importing materials needed for wartime production. It got ugly when Wallace trashed his colleague to newspapers, stopping just short of calling Jones an unpatriotic bonehead. He accused the secretary of "obstructionist tactics . . . [that] have been of major consequence in this job of waging total war." That same charge could have been leveled against Benedict Arnold. Public feuding among his Cabinet members was the kind of drama that sat squarely on Roosevelt's last nerve. Above all else, Roosevelt was a practical politician—a coded phrase for cold, calculating, and manipulative. He only addressed a dicey situation with candor when obfuscation failed. Eleanor Roosevelt said of her husband that he "always hopes to get things settled pleasantly."

An added drawback with Wallace was his disinterest in his duties as presiding officer of the Senate. He never made time to speak with senators. "The [Senate] majority leader, Barkley, advised Henry in a friendly way 'to give more attention to his work.' Wallace, for his part, continued to give no attention to the Senate. Barkley wryly noted that, 'he [Wallace] always took my suggestions in good spirit and thanked me for them, but it never seemed to make any impression.' Wallace preferred international missions."

A 1932 photo of Franklin Delano Roosevelt with *New York Herald* reporter Louis McHenry Howe. Howe acted as a political advisor to Roosevelt starting with Roosevelt's 1920 vice presidential campaign. After Roosevelt's successful 1932 presidential bid, Howe helped shape some of the early, popular New Deal programs such as the Civilian Conservation Corps.
COURTESY OF WIKIMEDIA COMMONS

Another blow to Wallace's reputation was being well regarded by Mrs. Roosevelt. Eleanor and Franklin were estranged, linked only by convention and political necessity. Over time, what had once been Franklin's grudging respect for his wife's keen-wittedness and social conscience transformed into irritation. To some observers, it seemed evident that if Eleanor lobbied for a person or policy, her husband was sure to be against it. Perhaps that factored in to the president's decision to scrap Wallace, but if it did, it certainly wasn't at the top of the list for a man whose first consideration was ever political calculation. By 1944, Franklin Roosevelt, despite fragile health, was convinced that only he could steer the Allied cause to a conclusion and realize America's new role as the preeminent power on the planet. It was heady stuff.

The president was not in the mood to continue with a vice president he often had to defend behind closed doors. He needed his strength for the great postwar struggles to come. Exactly when the cabal started its work to unseat Wallace is difficult to isolate, but the faction was rolling by early May 1944.

Sometime before May 20: Bob Hannegan, chair of the Democratic National Committee (DNC), met with Roosevelt. Hannegan, considered a straightforward guy by his contemporaries, delivered some unwelcome news. He'd been canvassing state Party leaders in preparation for the July Democratic Convention, and had heard a lot of unfavorable chatter about Wallace. Roosevelt told Hannegan to meet with the vice president and let him know what was going on. Before Hannegan got to Wallace, Wallace got to him. "The president," he said, "told me I should talk to you." Hannegan was direct. He told Wallace that he'd spoken to Democratic leaders across the country, and they were adamant the vice president needed to be off the ticket in the upcoming election.

Wallace was taken aback and unprepared. He questioned Hannegan about who was consulted, but said little else. Hannegan left the meeting believing Wallace would let the president know he didn't want the nomination. Wishful thinking. Whatever Wallace was turning over in his mind about the vice presidency, he didn't spill it before leaving on May 20 for a nearly two-month trip to Russia and China. It had been a long time in the making, the kind of goodwill tour Wallace savored.

Friday, June 2: On this date, a crucial meeting took place that marked the beginning of the end to Wallace's bid for the vice presidency. Among the three administrative assistants to the president was Jonathan Daniels, a dedicated note-taker. He recorded Roosevelt as saying that it was well known he was for Henry Wallace even though he'd been warned that it could mean a loss of one or two million votes. Roosevelt meandered around on some other subjects but, at last, got to the point. "I think one or two persons ought to go out and meet Wallace and tell him about this feeling about his political liability." The president also made it clear in this session that Wallace, in his estimation, had been the default running mate in 1940 when the man he really, really wanted, Jimmy Byrnes, a lapsed Catholic who opted for joining his wife in the Episcopal faith, was nixed by Cardinal Spellman. This was classic Roosevelt. Put the word out to enough people and hope it might filter back to the absent subject.

If the president was counting on Wallace getting the message, it didn't work. Somewhere near this meeting, Philip Murray, head of the labor union, the Congress of Industrial Organizations—the CIO in AFL-CIO—met with Roosevelt. He strenuously advocated for Wallace, well-liked by his union members. "Murray talked, Roosevelt puffed at a cigarette and looked at the ceiling. After Murray finished, FDR said, disconcertingly, 'Oh, you are talking about the Yogi Man.'" It was a sly, revealing comment. Roosevelt had no intention of supporting Wallace.

Sometime during the week of July 2: Roosevelt brought his special counsel, Sam Rosenman, into the plot. Wallace was due back in the States from his Russia-China junket on July 9, just ten days before the start of the DNC in Chicago. The president wanted Rosenman to meet the plane in Seattle, Washington, and return to Washington, DC, with Wallace. On the trip, Rosenman was to deliver the news that the renomination of the vice president would split the Party. Roosevelt, without any evidence, told his special counsel Wallace would never want to be in the middle of that fight and surely would step down. Rosenman knew that theory was junk as soon as he got in touch with Wallace's office and tried to get on the plane. No luck. To Rosenman, that was a clear signal Wallace was *not* going to quietly fade away.

Friday, July 7: The intrigue deepened with a meeting between the president, Rosenman, and Harold Ickes, Roosevelt's interior secretary. Ickes had been at the Department of the Interior since 1933. He was mostly seen as a liberal stalwart who reliably carried out Roosevelt's New Deal vision, especially as it translated into policy and practice with American Indians. Ickes entertained the idea of becoming Roosevelt's running mate. He was happy to jump into the fray with Wallace. A man who loved political gossip, Ickes was a tough, pugnacious, burly politician with the reputation of being a Washington insider. He and Rosenman—a slender, diffident, diplomatic man—seemed a decent combo to deliver the news to Wallace as soon as he got back to the nation's capital.

It was a mean-spirited move. The man had been away for almost eight weeks, and before he could get his bearings, Rosenman and Ickes were directed to get at him. Ickes wrote in his diary that they were instructed

A 1937 photo of Harold Ickes, longest serving US Secretary of the Interior, 1933 through 1946. One of Franklin Roosevelt's first cabinet nominations, Ickes was at Interior through the New Deal era and World War II.
COURTESY OF WIKIMEDIA COMMONS

to sweeten the deal by letting the vice president know Roosevelt "would make him Ambassador to China where he would fit in well."

Monday morning, July 10: Wallace was back in Washington. He had traveled 27,000 miles in fifty-one days. Brutal. At 10:00 a.m., the vice president called the White House and got on Roosevelt's schedule for that day. His appointment with the president was at 4:30 in the afternoon, which left plenty of time for a lunch meeting with Ickes and Rosenman.

Monday lunchtime: The deadly duo failed to deliver a knockout blow to Wallace. In Wallace's version of the events, Roosevelt's emissaries were unconvincing. Wallace either didn't believe or chose to ignore the meaning of the president's plea—that though *he* wanted Wallace, it didn't look as if Wallace would win at the convention, or be of any use in the election. Ickes and Rosenman left the meeting deflated after Wallace's icy comment that he wasn't about to discuss politics when he was scheduled to meet with Roosevelt that very afternoon. The count of demoralized presidential envoys now stood at three—Hannegan, Ickes, and Rosenman.

Monday afternoon, 4:30 p.m.: Wallace was at the White House with the president, who by then had gotten the report from Ickes and Rosenman that Wallace had shut them down. True to his political nature, Roosevelt went into a circuitous bit of sidestepping when, after debriefing the president about his trip, Wallace put the question of his nomination on the table. Roosevelt cautioned Wallace that what he was about to tell him was between the two of them. He assured Wallace that he supported his nomination and would make it public. Wallace wanted a commitment that Roosevelt would make an unequivocal statement of support. Roosevelt said he would, even though it wasn't going to be popular. The president pulled out the blackmail argument that Party bosses would only go along if Roosevelt put his nomination on the line as well, Wallace was quick to interrupt—if there was a better candidate, then Roosevelt should select that person.

Roosevelt never liked being in the role of "disappointer-in-chief." He countered with an argument that it wasn't about him; it was about not wanting to see Wallace or his family embarrassed at the convention by jeers and catcalls. It was a classic romance breakup conversation straight out of high school—you mean so much to me but I know I'll just hurt you if this keeps on. Wallace wasn't having it.

Roosevelt invited him back for round two the next day. But before that, yet another emissary was launched at Wallace. On Monday evening, Senator Joe Guffey of Pennsylvania got together with Wallace and a couple of the vice president's aides. Guffey laid out the situation. Wallace was going to have an impossible time winning the nomination. Wallace didn't buy it. His aides didn't buy it. Another Roosevelt messenger joined the ranks of the defeated. Ten days and counting until Chicago.

Tuesday morning, July 11: Before Wallace's scheduled luncheon with Roosevelt, Guffey called Wallace's office, where an aide read a draft of the support letter Wallace was requesting from the president. Guffey reported to Roosevelt that the language was something like, "we have made a team which pulls together, thinks alike and plans alike." Guffey told the aide that this language wouldn't fly, but he would pass along the request. The letter Roosevelt finally wrote on behalf of his vice president didn't come close to what Wallace wanted.

Soon after Guffey's phone call, Wallace met Roosevelt for lunch. The vice president was prepared. He said that by his count, at least 290 delegates were in his camp, and a Gallup poll showed him with 65 percent support among Democratic voters. Impressed for about a nanosecond, Roosevelt countered that Party bosses had told him that in some circles, the vice president was considered a communist. The criticism didn't shake Wallace. He was happy to take on the fight. Roosevelt didn't get the response he wanted, so he invited the vice president back for lunch on Thursday, July 13. The president and vice president were now in a food fight.

That evening, the Party power brokers and the president gathered to discuss how to get rid of the unsinkable Henry Wallace. While Roosevelt's inner circle understood that the president was done with Wallace, who would take Wallace's place was still up in the air. That was one of the agenda topics for Tuesday evening's White House meeting. The assembled men included Edward Flynn, Democratic leader in the Bronx whose handsome features, refined tastes, and long history with Roosevelt gave him standing; Frank Walker, Postmaster General; Edwin Pauley, treasurer of the DNC; Bob Hannegan, chair of the DNC; George Allen, secretary of the DNC; and Chicago mayor, Ed Kelly.

After cocktails—martinis mixed by Roosevelt, who liked showing off his bartending skills—and dinner, the men retired to the Oval Office and got down to it. Though a cut above the smoke-filled back room of a saloon, the meeting participants were about the same business— managing the successful nomination of the president's choice for a run- ning mate with a minimum amount of dissension in the delegate ranks.

Two names were quickly eliminated from the vice presidential sweep- stakes: Senate majority leader Alben Barkley of Kentucky was thought too old, and leader of the House Democratic Caucus, Sam Rayburn from Texas, wasn't likely to get the support of his own delegation. Jim Byrnes, a close assistant to the president and director of the Office of War Mobi- lization, was seriously discussed. Roosevelt liked the man. That Byrnes was once Catholic turned Episcopalian didn't bother the president, but Byrnes had another strike against him. Mayor Kelly and Ed Flynn thought Byrnes's decidedly Southern segregationist background would be

A 1961 photo of Speaker of the House, Sam Rayburn a twenty-four-term Congressman in the US House of Represen- tatives representing Texas's 4th Congressional District.
COURTESY OF WIKIMEDIA COMMONS

a serious turnoff for Black voters. Byrnes had also alienated the labor vote with his refusal to entertain wage increases for workers in war industries.

Two additional names that went up and down quickly were John Winant, ambassador to London and a former governor of New Hampshire, and Supreme Court justice William O. Douglas, who was mentioned often by Roosevelt as a running mate but considered a political neophyte by the assembled politicos.

Truman's name was also put on the table. He'd been a loyal Democrat but had baggage—he'd relied on the Kansas City political boss, Thomas Pendergast, when his Senate reelection ran into trouble. Pendergast was subsequently arrested for voter fraud and other assorted felonies related to running a political machine.

As the meeting waned, Roosevelt, turning to Truman's friend, Hannegan, announced that he would go with the senator from Missouri because that seemed to be a fellow the DNC chair could get behind. Assignments for delivering the bad news to hopeful men were made—Postmaster General Walker drew Byrnes; DNC treasurer Pauley was assigned to Rayburn; and the secretary of the Senate, who wasn't present, was drafted to speak with Senator Barkley. Hannegan drew Wallace—again.

Before he left, the DNC chair got Roosevelt to write down on a piece of scrap paper that Truman was his pick. The stage was set—so long as all the players cooperated.

Wednesday, July 12: Hannegan met with Wallace, but the vice president knew what to expect. He'd been tipped off that morning. In Wallace's words, "He [Hannegan] said he wanted to tell me that I did not have a chance. He said I ought to withdraw." The infighting was about to become public. Wallace was not backing down. He let Hannegan know that if the president wanted him off the ticket, the president would have to say this to him directly. Yet everyone who worked with Roosevelt, including Wallace, knew the president always used surrogates for unpleasant tasks. This avoidance of difficult confrontations face-to-face seemed a curious trait for a man who was leading the Allied cause in a global war effort.

Thursday, July 13: Roosevelt and Wallace had lunch. The president had yet another chance to be direct with Wallace, but he wasn't. When

Wallace offered to stand down if that's what Roosevelt wanted, the president demurred. He reiterated that he just wanted Wallace to know there were concerns about his nomination. Roosevelt also hinted that he had no appetite for a fight over Wallace. Later, the vice president wrote that when he was preparing to leave, "the president 'drew me close and turned on his full smile and a very hearty handclasp,' and said, 'While I cannot put it just that way in public, I hope it will be the same old team.' As he neared the door, the president ended with, 'Even though they do beat you out at Chicago, we will have a job for you in world economic affairs.'"

Henry Wallace had transformed into a political vampire, sucking the energy from the Democratic leadership, and the only person that could truly put a stake in his heart refused to do it. Again, Wallace refused to withdraw from the race even though he knew full well that's what Roosevelt wanted. He later wrote that he knew when he got back from his Far East tour that Roosevelt "wanted to ditch me as noiselessly as possible." Instead, Wallace chose to focus on the president's words and ignore the president's wishes.

Roosevelt piled on the confusion by finalizing a letter of support for Wallace's nomination, which was sent to Senator Samuel Jackson of Indiana, permanent chair of the DNC. Granted, the letter was tepid at best, but the president's confederates acted as if they were all suffering from a kind of collective amnesia. Didn't Roosevelt at the Tuesday-evening meeting declare Truman was in and Wallace was out? The letter was a non-endorsement endorsement that stated the president didn't want to dictate to the delegates what they should do. It was their job to size up all the candidates, and while Wallace was his friend and choice, he, Roosevelt, would nonetheless abide by the delegates' decision—no matter who they chose for the vice presidency. It was a pure duck-and-cover exercise.

Friday, July 14: Byrnes also refused to go quietly into the background. He wanted the nomination. This prompted another round of web-spinning and maneuvering on the part of Roosevelt. The president appeased Byrnes. He got Byrnes to agree with him that he, Roosevelt, couldn't directly repudiate Wallace. But the president assured Byrnes that if he was the man chosen by the convention—and Roosevelt thought that would happen—well, he would be quite tickled to have him as a running mate despite his political drawbacks with Black voters. Roosevelt knew the Party leaders were not about to let a Byrnes nomination get by. But Roosevelt also slipped into his conversation that the two men who would probably have the least baggage with voters were Truman and Douglas.

This was Roosevelt at his duplicitous best. Byrnes knew precisely what that meant, but he, like Wallace, decided to go with the words and not Roosevelt's intent. He contacted Harry Truman, who he knew was on the short list, and told him the president had given him, Byrnes, the signal to go for the nomination. He asked if Truman would place his name before the convention. It was a slick move designed to knock Truman off. Byrnes knew Truman was being courted but hadn't yet agreed to run.

Friday evening: Roosevelt boarded a train on Friday evening. He was off to the West Coast, where he would board a ship for Hawaii and a meeting with Admiral Nimitz and General MacArthur to talk over strategy in the Pacific. Roosevelt would stop in Chicago but not be at the convention. Reviewing where things stood with the vice presidential nomination, Roosevelt decided two things needed to happen quickly. Insistent, pushy Byrnes had to be ousted, and Truman had to commit to being in the race. These two matters consumed the president's limited energy between Saturday, July 15, and the following Wednesday, July 19, when the convention was convened.

Saturday, July 15: On that Saturday afternoon, the DNC chair, Hannegan, met with Roosevelt on his private train car, the *Ferdinand Magellan*, which was parked in the Chicago train yard, a maze of steel and iron. It was a warm summer day, not ideal for clambering around and over hot metal tracks, but Hannegan needed to see the president. Byrnes was telling everyone he'd gotten the nod from Roosevelt to seek the nomination. Hannegan pushed the president for a straightforward answer to a simple question: Did he want the convention to go with Byrnes? His next order of business was to get some changes made, if possible, on the president's letter of support for Wallace. Finally, Hannegan needed to get Roosevelt's scrap-paper commitment to Truman typed up on White House stationery.

That same afternoon, Jimmy Byrnes was on the edge of his chair in Washington, DC, waiting for a call. He knew Hannegan and Roosevelt were meeting. Finally, Mayor Kelly got in touch with him. Kelly reported the president's words: "Well, you know Jimmy has been my choice from the very first. Go ahead and name him.'" Roosevelt had now handed Wallace a letter of support, given the nod to Byrnes, and, as yet, not spoken to Truman. Mayor Kelly directed Byrnes to come to his Lake Shore Drive house the next day, Sunday, as soon as he arrived in Chicago. There was a lot to do.

So much for poor Hannegan's bid to be released from confusion. The web master was still spinning.

Saturday evening: Byrnes boarded a train at Union Station and headed for Chicago. He avoided questions from the press about his availability as a candidate for the vice presidency. While he sidestepped one error, Byrnes made another. He got the biggest suite in the convention hotel because of his status with the wartime administration. The suite had been reserved by Edwin Pauley, manager of the convention, for the

Robert E. Hannegan calls the 1944 Democratic National Convention to order in Chicago, Illinois
COURTESY OF WIKIMEDIA COMMONS

delegation from his own state, California. Byrnes's act irritated the Party treasurer. It was not an auspicious start to Byrnes's convention stay.

Sunday morning, July 16: A cheerful Jimmy Byrnes arrived at Lake Shore Drive to breakfast and plan with Kelly and Hannegan. Between talk of signs and delegations, Byrnes got the news that the president had one *teensy-weensy* caveat regarding Byrnes's nomination. Roosevelt wanted the leaders of the CIO to give their blessing to Byrnes. Neither Hannegan nor Byrnes expected a problem. In their estimation, the request was a mere formality. The order for signs went forward.

Sunday evening: A virtual victory celebration on Byrnes's behalf was pulled together at a borrowed apartment in the city. Friends and acquaintances of the putative nominee were rounded up. The Party power brokers, Hannegan, Kelly, and Walker, were there. During a lull in the chatter, Hannegan turned to Kelly and told him about the president's desire to have labor leaders Sidney Hillman and Philip Murray give their okay to the Byrnes nomination. Within a couple of days, it was evident that this Sunday-evening dinner was the high point of Byrnes's Chicago visit.

Monday morning, July 17: Bless his heart, the happy Byrnes moved his base of operations to the Blackstone Hotel so he and Hannegan could work together to get convention delegates lined up. But another sticky issue came charging at Byrnes with the arrival of the Bronx political boss, Ed Flynn. He was livid. Byrnes would cost at least two hundred thousand votes in his city, not to mention in other cities like Chicago. He enlarged the problem to a loss of the entire election if Byrnes was nominated. And by the way, whatever happened to Truman? But the real knockout blow came later with the *formality* of Hillman and Murray. The labor vote was crucial to Roosevelt's reelection.

Monday evening: Hillman and Murray were adamant that Wallace, not Byrnes, was their guy. Hillman was especially vocal in his opposition to Byrnes's nomination. The man had scuttled wage increases for his union members. What was wrong could not be made right. Later, Byrnes wrote about his bitterness with Roosevelt. He was certain the president had used that passing line about Hillman's approval to shut down Byrnes's bid. He believed the president had betrayed him in the worst way possible—by proxy. There was no proof Roosevelt had plotted this twist, but it certainly bore the hallmarks of a Roosevelt manipulation. In his diary, Ickes recorded that Rosenman, Roosevelt's special counsel, told him the president had relied on Hillman to stop Byrnes. Hillman confirmed the story. But who knows?

Roosevelt finally sent a direct message to Byrnes on Monday evening and didn't mince words. Byrnes was a liability to the ticket. It was official: Byrnes was finished. His signs were yesterday's trash before the ink had even dried. On the call with Roosevelt and Byrnes were Hannegan, Walker, and Kelly, whom Roosevelt told to go all out for Truman.

Monday, July 17 through Wednesday, July 19: Truman was in Chicago and took the position he was not in the vice presidential race. For one thing, he didn't trust Roosevelt when it came to loyalty. The man had great strengths but was also dismissive, irascible, and short on memory when it came to who was a steadfast supporter. Hannegan told Truman he was the president's choice, but Truman was still wary. Roosevelt had been like a ping-pong ball bouncing from one name to the next. He could bounce again. Truman told his elderly aunt Ella, before he left Independence, Missouri for Chicago, "I'm going to the convention to defeat myself; I don't want to be vice president." Anyone who inquired of Truman about his ambitions got the same answer—golly, he liked being a senator.

But there were other, very personal reasons Truman was reluctant to be in the limelight. Though concerned about the Pendergast connection being dredged up, but he was more concerned about his wife and sister. He'd put them both on his Senate payroll, an embarrassing situation if it was revealed. Bess had an annual salary of $4,500, a tidy sum in 1944, though she rarely stepped foot in Truman's offices. As for his sister, she was in Missouri, caring for their elderly mother.

Truman certainly wasn't the first—or the last—politician to engage in nepotism, but the behavior is curious given his upright, downright, forthright Midwestern values and penchant for honesty. He was *not* a pretentious man. But he was beset by money problems his entire political life. When he left office in 1953, he had to borrow money to move back to Independence.

Truman also knew that Roosevelt was likely to die sooner rather than later. If he were vice president, he and Bess would then be in the White

House, and his wife seemed to have a profound antipathy for that address. He didn't know if her dislike for the residence was related to her disapproval of the Roosevelts—all their children were divorced—or something more visceral. Truman was also worried for himself should Roosevelt die. He didn't relish the idea of being compared to the president, fearful he'd come up short, a "little man trying to fill big shoes." His first couple days in Chicago, Truman spent his time testing out his speech to nominate Jim Byrnes.

Tuesday morning, July 18: Byrnes still held on to hope despite the message he'd received on Monday evening. He put a call through to Roosevelt and asked him what the story was on the political liability remark. Roosevelt danced around the issue, claiming that he'd merely repeated the objections the Party bosses had given to him concerning Byrnes. Confused and terribly hurt, Byrnes got in touch with Hannegan. Though he never said the president had lied, Hannegan did say that Byrnes was toast. Mayor Kelly also talked to Byrnes and gave him the same message.

At last, Byrnes capitulated. Two obstacles remained to getting Truman's nomination in place. Wallace was still in the running, and Truman had not yet agreed to run.

Truman had a breakfast meeting with Sidney Hillman and asked Hillman to endorse Byrnes. Truman hadn't gotten the memo on Hillman's dislike of Byrnes. Anyway, Hillman refused and said he was a Wallace supporter. Then he added that if it didn't work with Wallace, labor would throw support to Truman. That was the signal. Truman realized Byrnes was down. He, Harry S. Truman, was the president's man. Whatever prompted Hillman to move from liberal Wallace to conservative Truman is a mystery. Hillman died in 1946 without a memoir. It's possible he, like so many others, was simply doing the president's bidding.

Wednesday morning, July 19: Byrnes announced at 11:15, through a letter to Senator Burnet Maybank of South Carolina, that he was *not* a candidate for the vice presidential nomination.

Wednesday, 12:04 p.m.: The 1944 DNC was under way. Party business, including the presentation of a dismal financial report, filled the first hours. The significant events weren't scheduled until the evening session.

Wednesday afternoon: Phil Murray, Sidney Hillman's colleague, took a meeting with Truman, who had decided to run. Murray told him he supported Wallace. "'I think you should not be a candidate for vice president,' he told Truman." The reluctant nominee replied that it wasn't his choice. He was drafted. And with that, Truman left the meeting.

Meanwhile, Henry Wallace had not been idle in the weeks before the convention. He and his closest supporters had organized a bold maneuver that had met with success at past political conventions—the stampede. When Wallace arrived in Chicago on Wednesday, he was buoyed by the welcome. Though two hours later than expected, two thousand people cheered and sang him into the hotel. Wallace made it clear to everyone he was there to win renomination. He wasn't dismayed when Roosevelt's lukewarm letter to the convention chair was released, and chose to frame it as a positive development. If anything, his delegate supporters dug in their heels with greater enthusiasm after reading the president's tepid letter. He took heart when Byrnes dropped out. And though Truman had decided to enter the contest, it didn't appear he was organized for a fight. Wallace intended to put his stampede strategy into action Thursday evening after the president's renomination was over, and before the Party bosses could mount a strenuous campaign against him.

Wednesday, late afternoon: Truman, sitting on a twin bed in a hotel room with convention managers, got the president's endorsement over the phone. It was classic Roosevelt. "He asked if Hannegan had gotten 'that fellow' lined up. The chairman said no, he was acting like a damned Missouri mule. 'Well,' came the response, 'tell him if he wants to break up the Democratic Party in the middle of a war that's his responsibility,' and banged down the receiver." The Chicago Stadium, a colossal structure that could seat 24,000 people, with room for another 10,000 standing in aisles and balconies, was the setting for the last act in the Wallace/Truman dramedy.

Wednesday evening: When Vice President Wallace entered the hall that night to take his seat with the Iowa delegation, he was greeted by several minutes of enthusiastic applause, cheers, and whistles. He welcomed the support. The evening session opened at 9:05 p.m. Keynote speeches lasted until 10:47 p.m., when a surprise announcement from

Tokyo had all the delegates in an uproar. The Tojo Cabinet had resigned. It was *the* highlight of the evening.

Thursday evening, July 20: Senator Alben Barkley gave a rousing speech when he placed Franklin Roosevelt's name in nomination for president. It was a noble act on Barkley's part. He was still thoroughly angry and dismayed after what had occurred the night before, when he learned the president had thrown his support to Harry Truman. When Barkley finally said the president's name, several accolades into his speech, the crowd went wild. Twenty thousand people stood, cheered, danced, clapped, threw confetti, marched, and cartwheeled. Organ music thundered through the sound system. Flashbulbs popped. It was happy mayhem.

When the crowd came back to their collective senses and the seconding speeches were done, the vote broke as expected. Franklin Delano Roosevelt garnered all but ninety votes. From San Diego, the familiar presidential voice came over the wire and filled the hall. Roosevelt's acceptance speech was blessedly short, but it conveyed the theme that would dominate his reelection bid—his experience as a wartime leader, a necessary requirement for a nation still at war. When Roosevelt finished, the fireworks started.

Wallace got an ovation when he reached the podium to offer a second to Roosevelt's nomination. In the minutes before he went onstage, the vice president stood in a small office under the stage. He happened to interrupt a phone conversation between the DNC treasurer, Ed Pauley, and the president. Just as Wallace walked in, Pauley was giving a progress report on efforts to thwart Wallace's nomination. Awkward probably doesn't get close to describing the atmosphere in the cramped, sticky space at that moment. Wallace stared, then told Pauley he, Wallace, was about to give a speech that would launch his campaign as well as endorse Roosevelt. Wallace pulled a sheaf of papers from his briefcase, left the case in the office, and headed to the stage. That was it. Later, Pauley said Wallace gave the most inspiring talk he'd ever heard from the man.

Thursday evening, July 20—The Rush: Wallace supporters slipped into the convention unnoticed on Thursday evening. Tickets were closely monitored. To gain entrance to the floor, an attendee had to present a ticket that carried the right date and session. But the organizers had not color-coded the tickets. All tickets for all events looked alike. When a crush was on, convention staff took tickets but didn't carefully examine them. It made a stampede easier.

Thousands of Wallace people packed the hall. Banners were quietly placed everywhere, and signs were readied. It looked like a Wallace campaign rally, which was the point. At 10:35 p.m., the president's acceptance speech ended. By then, the hall was beyond full. Police said they'd never seen such a crowd at past conventions. The crowd cheered for about three minutes before the chairman led the throng in a rousing rendition of the National Anthem. When that ended, the Wallace throng went into action.

First came the chant, "We want Wallace." The organist joined in and played the Iowa state song. A parade of gyrating, dancing supporters moved through the aisles, signs were raised and banners unfurled that read "Roosevelt and Wallace." The Party bosses were in a state of shock and awe. What the hell was happening, and who the hell was running the convention? Unsure of what the Wallace enthusiasts might do, and highly incensed at their disregard for protocol, DNC leaders moved quickly to shut down the jubilant melee.

First, Pauley screamed over the din at his assistant, Neale Roach, and told him to stop the organ. Roach tried to get the organist's attention. It didn't work. The organist ignored him. Pauley commanded Roach to get an ax and cut the organ's cable. Whether he cut something, threatened the organist, or just pulled a plug, the instrument was silenced. Mayor Kelly informed Hannegan, that he, Kelly, had the right to declare the hall an overcrowded fire hazard and shut the place down. Hannegan, using threats and stink-eye looks, forced the convention chair to get to the microphone and introduce Mayor Lawrence, who would move for an adjournment of the session.

Everybody hopped to it. The convention chair, Jackson, was barely audible above the din. He made some schlocky statement about it being a great night with more to look forward to on the next day, then got Lawrence to the microphone. Mayor Lawrence, a reliable ambassador for Hannegan, moved to adjourn. It was 10:54 p.m. Jackson then called for a voice vote on the motion. Ayes and nays came at the hapless Jackson from all sides. No one was counting. Jackson declared the motion carried and the convention adjourned until 11:30 the following morning. It was pandemonium. A Hannegan aide motioned for the spotlights to be cut, and the microphones were turned off.

Years later, Claude Pepper, a Wallace supporter, claimed he'd fought his way through the jammed aisles and was just nine feet from the stage, ready to put Wallace's name in nomination, when the stage was plunged into semidarkness. The fate of the American presidency was decided in a twenty-minute span of bedlam. It seemed that some of the finer details of the stampede—like stationing someone near the stage to put Wallace's name in nomination—had either been forgotten, ignored, or never spelled out. Anyway, it was over. The stampede was stamped out.

Friday morning, July 21: Thursday, before the evening session, had been busy for the Party bosses. There were many strategy sessions, discussions with Truman, conversations with delegates, and more strategy sessions, all in service to securing Truman the vice presidential nomination. On Friday morning, the crucial argument for why delegates should throw their support to Truman was fine-tuned. Roosevelt's surrogates spread out to all the delegations. They hammered home the message that the president wanted the Missouri senator because he would *lose* fewer votes for the Democrats in the general election than any of the other candidates. That was it. The canvassing and corralling and cajoling lasted all day. Hannegan was not convinced he and the others could pull off this massive persuasion campaign with so little time. They knew that in addition to Wallace, Justice William O. Douglas's name would be put in nomination for the vice presidency. But Douglas was a liberal. He wouldn't get any traction while Wallace was in the contest. That left only Truman as a viable alternative to Wallace.

Friday afternoon, Chicago Stadium: Twelve speeches were delivered in the afternoon session. Wallace, Truman, Barkley, and favorite son candidates were nominated and seconded. Jackson, recovered from the previous night's travails, immediately moved to a roll-call vote. The convention managers wanted to keep the session moving. They didn't want the nomination process dragged into another evening event. Delegation leaders were told *not* to lobby for Truman with their members, at least for the first ballot. Delegates could vote as they wished. There were enough candidates put forward to block Wallace from the nomination on round one.

Wallace managed to garner 429 votes, close to the 589 needed. Truman pulled a respectable 319 votes. On the second ballot, delegation chairs twisted arms and pulled their members into line. Except for California and Alabama, all the delegations voted as a unit for the president's favored son, Harry Truman. It was a stunning landslide. Truman amassed 1,031 votes to Wallace's 105. Roosevelt had done it. He'd woven the net and then pulled it tight. Wallace was caught, then quietly sliced and diced by the president's henchman. July 21 was the vice president's Ides of March. The drama was over in a matter of minutes. When the Iowa delegation was called, Wallace voted for Truman. The rest, of course, is history.

Epilogue: At the 1944 DNC, delegates consumed more than 50,000 hot dogs, 125,000 bottles of soda, 80,000 bottles of beer, and 300 quarts of bourbon, rye, and scotch. It was a banner year for hard liquor—more

In an upset victory engineered by President Roosevelt, Harry S. Truman won the vice presidential nomination in 1944 ousting the sitting vice president, Henry Wallace. The selection of Truman not only changed the man's life, it also dramatically shifted American foreign policy in the post–World War II era.
COURTESY OF WIKIMEDIA COMMONS

than three times the amount was imbibed than at any previous national convention, Republican or Democrat.

April 12, 1945: On this date, Harry S. Truman's worst fear was realized when he was sworn in as the thirty-third president of the United States of America. Roosevelt had survived only weeks into his fourth term. The world is still waiting for Henry Wallace's "Century of the Common Man."

Frederick Joubert Duquesne

Passing Intelligence

There are three things to consider in the story of Frederick "Fritz" L'Huguenot Joubert Duquenne (he changed the spelling to "Duquesne" in America): For a start, his life is the definition of adventurous, so outrageous in its boldness that it's easier to imagine him as a movie character than a flesh-and-blood being. Next, he was a committed deceiver whose aliases, at least those the FBI knew about, numbered more than forty. Teasing out the actual man from his embellished personas is challenging. Finally, although it's engaging to read about his bon vivant lifestyle, imprisonments and escapes, brushes with power, and multiple professions—journalist, author, big-game hunter, soldier, explorer, and more—there was a singular life experience, a crushing loss, that drove Fritz's choices for more than five decades, and shaped his later notoriety with the Anglo-Boer War, World War I, and J. Edgar Hoover's FBI. Though not a churchgoer, the last fifty years of Fritz Duquesne's life was an homage to the Biblical injunction found in Genesis, chapter 9, verse 6: "Whoever sheds the blood of a human, by a human shall that person's blood be shed; for in his own image God made humankind." To be fair, the man also had a wry sense of humor, and an appreciation for the absurd, qualities that enhanced his charm—and deadliness.

IN 1910 A UNITED STATES CONGRESSMAN NAMED ROBERT F. BROUS-sard was certain that a national meat shortage loomed on the American horizon. His alarm, shared by others, was not that far-fetched. The country's human population had been growing at a fast clip while its animal population, the mega meat producers like buffalo, had been hunted to near extinction. Congressman Broussard proposed that Congress approve an appropriation of a quarter of a million dollars "to import wild and domestic animals into the United States." To corral support for his measure, the congressman held a hearing on the benefits of supporting the bill, nicknamed the "American Hippopotamus Act."

One of Broussard's expert witnesses, an advocate of the hippo scheme, was Frederick Joubert Duquesne, a handsome South African and big-game hunter who looked like he'd been sent from central casting. Another witness was Frederick Russell Burnham, also an ardent supporter of hippo importation, who was central casting's pick for handsome, pugnacious cowboy-searching-for-a-brawl, in or out of a barroom. Burnham and Duquesne had indeed shared a brawl, of sorts. "He was one of the craftiest men I ever met," said Burnham about Duquesne. "He had something of a genius of the Apache for avoiding a combat except on his own terms; yet he would be the last man I should choose to meet in a dark room for a finish fight armed only with knives." The mercurial Duquesne returned the sentiment: "To my friendly enemy, Major Frederick Russell Burnham, the greatest scout of the world, whose eyes were that of an Empire. I once craved the honour of killing him, but failing that, I extend my heartiest admiration."

The frenemies first took an appreciative dislike to each other during the Second Boer War, a conflict they shared—on opposing sides. This was the seminal event that launched Duquesne into a life of subterfuge and sabotage against Britain, and by extension, any nations allied with England, including the United States.

Frederick Duquesne was a liar of the first order—sometimes. He also told the truth—sometimes. His unreliability made it challenging for any biographer to produce a trustworthy account of the man. Writing a book is its own form of peculiar torture without adding further obstacles. Still, two biographies of note have been published about Duquesne. One, *The Man Who Killed Kitchener* by Clement Wood, appeared in 1932. Despite the lack of footnotes or bibliography, much of the information in it has been incorporated into other narratives on the man. Nothing was verified by Wood, though verifiable incidents are recounted. As one reviewer observed, it seems the author wrote a "fictionalized biography." Wood said he got his material from a mysterious man with a cache of papers and photos who paid him a visit. Despite the fact that Fritz was still alive and vigorous when Wood undertook the project, he never interviewed his subject, an odd exception for a biographer. There's every reason to assume that *The Man Who Killed Kitchener* is really a vanity project engineered by Duquesne and happily indulged by Clement Wood.

Counterfeit Hero, by Art Ronnie, was released in 1995. Written sixty years after *The Man Who Killed Kitchener*, fifty years after Duquesne was arrested by the FBI, and forty years after Fritz's death, Ronnie's more-measured work provides a sober, well-researched account. Read together, these books describe a charming pretender, a dashing adventurer—and an assassin who relished the shadowy world of espionage.

Fritz Duquesne's life started in East London, a region on the southeast coast of southern Africa, in what was then the British-controlled Cape Colony. The Duquesne family, Catholics of French Huguenot descent, moved when Fritz was a small boy to a farm in the Nylstroom region of the Transvaal Republic, an independent Boer (the Dutch word for "farmer") nation in the northern reaches of modern-day South Africa. The household included Fritz's father, Abraham Duquesne, his mother, Minna Joubert, a younger sister, Elsbet, a younger brother, Pedro, and Fritz's blind, elderly great-uncle, Jan Duquesne. A hunter and trader, Abraham was gone for long periods of time, leaving the farm operation to his wife and uncle.

Aside from the punishing physical labor intrinsic to farming, life on a Transvaal spread was isolated and dangerous. Tensions between the White and Black populations in the Boer republics were never more than a wrong gesture or careless word from boiling into lethal confrontations. It was on one such occasion that Fritz, aged twelve, killed his first man, a Zulu who had arrived at the Duquesne farmhouse to sell some items. One room of the home was set aside as a trading outpost. Abraham was away, leaving Minnie to oversee operations. In the bartering that followed, the man became agitated and attacked Minnie when she refused to meet the price he wanted for his goods. Fritz, standing nearby, grabbed the short spear the man carried in his waistband and plunged it into the attacker's stomach.

Other stories from Fritz's youth attest to his marksmanship and fearlessness when it came to using weapons against wild game—or men. In later life, his boyhood reminiscences were veiled in contented nostalgia. At thirteen, the lad was sent by his parents from the Transvaal frontier to be educated in England. How Fritz spent the next four years after he finished his schooling depends on who is telling the tale. What's indisputable is that in 1899, he returned to the Transvaal—and war—at the urging of his father.

This grimy episode of British imperialism, the Anglo-Boer or Second Boer War, was characterized by particularly bloody and horrific proceedings. England was determined to bring the Boer republics under British rule. During the conflict, British forces, under the command of Herbert Kitchener, 1st Earl Kitchener, pioneered the use of mass incarceration of a civilian population as part of a scorched-earth strategy. Kitchener checked all the boxes for how a general of the late British Empire ought to look. Mustachioed with slicked-down brown hair, parted in the middle, and a perpetually furrowed brow, the

Captain Duquesne, Boer Army photo, circa 1900

never-smiling soldier was the embodiment of brusque disapproval. He was, of course, more complicated and nuanced than he appeared, but the consequences of his orders in the Boer campaign are staggering in their loathsomeness.

Kitchener's goal was to deprive the Boer fighters of any food, shelter, supplies, or sustenance, including the support of family. What he underestimated was how his policies would be interpreted as a license for terrorist actions of rape and murder by contingents of British soldiers on search-and-destroy missions. Kitchener also failed to provide for the proper administration of the internment camps he established. In less than three years, more than 26,000 camp prisoners died, mostly women and children. The incarcerated Boers perished from infectious diseases spread through abysmal sanitation conditions, crowding, and starvation. One estimate puts the number of child deaths at 80 percent of the total count. By every measure, the British campaign of destruction and internment in the Anglo-Boer War fit the definition of genocide. For Duquesne, Kitchener's policies precipitated a personal tragedy that focused Fritz's purpose for the remainder of his life.

The Boer resistance to the British transformed within a year into a guerrilla operation. The Boers lacked the manpower, weaponry, and logistical support to effectively confront the British Army straight up. There's been speculation that Duquesne was a soldier of fortune who later fabricated his story of being raised in the Transvaal Republic, but that's just one in a slew of rumors that swirl about the man. Commissioned a lieutenant, Fritz was assigned to the staff of commander Piet Joubert. After taking a bullet in the shoulder during the Battle of Lombard's Kop, a win for the Boers, Duquesne was promoted to captain of artillery.

An early and tenacious legend that attached itself to Duquesne involved his intercepting a wagon train of thirty ox-drawn carts loaded with gold and papers being sent to the coast for safekeeping by the Transvaal president, Paul Kruger, before his exile from the continent. The destination was Mozambique, where the shipment would be taken by steamer to Europe. According to the legend, along the route, Fritz rendezvoused with the caravan, killed the four white soldiers who were planning to make off with the treasure, and ordered the native guards to bury the gold in caves near the Drakensberg Mountains. The guards did as they were told, only to be promptly massacred by local tribesmen. Where the golden cargo was stashed is a tantalizing mystery that persists to this day—despite *no* evidence the incident ever happened.

It's no wonder myths surround Duquesne. The corroborated war stories of his captures and escapes, the number of British he killed, his successful sabotage missions as a commando leader, and his nickname, Black Panther of the Veld, have earned him kudos and loathing, fame and infamy. While running his own commando unit, Fritz specialized in vexing Kitchener's scouts, who were led by the American Frederick Russell Burnham, the man who later testified at the congressional hippo hearings. "There were only two men on the veld I feared, and one was Duquesne," Burnham admitted in his memoir. "Much has been written about Duquesne, most of it rubbish. Yet his real accomplishments were so terrible . . . they make the yellow journal thrillers about him seem as mild as radio bedtime stories." High praise coming from a man targeted by Fritz for kill or capture. Of course, Burnham was charged with doing the same to Duquesne.

But all the war drama paled next to the singular atrocity that held Fritz hostage for the rest of his days.

While operating as a courier, Duquesne slipped into the Nylstroom region and made his way to his family's farm. The vivid description of what he found there, as recounted in Ronnie's book, is challenging to read, and appalling to ponder. It makes clear why Fritz's vitriolic reaction to all things English never abated.

Arriving at the spot where the Duquesne homestead had been, Fritz was confronted with "fire-blackened ruins." House, *kraals* (livestock pens), and crops were all ravaged—and there was worse news. An elderly servant, a Mponda man named Kanya, told him that a contingent of British soldiers, following Kitchener's slash-and-burn policies, had swept through the area. Kanya reported that "old Uncle Jan had been hanged from a telegraph pole with a cow rope, and as his face turned black, the soldiers 'stuck him with the shiny knives on the ends of their guns.'" Elsbet, Fritz's sister, was raped by three tormentors who held her down. When they let her up, she ran, only to be shot in the back.

Fritz's mother was also raped, by how many, the elderly man could not say, as it had happened behind the house, but Kanya watched as the "mother misses" was led off, her dress ripped and dirty, her hands tied.

If Fritz Duquesne dropped to the ground and sobbed, screamed, or shot his rifle into the air, it's not revealed. He left his former home wearing a purloined British military uniform, and found the nearest internment camp several days away, in Germiston, near Johannesburg. There, he informed the camp commandant he was looking for a Boer woman named Duquesne, rumored to have "valuable information." He found his mother in a "barbed-wire kraal, starving and dying from syphilis and holding a seven-month-old baby boy in her arms." There was no saving his mother or the infant. It was too late; the starvation and disease were too advanced.

Fritz's parting whisper to his mother was a covenant: "As long as I live I will never draw one breath but to pay back the English for what they have done. . . . I pledge my soul that for every drop of rotten, poisoned blood in your body I will kill one hundred Englishmen." Perhaps the bitter, anguished oath was a comfort to the desolate woman clutching a wasted baby. Or perhaps the woman's mind, knowing the body it inhabited would soon collapse, had already left, taking comprehension with it.

However it was, Fritz and Minna never saw each other again. Seething and heartbroken, Duquesne retraced his steps through the overcrowded, wretched camp, mounted his horse, and rode off.

His first act of vengeance came quickly. "A score of miles away, on the burned-over veldt, he passed two officers, an English captain and a Cape lieutenant, chatting amiably together. He saluted, and they saluted. He turned back as soon as he had passed, and drilled both of them clean through the heart from behind—it was nothing for him, who had shot lions leaping—and watched them as they toppled slowly from their horses, and the frightened little horses galloped away in a cloud of ashy dust."

The episode concluded with Fritz walking over to the dead men and crushing each one's face with a well-placed kick of his booted foot. For good measure, he slammed the butt of his rifle into each man's torso. It was just the beginning.

A list of provocative missions, arrests, and escapes from British authorities continued to the end of Fritz's tenure as a Boer fighter. He finally wound up in a British penal colony on Burt's Island in St. George's Harbour, Bahamas. It was here he met the only woman he ever married. Alice Wortley, seven years younger than Duquesne, was eighteen years old at their first meeting. Fritz's later claims that Alice's family had "vast plantations in the British West Indies," and were directly related to Lady Mary Wortley Montague, a British aristocrat, was straight-up nonsense. Alice's father, Samuel Short Wortley from Akron, Ohio, was the American director of agriculture in Bermuda. He was also a building contractor and civil engineer who oversaw the construction of docks in the island nation.

Duquesne not only lied about the Wortley family, he also put several nasty little twists on his lies about Alice. In some quarters, he bragged that he had seduced her for the pleasure of defiling a woman with British blood in her veins. He also claimed that she was so captivated by his lovemaking that she helped him escape from Burt's Island. The former is repugnant. The latter is make-believe. How Alice and Duquesne met wasn't conventional, but it hardly rose to the level of bodice-ripper romance.

During a rest period one afternoon, while on a prison work detail, Fritz was sitting in the shade, shackled to his fellow inmates. A tennis ball, chased by a young woman, rolled to a stop at his feet. So did the young woman. Duquesne called out, "Don't be afraid; we won't eat you," and kicked the ball in her direction. The scene ends with the gallant prisoner getting to his feet and introducing himself. Alice did likewise. Family legend has it the disheveled but strikingly good-looking Fritz and the comely Miss Wortley were immediately taken with each other. From then on, whenever she saw him—which was often, as the prisoners routinely worked along the roadways—she would make excuses to go and speak with him. But Alice didn't help him escape, nor is it credible that they shared sexual trysts amid a work gang or within the prison enclosure on Burt's Island. Fritz did manage to escape from the island, but it was six years before he and Alice were in the same place at the same time long enough for a courtship to evolve. And it was another two years after that before they married.

Duquesne's journey from Burt's Island to America started on the rainy evening of June 25, 1902, when he got past guards, a fence, and more than a mile-long swim through shark-laced waters to reach Bermuda's main island. Luck was kind, and Fritz made it to the home of a Boer sympathizer who gave him clothes, food, money, and passage on a skiff to Bermuda's capital, Hamilton. The fugitive melted into the dodgy slums near the Hamilton town wharves. For a short stint, he worked as a pimp for a local prostitute, Vera, splitting the take with her from sailors he pushed in her direction. But when he discovered one of the customers he collared was a steward on the luxury yacht, *Margaret*, bound for Baltimore, Maryland, he took the opportunity to bolt.

The ruse was simple: Fritz plied the hapless steward with alcohol until he passed out, then he dressed in the man's clothes and staggered onto the boat. The switch was discovered the next morning, but by then it was too late. *Margaret* was already at sea. Threatened with being handed over in Baltimore to immigration authorities, Fritz went overboard when the ship entered the Chesapeake Bay. He got to shore and through his own cunning, along with assistance from a network of Boer sympathizers, he made it to the city that ran on immigrants, legal or otherwise—Manhattan.

In the fall of 1902, after a series of undistinguished jobs arranged by Fritz's Boer connections, the dashing ex-fighter landed himself in the teeming world of New York City journalism. Over the next twelve years, Duquesne wrote three novels and three plays while working for some of the largest, most prestigious newspapers in the country, starting with the *New York Herald* and moving to the *Sun* and the *World*. He perfected his upper-class British accent, recognizing its allure to American audiences, and honed his storytelling skills. He was known as a mellifluous raconteur. Yet even when he was successful at winning attention with true tales of his boyhood and war experiences in South Africa, he couldn't resist adding pretty prevarications to his résumé. Included in the *Who's Who in New York City and State* between the years of 1904 to 1909, Fritz claimed status as a special correspondent for different papers. His assignments, he said, took him to Port Arthur in China, Paris, Macedonia, Tangier, the Congo Free State, and Australia, where he served as the foreman for "the Eldu expedition for Sir Arthur Jones," an event that never happened.

Committed to embellishing the truth, Duquesne was rarely—if ever—challenged on the details of his life or accomplishments.

There were, however, two endeavors during his journalism days that were particularly salient to Fritz's future: public lectures, and the publication of his adventures as an African big game hunter.

The significant event on the lecture front occurred when Fritz gave a talk at Manhattan's Cooper Union. Alice Wortley, the young woman from his Burt's Island days happened to be in the audience that night. They reconnected and married in 1910.

On the story front, Fritz's gripping tales of stalking and bagging wild game earned him a White House invitation to meet with President Teddy Roosevelt. On January 25, 1909, the two men visited and talked for nearly two hours. Roosevelt was in a frenzy over preparations for a planned hunting safari in East Africa, scheduled to take place soon after he left office in March. Fritz was one of several renowned hunters and explorers the president consulted. Despite what some sources suggest, Duquesne was not the president's shooting instructor—though they certainly spoke about equipment, including guns and ammo—nor did he accompany Roosevelt on this safari. Still, an invitation and lengthy chat with the US president looks fantastic on the résumé.

The last half of 1913 opened another chapter for Duquesne. In the summer of that year, after losing his 1912 bid for the presidency, Teddy Roosevelt embarked on a punishing expedition to South America, where he intended to chart the mysterious, unexplored route of a tributary that spilled into the Amazon River. Fritz, who had worked on Roosevelt's Bull Moose campaign, saw the former president's adventure as a fund-raising opportunity to support his own wanderlust. He approached Goodyear Rubber Company of Akron to finance a South American trip in search of indigenous rubber plants that could be sourced for Goodyear's purposes. According to the book, *Throttled!*, published in 1919 by Captain Thomas J. Tunney, head of the bomb squad for the New York City Police, Fritz had established a friendship with Goodyear's cofounder, Frank Sieberling. In 1911, Sieberling, along with Thanhouser Film Company, financed Fritz to make a documentary film record of his explorations in Central America. For his latest venture, in addition to Goodyear, Fritz also secured a contract with another film company to produce a documentary record of Roosevelt's trip. This arrangement netted him nearly $80,000 in film and negatives. There's no indication he planned to actually film Roosevelt's expedition but if he did shoot footage for that purpose, later events showed it was pointless. Before leaving the States, Fritz took out an insurance policy on the movie supplies, which he carefully packed in a dark green metal trunk. He and Alice departed near the end of December 1913. Both traveled on American passports, Fritz having been granted naturalized citizenship thanks to a combination of celebrity, luck, lying, and lax scrutiny.

What happened next eventually turned their lives inside out.

In July of 1914, war broke out in Europe. Fritz and Alice were in Manaus, capital of Brazil's Amazonas state, at the start of World War I. Unsure of the implications for steamship travel, Fritz sent Alice home immediately. Quite sure of the implications for his own agenda, the destruction of all things British, he presented himself at the German consulate. Fritz intended to spy for the Kaiser. And here was luck! His nemesis, Lord Kitchener was brought into the government as Britain's secretary of state for war. Frustrating the Secretary's efforts would be a supreme pleasure for Frederick Joubert Duquesne.

Duquesne, in the employ of Germany, took on the role of master saboteur. Using assumed names, he dogged ports in the northern regions of South America, wherever large crates of materials were being shipped to Europe—specifically, Britain. His goal was to disrupt the British supply chain by planting incendiary devices on the supply ships timed to explode when the boat was at sea. Duquesne bragged that he sank twenty-two ships in this fashion, a number Clement Wood repeated in his biography of the man. But Art Ronnie—the spy's later biographer who made it a point to research and document sources—suggested the number was considerably less. Regardless of the amount, Duquesne had no qualms when it came to blowing up people and property.

The British, however, got wise to the Boer veteran's activities, and in 1915 attempted to nab him in a Brazilian port. It was a close call but he got away from a contingent of British agents by scrambling over the rooftops. His set his last bomb in 1916, on a British ship, the *Tennyson*, bound for the United States from Brazil. The boat's cargo included Duquesne's green trunk loaded with film and equipment plus sixteen boxes of supposed minerals. When the craft was halfway to Trinidad, a large explosion occurred killing three sailors.

The British opened an intense manhunt for Fritz, so intense that he concluded his only escape was to die before he was captured. He had no doubt that would be his fate if the British nabbed him. His next, he soon regretted. To throw off his pursuers, Duquesne cabled a "press release" to the *New York Times* announcing his death at the hands of hostile Indians while leading an expedition in Bolivia. Seventeen days later, he changed the story. He remembered he was traveling on an American passport, a protection against British prosecution, so he planted a piece with the Associated Press wire service that changed the outcome of his fight with the Indians from being killed to being badly injured. Bolivian soldiers, he lied, had rescued him.

His ploy worked.

In April of 1916, he showed up, briefly, in New York to execute an insurance scam. Using the alias Frederick Fredericks, he purchased $24,000 of film with money he had raised in Argentina for another scam movie project. Once acquired, he placed the film in a Brooklyn warehouse. When the warehouse exploded two weeks later, he got his unsuspecting wife to file two insurance claims—one in Fredericks's name for the Brooklyn loss, to the tune of $33,000; and the other, an $80,000 claim for the loss of film suffered by the fictitious Mr. George Fordham, when the *Tennyson* blew. Alice Wortley dutifully carried out her husband's directions, not realizing insurance fraud was one way Fritz financed his espionage operations. The scheme came back to bite him three years later. In the meantime, he disappeared again in May of 1916. The story he told later was that he left Manhattan to carry out an assassination plot against England's "most illustrious soldier."

As the trench warfare dragged on in Europe, Prime Minister Asquith's government grew concerned that Tsar Nicholas II of Russia would capitulate to the forces in his bedraggled country clambering for withdrawal from the war. Asquith decided a mission should be dispatched "to Russia to strengthen that country's resolve and to discuss supplying weapons and munitions." Lord Kitchener received permission to lead the delegation. On June 5, 1916, he boarded the HMS *Hampshire* in Scapa Flow, home to the main British Fleet, located in the Orkney Islands off Scotland. "British intelligence believed the route selected had been swept clear of mines, unaware that on 28 May the German submarine U-72, commanded by Lieutenant Commander Curt Beitzen, had laid a series of mines . . . along Kitchener's precise route."

At 7:30 p.m., when the *Hampshire* was past the guarded waters of the Scapa Flow basin, a colossal explosion ripped a hole between the ship's bow and bridge. It took fifteen minutes for the craft to sink, bow first; then, with stern high in the air, the ship turned over and disappeared beneath the water. Wildly tumultuous seas prevented lifeboats from being lowered, although a few sailors managed to get away from the vessel in a rubber raft. One of the twelve survivors said he "last saw Lord Kitchener walking calmly from his cabin to the quarterdeck, where he waited with equal calm for the inevitable." The British secretary of state for war was drowned, as were 736 other persons. Kitchener's body was never recovered.

There were many nominees rumored to be itching for Kitchener's death. One very nasty whisper was promulgated by Oscar Wilde's lover, Lord Alfred Douglas. He suggested the Jews had engineered the murder and involved Winston Churchill in the plot, all for the benefit of a Jewish financier. Lord Douglas got sued by Churchill and received six months in prison for his gossip. Irish Republicans were also credited with the act, as were Russian communists, German intelligence officers, and British secret service. But Duquesne's version of how the old warhorse was eliminated was by far the raciest and most enduring of the tales.

In Fritz's story, he claimed to have made his way to the Netherlands from South America where he contacted a group called the Boer Revolutionary Committee. He said he was informed by the Committee that a Count Boris Zakrevsky was dispatched by Russia to accompany Kitchener from England to Petrograd. German intelligence got wind of this arrangement from Zakrevsky's fiancée, who was a German spy. The German government wanted him, Duquesne, to impersonate the count. The assignment was simple—kill Kitchener.

Fritz claimed the Russian envoy was kidnapped and thrown into a German prison, clearing the way for him to pose as Count Zakrevsky. In his assumed disguise, Fritz rendezvoused with Kitchener in London. The men then traveled by train, car, and a destroyer, to reach the *Hampshire*. On his first night at sea, Duquesne tossed self-igniting flares out the porthole in his cabin to signal waiting German submarines to attack. Once the flares were tossed, around 7:45 in the evening, Fritz put on a life jacket and grabbed his pistol.

When the explosion occurred, a violent shudder sent Fritz into the passageway. He spotted Kitchener and followed him onto the quarterdeck where, not twenty feet from his prey, he waited for an opportunity to shoot his target. A large wave, however, carried the old soldier overboard before Fritz could fire. Duquesne jumped overboard, into the pounding waters, and frantically swam through a Force 9 gale to a waiting German craft. By stealthy means, he entered Germany where he was feted by all the Central Powers. Fritz ended this fabulous, fabricated tale with a flourish. In gratitude for his service under such treacherous conditions, he was awarded the German Iron Cross with gold leaves along with the Diamond Crescent of Turkey. Wow!

Although this account seems absurd on the face of it, Fritz's verified escapades were often harrowing and outlandish. After his arrest, years later, authorities found a photo in Duquesne's effects that showed him dressed in a German military uniform sporting an Iron Cross and medals from Bulgaria, Austria, and Turkey. Of course, Fritz was a master of disguise and costume and could easily have acquired the outfit and pins. There's never been any credible evidence put forward to corroborate Kitchener's death at the hands of Duquesne, but he never stepped away from the story. Haunted by the deaths of his mother and sister, in his heart and head he'd been butchering Kitchener for fifteen years by the time the old man perished. If nothing else, Fritz had willed the field marshal's death into existence.

It was July 1917 before Fritz surfaced again in the public record. In *Throttled!*, Captain Tunney quoted a lengthy excerpt from a speakers' bureau pamphlet—possibly Pond Lyceum Bureau—advertising lectures on war by the fictitious Australian officer Captain Claude Staughton formerly of the equally bogus West Australia Light Horse Brigade. With America now in the war, Fritz's fertile imagination concocted a daring war record filled with brave exploits for his Staughton persona. In this guise, he became a favorite on the public lecture circuit. In deference to his character, he vigorously supported US war bond drives and refrained from his activities on behalf of Germany.

As for his bogus insurance claims for Frederick Fredericks and George Fordham, the companies were dragging their bureaucratic feet on paying. Instead, they decided to dig into the cases. The best clue leading to Duquesne was that it was his wife who'd filed the claims. Since an explosion in a Brooklyn warehouse was involved, two seasoned investigators, Thomas P. Brophy, New York's chief fire marshal, and the already mentioned Thomas J. Tunney, head of the New York City Police bomb squad, got involved. They caught a break when Fritz, posing as Staughton, slipped a few pro-German comments into a conversation with a woman who promptly reported him to the FBI. Asked to look through mug shots, she identified Staughton as Duquesne.

That did it. Bomb squad detectives raided Fritz's apartment on December 7, 1917. It was a gold mine of incriminating evidence, including an invoice for the *Tennyson* film shipment. Arrested and charged with insurance fraud following suspicious explosions, Fritz also knew the British authorities were lurking like dogs eyeing a juicy bone, waiting to get at him. His first ploy after being arrested was to feign insanity. An accomplished actor, he fooled psychiatrists and won himself a stay in New York's Matteawan State Hospital.

Eight bumpy years of marriage, most of it spent apart from her husband, were enough for Alice. She threw in the towel and divorced Fritz. She went on to marry a mechanic from Buffalo and have a son, Lyle. The family relocated to California, where Alice died in 1966 at the respectable age of eighty-one.

The insanity ruse lasted for about five months, at which point Fritz had a miraculous recovery and petitioned the court for a hearing on the insurance charges. He pleaded guilty on the Brooklyn warehouse scam but offered nothing on the *Tennyson* explosion. The British were eagerly trying to extradite him for the *Tennyson* affair to stand trial in England for murder. On December 23, 1918, at a deportation hearing, Fritz pulled out another ploy. He collapsed in the courtroom, overcome by sudden paralysis below the waist. After a grueling examination by several doctors, he was pronounced paralyzed and unable to travel.

He retired to the prison ward of Bellevue Hospital. Five months later, on May 19, 1919, another deportation hearing was held. The judge pulled an unexpected move and granted the British petition. In the early-morning hours on the day he was scheduled to sail away to his sure death in England, Fritz escaped from Bellevue. Just past midnight on May 26, "he broke out two window bars, fell to the ground from the second-story window, and staggered away into the night. No one helped him."

Unbelievable. The London *Daily Mail* ran the following item on May 27:

> *Col. Fritz du Quesne, a fugitive from justice, is wanted by His Majesty's government for trial on the following charges: Murder on the high seas; the sinking and burning of British ships; the burning of military stores, warehouses, coaling stations, conspiracy, and the falsification of Admiralty documents. He carried on hostile operations against the British government in various parts of the world under the following names: Fred, Fredericks, Capt. Claude Staughton, Col. Bezan, von Ricthofen, Piet Niacud, etc. His correct and full name is Fritz Joubert Marquis du Quesne. Prior to the war he was known as Capt. Fritz du Quesne, a big-game hunter, author, explorer, and lecturer.*

For thirteen years the lucky and elusive Fritz remained free, living a good life and working in Boston under yet another assumed name, Major Frank Craven. But in May 1932 he was apprehended by the New York City Police Department's Alien Squad and escorted at gunpoint from his workplace. Clement Wood was pulled in by the cops to identify Fritz. He insisted the man in custody was the Major Craven he'd known since 1927—one more reason Wood was not a reliable reporter.

Charged with murder and unlawful escape, Duquesne had the services of a crackerjack defense lawyer, Arthur Garfield Hays, a veteran of the high-profile cases of Sacco and Vanzetti, the Scottsboro Boys, and

John Scopes. Britain, however, had lost interest in pursuing the murder charges and dropped their extradition request. The unlawful escape charges were dismissed. Fritz Duquesne walked free. When it came to being held accountable by the law, the man seemed to be coated in Teflon and dressed in shamrocks.

Within a decade of his escape from extradition, the talented Mr. Duquesne was once again in the crosshairs of the FBI. His final campaign started in 1934 when Fritz, ever faithful to his anti-British credo, accepted a job as an intelligence officer with the Order of 76, one of the many small, fringe, pro-Nazi groups that had popped up in America since Hitler's ascendancy as chancellor of Germany. Affiliated with the better-known Silver Shirts organization, there's no solid information on what Duquesne's duties were at the Order of 76, and by 1935, he was gone from the organization.

But in 1937, authentic German Nazis came knocking on Fritz's door.

Germany's military intelligence division, the Abwehr, was headed by Admiral Wilhelm Canaris, who was familiar with Fritz's espionage work in South America from the First World War. Canaris, eager to develop a sophisticated intelligence-gathering network in America, selected a Colonel Nikolaus Ritter, who had returned to Germany after thirteen years of living and working in the States. Ritter went back to the United States with orders to contact Duquesne, among others.

Ritter also knew Fritz, having met him in 1931 through a mutual friend, Colonel Uldric Thompson. He recalled Fritz as "being in his early forties, with a small intelligent face and aristocratic nose, gray eyes [his eyes were in fact steel blue], and graying hair. . . . Ritter always admired him for the way he managed to move in the best circles despite his lack of funds . . . he was innately charming. Ritter admitted that even he was charmed." In December 1937, Ritter and Fritz met again, this time to discuss Fritz's recruitment as one of Ritter's agents.

With his US network in place, Ritter sailed for Germany in early 1938. For two years, Ritter's spies, including Fritz, operated in isolation from each other, passing information to the Abwehr as instructed. Ritter, through his network, was responsible for two remarkable intelligence scoops falling into German hands—the Norden bombsight schematics, passed along by Hermann Lang, and the Sperry gyroscope plans, delivered by another agent, Everett Roeder. The intel was acquired before America's entrance into World War II.

Absurdly, Ritter was also responsible for the demise of his carefully crafted stateside web. The network unraveled under the leadership of William Sebold, dispatched by Ritter, to be the primary contact for his US operation. In a sting scheme that the author, Ronnie, called "unusual and letter perfect," the FBI successfully crushed Ritter's organization with Sebold's assistance. Though the ring was not of Duquesne's making, the Bureau tagged him as the leader of the gang. The FBI case file is entitled "Duquesne Spy Ring." Based on that file, here's a condensed version of how the operation unfolded.

William Sebold, a naturalized American citizen of German birth, made a trip home in February 1939 to Mulheim, Germany, for an overdue visit with his mother and other family members. He drew the interest of the Gestapo likely because of his American employment as an airplane mechanic. Sebold ignored the first two letters he received from the Gestapo's Dr. Gassner, requesting a meeting. But Gassner forced the issue by visiting Sebold in his home where he pressed the hapless man to work as a spy on behalf of Germany's intelligence services, headed by Ritter. Ritter also visited Sebold, and between the two men and threats of reprisals against his family, Sebold agreed to serve. He was so convincing that Ritter never doubted his sincerity, even when the man used some pretext to visit the American consulate offices in Cologne. At the consulate he revealed his recruitment as a spy and said he wished to cooperate with the FBI once he was back in the States.

Keeping with Abwehr protocol, Sebold was sent to Hamburg, Germany, for espionage training, and in 1940 he sailed for the States from Genoa, Italy, under the name Harry Sawyer. His task was to consolidate and expand the Ritter network. On February 8, 1940, he stepped off the gangplank in New York. The Bureau, having advance warning of Sebold's arrival, his mission, and his desire to work with them, was not surprised when he showed up at their offices.

Under the guidance of an FBI agent, who moved in with him for two months, Sebold found an apartment and set up an office under his

The 33 convicted members of the Duquesne Spy Ring

FBI mug shots of the thirty-three convincted members of the Duquesne Spy Ring

assumed name of Harry Sawyer. The office served as a location for meetings with other members of Ritter's network. It also allowed the FBI to set up a sham shortwave radio station and design a covert filming operation using a 16mm camera camouflaged by a one-way mirror. The shortwave transmissions were controlled from a rented house on Long Island where the Bureau staffed a transmitter using German-speaking agents, and conveyed "Sawyer's" information, in heavily redacted but not totally fictitious form, to Germany.

Though Fritz began sending enormous amounts of information to the Abwehr through Sawyer, most of it was easily available from public sources, newspapers or company brochures. At some point, German officials sent a message to Fritz through Sawyer that said, "Tell Duquesne that we are not interested in information that has been published several weeks ago in the *New York Times* and the *Herald Tribune*." Fritz did manage to secure some meaningful intel; for example, he knew that Washington was handing over the Norden plans to the British. On occasion, he also reported on where naval battle fleets were being deployed. But usually his "secrets" were of low value. While he met with Sawyer often, Fritz wouldn't step foot in the man's office, preferring to play it safe.

And then one day, he let down his guard. On June 25, 1941, he walked into a trap. The FBI captured him on film meeting with Sawyer and handing over written notes pulled from his sock. Four days later, the feds lowered the boom. Nineteen German spies were arrested in New York City and another four were nabbed in New Jersey. The total number of German agents arrested and charged ballooned to thirty-three.

The government's cat-and-mouse game lasted for sixteen months. It consumed the time of ninety-three FBI agents and resulted in three hundred messages being transmitted to Germany and two hundred messages being received through the shortwave radio masquerade. Fritz was arrested in his apartment. He had been under surveillance by an agent posing as a friendly neighbor. Given his ego, Fritz may have taken some small comfort in being branded by J. Edgar Hoover as the "most important" of the defendants.

Duquesne was one of fourteen out of the initial group of twenty-four to opt for a trial. He was the first to testify in a six-week marathon trial that started in September 1941, beguiling the jury and courtroom attendees with his exquisite storytelling skills and fantastic adventures. He also fabricated to his heart's content, claiming he was responsible for Kitchener's death and had been rescued from Bellevue by members of the Irish Republican Army. He testified that the only person in the ring that he knew was Sebold (aka, Sawyer). That was likely a bit of truth splashed like a raindrop into the garden of fantasies he had so carefully cultivated. Despite the overwhelming evidence of his spying activities, Fritz remained steadfast in his assertion that he *was not* a spy. He intimated he'd just been stringing Sebold along for the money. "I sold him a code," he said, "used by Benedict Arnold in the war between England and the United States in 1776."

By happenstance, the attorneys for the defense presented their closing arguments to the jury on December 8, 1941, the day after Japan attacked Pearl Harbor. The timing couldn't have been worse. All the defendants were found guilty. It took the jury a mere eight hours to reach the verdicts. Sentences ranged from a few months to eighteen years for Hermann Lang of Norden bombsight fame and Fritz Duquesne. This time, there would be no miraculous escapes, and he knew it. Still, he engaged in a last act of melodrama. "Long live America!" Fritz shouted as he was led down the courthouse hallway.

Of all the convicted men, Duquesne remained in prison the longest: twelve years, seven months, and sixteen days. Prior to his release on September 19, 1954, the indomitable Boer filed one last lawsuit against the FBI, claiming that when arrested, "valuable properties and monies" were taken from him. "The property included three bags of uncut diamonds worth $3 million, two albums of stamps worth $150,000, an original history of the Boer War valued at $40,000, and various rings, watches, and cameras. The appeal was dismissed."

Seventy-seven years old when he was paroled, Fritz had suffered a stroke in prison that left him partially paralyzed, his once movie-star looks distorted, his voice, faint and slurred. He walked unsteadily with a cane, but still had "wavy, jet-black hair." He spent the last twenty months of his life in Manhattan, checking in with parole officers and on welfare. First placed at the London Arms Nursing Home, then relocated to Pelham Manor, Fritz finally got his wish to have his own apartment, a

1941 mug shot of Fritz
Duquesne from his FBI
file
COURTESY OF FBI.GOV

walk-up at 526 East 83rd Street. While happier in his new surroundings, he was also more vulnerable to falls and missteps. A bad tumble in his apartment put him in City Hospital on Welfare Island with a fractured hip. He recovered enough to be scheduled for rehabilitation services, he was slammed by a fatal stroke on May 24, 1956.

Frederick Joubert Duquesne was seventy-eight years old when he died. He was cremated, his ashes at last scattered in the Bay of Fundy in 1984, a place far from South Africa where they were meant to be. It turned out wanderlust was Fritz's companion even in death. It's a good bet Frederick Joubert Duquesne would be impressed that he's still in the spotlight on the FBI website under the tab "Famous Cases & Criminals." In a century marked by spyware, schemes, and scams that not even Duquesne's fantastical imagination could have conceived, he's still a notorious celebrity with the US Department of Justice. He never stopped loathing all things British.

Sources

BEGGED

Kennewick Man: Skeleton Seizure

Bones of Contention. PBS, Public Broadcasting Service, June 19, 2001, www.pbs.org/news hour/show/bones-of-contention.

"Bryan and Darrow Wage War of Words in Trial Interlude." *New York Times*, July 19, 1925.

Chatters, James C. *Ancient Encounters: Kennewick Man and the First Americans*. New York: Simon & Schuster, 2002.

———. "Kennewick Man." *Kennewick Man*, Smithsonian Institution, 2004.

Deloria Jr., Vine. *Indians of the Pacific Northwest: From the Coming of the White Man to the Present Day*. Golden, CO: Fulcrum Publishing, 2016.

Deloria Jr., Vine, et al. *Spirit & Reason: The Vine Deloria Jr. Reader*. Golden, CO: Fulcrum Publishing, 1999.

Egan, Timothy. "A Skeleton Moves from the Courts to the Laboratory." *New York Times*, July 19, 2005.

Fort, John. "Bryan vs. Darrow, Battle of Giants." Newspapers.com, Ancestry, July 10, 1925.

Goldberg, Steven. "Kennewick Man and the Meaning of Life." *Georgetown Law Faculty Publications and Other Works*, 2006, https://scholarship.law.georgetown.edu/facpub /448.

Green, Sara Jean. "'A Wrong Had Finally Been Righted': Tribes Bury Remains of Ancient Ancestor Known as Kennewick Man." *Seattle Times*, February 20, 2017.

Hegde, Sushmitha. "Who Is the Kennewick Man?" Kennewick Man: History, Facts and Controversy, *Science ABC*, April 30, 2019, https://www.scienceabc.com/social -science/who-is-kennewick-man.html.

"Kennewick Man: The Ancient One and Repatriation." OSU—School of History, Philosophy and Religion, May 17, 2017, https://www.youtube.com/watch?v= Hzb4fz2JFlA.

Linder, Douglas O. "*Epperson v. Arkansas*: Supreme Court of the United States (1968)." Famous Trials, University of Missouri–Kansas City School of Law, 2005.

Mihesuah, Devon A., ed. *Repatriation Reader: Who Owns American Indian Remains?* Lincoln: University of Nebraska Press, 2000.

Native American Graves Protection and Repatriation Act (NAGPRA). *A Quick Guide for Preserving Native American Cultural Resources*. US Department of the Interior, National Park Service, 2012.

Owen, Russell. "From Monkey Trial to 'Atomic Age.'" *New York Times Magazine*, July 21, 1946.

Preston, Douglas. "The Kennewick Man Finally Freed to Share His Secrets." *Smithsonian Magazine*, Smithsonian Institution, September 1, 2014, https://www.smithson ianmag.com/history/kennewick-man-finally-freed-share-his-secrets-180952462.

Rasmussen, Morten, et al. "The Ancestry and Affiliations of Kennewick Man." *Nature*, US National Library of Medicine, July 23, 2015, https://www.nature.com/articles /nature14625.

Samuel, Sigal. "What to Do When Racists Try to Hijack Your Religion." *The Atlantic*, November 2, 2017.

Thomas, David Hurst. *Skull Wars: Kennewick Man, Archaeology, and the Battle for Native American Identity*. New York: Basic Books, 2002.

Westneat, Danny. "Kennewick Man Panel Hears Both Sides—Tribes, Scientists Continue to Disagree Over the Study of Ancient Man." *Seattle Times*, June 11, 1998.

James Armistead Lafayette: Snatching Secrets

"The American Revolution." National Parks Service, US Department of the Interior, December 4, 2008.

Ellis, Joseph J. "Washington Takes Charge." *Smithsonian Magazine*, Smithsonian Institution, January 1, 2005, www.smithsonianmag.com/history/washington -takes-charge-107060488.

Kaplan, Sidney. *The Black Presence in the Era of the American Revolution*. Washington, DC: National Portrait Gallery, Smithsonian Institution, 1973.

Kaplan, Sidney, and Emma Nogrady Kaplan. *The Black Presence in the Era of the American Revolution*. Amherst: University of Massachusetts Press, 1989.

Klein, Christopher. "The Ex-Slaves Who Fought with the British." History.com, May 24, 2016, www.history.com/news/the-ex-slaves-who-fought-with-the-british.

Nash, Gary B. *The Unknown American Revolution: The Unruly Birth of Democracy and the Struggle to Create America*. London, UK: Jonathan Cape, 2006.

Rogers, J. A. *Africa's Gift to America: The Afro-American in the Making and Saving of the United States*. Middletown, CT: Wesleyan University Press, 2014.

Witherbee, A. "James Armistead Lafayette." EBSCOhost, August 2017, search.ebsco host.com/login.aspx?direct=true&db=f5h&AN=25160572&site=ehost-live.]

John Sutter: Stolen Land and Golden Greed

Blakemore, Erin. "The Enslaved Native Americans Who Made the Gold Rush Possible." History.com, January 24, 2018, https://www.history.com/news/the-enslaved -native-americans-who-made-the-gold-rush-possible.

———. "California Slaughtered 16,000 Native Americans: The State Finally Apologized for the Genocide." History.com, June 19, 2019, https://www.history.com /news/native-american-genocide-california-apology.

Field, Margaret A. "Genocide and the Indians of California, 1769–1873." ScholarWorks at UMass, 1993, Graduate Master's Theses, Paper 141.

Hurtado, Albert L. "California Indians and the Workaday West: Labor, Assimilation, and Survival." *California History*, vol. 69, no. 1 (1990).

"John Sutter and California's Indians." HistoryNet.com, www.historynet.com/john -sutter-and-californias-indians.htm.

Koster, John. "John Sutter's California Dream Became His Worst Nightmare." *History Net*, https://www.historynet.com/john-sutters-california-dream-became-his-worst -nightmare.htm

Landry, Alysa. "Native History: California Gold Rush Begins, Devastates Native Population." *IndianCountryToday.com*, National Congress of American Indians, September 17, 2017, https://indiancountrytoday.com/archive/native-history-california -gold-rush-begins-devastates-native-population-WI8OlTnZ7U-i66nhfbWhfA.

Rawls, James J. *Indians of California: The Changing Image*. Norman: University of Oklahoma Press, 1986, p. 177.

Shoup, Kate. *The California Gold Rush*. New York: Cavendish Square Publishing, 2015, p. 28.

Trafzer, Cliff E., and Joel R. Hyer, eds. *Exterminate Them: Written Accounts of the Murder, Rape, and Enslavement of Native Americans During the California Gold Rush*. East Lansing: Michigan State University Press, 1999.

SCHILLINGER V. UNITED STATES: CAST IN CONCRETE

California Artificial Stone Paving Co. v. Molitor, 113 U.S. 609 (1885).

California Paving Co. v. Schalicke, 119 U.S. 401 (1886).

"Defining the AOC." Architect of the Capitol, www.aoc.gov/defining-aoc.

"*Hurlbut v. Schillinger*, 130 U.S. 456 (1889)." *Justia Law*, supreme.justia.com/cases /federal/us/130/456.

Official Gazette of the United States Patent Office, vol. 41, US Patent Office, January 1, 1888.

"*Schillinger v. United States*, 155 U.S. 163 (1894)." *Justia Law, Justia*, supreme.justia.com /cases/federal/us/155/163.

Supreme Court Reporter, vol. 9 (January 1, 1889).

Tucker, Charles Cowles, and Franklin Hubbell Mackey. *Reports of Cases Argued and Adjudged in the Supreme Court of the District of Columbia: Sitting in General Term, from June 14, 1880, to [June 20, 1892]*. United States: J. L. Ginck, 1891.

United States Reports: Cases Adjudged in the Supreme Court at . . . and Rules Announced at . . ., vol. 130, US Supreme Court, John Chandler Bancroft Davis, Henry Putzel, Henry C. Lind, Frank D. Wagner. Edited by John Chandler Davis, et al., Banks & Bros., Law Publishers, January 1, 1889.

"US Court of Federal Claims." US Department of Justice, www.uscfc.uscourts.gov.

Watts, Jonathan. "Concrete: The Most Destructive Material on Earth." *The Guardian*, February 25, 2019.

EDISON, TESLA, AND WESTINGHOUSE: THE WAR OF THE CURRENTS

Carlson, W. Bernard. *Tesla: Inventor of the Electrical Age*. Princeton, NJ: Princeton University Press, 2015.

Decherney, Peter. "Copyright Dupes: Piracy and New Media in *Edison v. Lubin* (1903)." *Film History: An International Journal*, vol. 19, no. 2 (2007), 109–24. *Onesearch*, doi:10.2979/fil.2007.19.2.109.

———. Hollywood's Copyright Wars: From Edison to the Internet. New York: Columbia University Press, 2013.

Josephson, Matthew. *Edison: A Biography*. New York: McGraw-Hill, 1959.

Miller, Francis Trevelyan. *Thomas A. Edison, Benefactor of Mankind*. New York: Winston, 1931.

"My Inventions." Nikola Tesla's Autobiography at Age 63, Nikola Tesla Tells Story of His Creative Life, WanttoKnow.info, www.wanttoknow.info/energy/nikola _tesla_autobiography.

Seifer, Marc. *Wizard: The Life and Times of Nikola Tesla*. New York: Citadel Press, 2016.

Stross, Randall E. *The Wizard of Menlo Park: The Life and Times of Thomas Alva Edison*. New York: Crown Publishers, 2007.

"Survived a Death Shock." *Chicago Tribune*, June 12, 1889, p. 9. *Newspapers.com*, Tesla, Nikola.

BEN-HUR: STOLEN STORYLINES

Balio, Tino. *The American Film Industry*. Madison: University of Wisconsin Press, 2011.

"*Ben-Hur:* A Tale of the Christ." General Lew Wallace Study & Museum, www.ben -hur.com/meet-lew-wallace/ben-hur.

"*Ben-Hur:* A Tale of the Christ." Wikipedia, January 25, 2020, https://en.wikipedia.org /wiki/Ben-Hur:_A_Tale_of_the_Christ.

"*Ben-Hur* Trivia." *IMDb*, www.imdb.com/title/tt0052618/trivia?ref_=tt_ql_2.

Hagiopian, Kevin. *Film Notes: Ben-Hur*, www.albany.edu/writers-inst/webpages4/film notes/fnf98n5.html.

Holmes, Oliver Wendell, and Supreme Court of the United States. US Reports: *Kalem Co. v. Harper Bros.*, 222 U.S. 55. 1911. Periodical. Retrieved from the Library of Congress, www.loc.gov/item/usrep222055.

"Injunction Asked Against Roman Spectacle." *Motion Picture World*, March 7, 1908.

"*Kalem Company v. Harper Brothers L*, Opinion of the Court." Wikisource, December 20, 2017, https://en.wikisource.org/wiki/Kalem_Company_v._Harper_Brothers_L.

Kanin, Garson. *Hollywood: Stars and Starlets, Tycoons and Flesh-Peddlers, Moviemakers and Moneymakers, Frauds and Geniuses, Hopefuls and Has-Beens, Great Lovers and Sex Symbols*. New York: Limelight Editions, 1984.

Lahue, Kalton C. *Continued Next Week: A History of the Moving Picture Serial*. Norman: University of Oklahoma Press, 1969.

Motion Picture magazine. February 1925, vol. XXIX no. 1, 100.

"Must Pay Royalties on Moving Pictures." *New York Times*, May 6, 1908, https://times machine.nytimes.com/timesmachine/1908/05/06/104724490.html?pageNumber=5.

Ramsaye, Terry. *A Million and One Nights: A History of the Motion Picture through 1925.* New York: Simon & Schuster, 1986.

Solomon, Jon. "The Kalem *Ben-Hur* (1907)." *The Ancient World in Silent Cinema,* edited by Pantelis Michelakis and Maria Wyke. Cambridge: Cambridge University Press, 2013.

Swansburg, John. "The Passion of Lew Wallace," http://www.slate.com/articles/life/his tory/2013/03/ben_hur_and_lew_wallace_how_the_scapegoat_of_shiloh_became _one_of_the_best.2.html.

BORROWED

FERDINAND WALDO DEMARA JR: A PRETENTIOUS PETTIFOGGER

Crichton, Robert. *The Great Impostor.* New York: Random House, 1959.

Konnikova, Maria. *The Confidence Game: Why We Fall for It . . . Every Time.* New York: Viking, 2016.

McCarthy, Joe. "The Master Imposter: An Incredible Tale." *Life,* January 28, 1952.

Williams, Roger M. *The Super Crooks: A Rogues' Gallery of Famous Hustlers, Swindlers, and Thieves.* Chicago: Playboy Press, 1973.

PAUL JORDAN-SMITH: THE ART WORLD'S TALENTED TRICKSTER

"Architectural Exhibition Is Opened, Many Arts Represented in the Show." *San Francisco Chronicle,* https://www.newspapers.com/image/27396434.

Bulliet, C. J. "No-Jury Show a Glowing Surprise." *Chicago Evening Post,* January 26, 1926, http://ecclesiastes911.net/disumbrationism/pictures/jerdanowitch-chicago -evening-post.jpg.

Chambers, Robert. "Mock Modernism: An Anthology of Parodies, Travesties, Frauds, 1910–1935." *Clio,* vol. 44, no. 2, Indiana University–Purdue University, April 1, 2015.

Crosse, John. "Southern California Architectural History." *Southern California Architectural History,* June 22, 2013, https://socalarchhistory.blogspot.com/2013.

"Ethel Sloan Park." *Park Family Reunion.net,* 2005, www.parkfamilyreunion.net/Ethel SloanPark.htm.

Jordan-Smith, Paul. *Soul of Woman: An Interpretation of the Philosophy of Feminism.* San Francisco, CA: Paul Elder & Co., 1916.

———. *The Road I Came: Some Recollections and Reflections Concerning Changes in American Life and Manners since 1890.* Caldwell, ID: Caxton Printers, Ltd., 1960.

"Letter to Paul Jordan Smith from his new bride, Ethel Sloan Park Smith," *Park Family Reunion.net,* October 12, 1904, http://www.parkfamilyreunion.net/Assets/ESPto PJS.pdf.

Lezard, Nicholas. "The Book to End All Books." *The Guardian,* August 17, 2001, https:// www.theguardian.com/books/2001/aug/18/history.philosophy.

"Minister's Wife Gets Decree on Cruelty Plea." *Chicago Examiner,* p. 3, http://digital .chipublib.org/digital/collection/examiner/id/42441/rec/1408.

Murphy, Colin. *Fierce History: 5,000 Years of Startling Stories from Ireland and Around the Globe*, eBook edition. Dublin, Ireland: O'Brien Press, 2018, p. 9.

Simkin, Mikhail. "Disumbrationist School of Painting: A Hoax that Embarrassed the Art World." Reverent Entertainment, *Ecclesiastes911.net*, May 1, 2006, http://eccle siastes911.net/disumbrated_art.html.

Warren, Beth Gates. *Artful Lives: Edward Weston, Margrethe Mather, and the Bohemians of Los Angeles*. Los Angeles, CA: J. Paul Getty Museum, 2011.

Whittaker, Alma. "International Art Hoax Bared." *Los Angeles Sunday Times*, August 14, 1927, p. 25.

Zindel, Timothy. "History—Material Dreams: Southern California through the 1920s by Kevin Starr." *Library Journal*, vol. 114, no. 20, December 1, 1989, p. 144.

THOMAS PAINE: PATRIOT PULLED FROM THE GRAVE

"A Biography of Thomas Paine (1737–1809)." Biographies, American History: From Revolution to Reconstruction and Beyond, Scribd.com, https://www.scribd.com /document/254194449/A-Biography-of-Thomas-Paine-1737-1809-Biographies -American-History-From-Revolution-To-Reconstr.

Chen, David W. "Rehabilitating Thomas Paine, Bit by Bony Bit." *New York Times*, March 30, 2001.

Chesterton, G. K. *William Cobbett*. London, UK: Hodder & Stoughton, 1925.

Cole, G. D. H. *Life of William Cobbett*. Abingdon, UK: Routledge, 2017.

Conway, Moncure. "The Adventures of Thomas Paine's Bones by Moncure Conway." *Thomas Paine National Historical Association*, thomaspaine.org.

Foner, Philip S. "Foner's Introduction to the Collected Works." *Thomas Paine National Historical Association*, thomaspaine.org.

Grimm, Kevin. "Thomas Paine." George Washington's Mount Vernon, 2020, https:// www.mountvernon.org/library/digitalhistory/digital-encyclopedia/article/thomas -paine.

Janz, Denis. *A People's History of Christianity*. Minneapolis, MN: Fortress Press, 2014.

Keyes, Pam. "Cobbett the Body-Snatcher, or What Happened to Thomas Paine's Corpse." *Historia Obscura*, October 27, 2014, http://www.historiaobscura.com /2014/10.

Landry, Peter. "William Cobbett (1763–1835), The Poor Man's Friend." Biographies, Blupete.com, 2011, http://www.blupete.com/Literature/Biographies/Reformers /Cobbett.htm.

"Moncure Daniel Conway (1832–1907)." Dickinson College, Archives & Special Collections at Dickinson College, 2018, http://archives.dickinson.edu/people /moncure-daniel-conway-1832-1907.

Nelson, Craig. *Thomas Paine: Enlightenment, Revolution, and the Birth of Modern Nations*. New York: Viking, 2006.

Osborne, John W. *William Cobbett: His Thought and His Times*. Westport, CT: Greenwood Press, 1981.

Philp, Mark. "Thomas Paine." *Stanford Encyclopedia of Philosophy* (Winter 2019), Edward N. Zalta, ed., https://plato.stanford.edu/entries/paine.

"Reign of Terror." *Encyclopedia Britannica*, January 24, 2020, https://www.britannica.com/event/Reign-of-Terror.

Walt Whitman: The Case of the Nabbed Notebooks

Birney, Alice L. "Missing Whitman Notebooks Returned to Library of Congress." *Walt Whitman Quarterly Review*, vol. 12 (Spring 1995).

Blake, David Haven. *Walt Whitman and the Culture of American Celebrity*. New Haven, CT: Yale University Press, 2006.

Debczak, Michele. "11 Facts About the Library of Congress." *Mental Floss*, updated April 24, 2019, https://www.mentalfloss.com/article/92655/11-well-read-facts-about-library-congress.

Hutchins, Aaron. "Closing the Book on John Mark Tillmann's Stolen Antiques." *Macleans.ca*, December 14, 2015, https://www.macleans.ca/news/canada/closing-the-book-on-john-mark-tillmanns-stolen-antiques.

Pollack, Barbara. "Anything Can Break Bad: An FBI Special Agent Has Learned the Difference Between the Art World and the Mafia." *ARTnews.com*, November 18, 2019, https://www.artnews.com/art-news/news/anything-can-break-bad-an-fbi-special-agent-has-learned-the-difference-between-the-art-world-and-the-mafia-6397.

Stovall, Floyd. "Dating Whitman's Early Notebooks." *Studies in Bibliography*, vol. 24 (1971), pp. 197–204.

Szekely, Peter. "FBI's 'Art Cops': In Hot Pursuit of Renoirs, Rembrandts and Ruby Slippers." Reuters, April 10, 2019, https://www.reuters.com/article/us-crime-art-fbi-feature/fbis-art-cops-in-hot-pursuit-of-renoirs-rembrandts-and-ruby-slippers-idUSKCN1RM14F.

Ten Notebooks and a Cardboard Butterfly Missing from the Walt Whitman Papers. Washington, DC: Library of Congress, 1954.

"Whitman's Missing Notebooks and the Cardboard Butterfly," http://jessicaa.lookingforwhitman.org/2009/10/15.

Wylly, Marion Johnston. "Motives of Art Theft: A Social Contextual Perspective of Value" (2014). Florida State University, PhD dissertation.

John Scott Harrison: A Case of Body Snatching Most Foul

"A Body-Snatching Horror." *Ottowa Free Trader*, June 8, 1878, p. 2.

Drusus, Livius. "The Body-Snatching Horror of John Scott Harrison." *Mental Floss*, May 21, 2015, www.mentalfloss.com/article/64221/body-snatching-horror-john-scott-harrison.

Edwards, Linden. "Body Snatching in Ohio." *Internet Archive*, Ohio Historical Society.

Fanebust, Wayne. *The Missing Corpse: Grave Robbing a Gilded Age Tycoon*. Westport, CT: Praeger, 2005.

Frank, Julia Bess. "Body Snatching: A Grave Medical Problem." *Yale Journal of Biology and Medicine*, vol. 49 (March 3, 1976), pp. 399–410.

"The Grave Robbery." *Cincinnati Enquirer*, June 7, 1878, 8.

Shultz, Suzanne M. *Body Snatching: The Robbing of Graves for the Education of Physicians in Early Nineteenth Century America.* Jefferson, NC: McFarland & Co., 2005.

Sievers, Harry Joseph. *The Harrison Horror.* Public Library of Fort Wayne and Allen County, 1956.

STOLEN

Frank Norfleet: From Chump to Chastiser

Barnum, P. T. *The Humbugs of the World: An Account of Humbugs, Delusions, Impositions, Quackeries, Deceits and Deceivers Generally, in All Ages.* Los Angeles: HardPress Publishing, 2012.

"'The Big Con': If You Can't Avoid It, Avenge It." *NPR*, March 24, 2012, https://www.npr.org/2012/03/24/149148112/the-big-con-if-you-cant-avoid-it-avenge-it.

Block, Lawrence. *Gangsters, Swindlers, Killers, and Thieves: The Lives and Crimes of Fifty American Villains.* Oxford, UK: Oxford University Press, 2004.

Dillon, John J. *Hind-Sights or Looking Backward at Swindles.* London, UK: Forgotten Books, 2015.

Glasrud, Bruce A. "Eavesdropping on Texas History," edited by Mary L. Scheer. *Southwestern Historical Quarterly*, vol. 121, no. 2 (2017), pp. 227–28, doi:10.1353/swh.2017.0056.

Hendley, Nate. *The Big Con: Great Hoaxes, Frauds, Grifts, and Swindles in American History.* Santa Barbara, CA: ABC-CLIO, 2016.

"J. Frank Norfleet: The Sucker, the Sting, the Sweet Revenge." *Hometown by Handlebar*, October 15, 2019, https://hometownbyhandlebar.com/?p=2028.

Johnson, Scott, and Craig Johnson. "J. Frank Norfleet." *Blonger Bros.—The Grafters Club*, http://www.graftersclub.com/bios/Norfleet.asp.

Norfleet, J. Frank, and Gordon Hines. *Norfleet: The Amazing Experiences of an Intrepid Texas Rancher with an International Swindling Ring.* Sugarland, TX: Imperial Press, 1927.

Reading, Amy. *The Mark Inside: A Perfect Swindle, a Cunning Revenge, and a Small History of the Big Con.* New York: Vintage Books, 2013.

———. "The 9 Stages of the Big Con." Amyreading.com, http://www.amyreading.com/the-9-stages-of-the-big-con.html.

Klaus Fuchs: Explosive Secrets

"The Costs of the Manhattan Project." Brookings, April 14, 2017, https://www.brookings.edu/the-costs-of-the-manhattan-project.

Goodman, Michael S. "Who Is Trying to Keep What Secret from Whom and Why? MI5-FBI Relations and the Klaus Fuchs Case." *Journal of Cold War Studies*, vol. 7, no. 3 (Summer 2005), pp. 124–46.

Martin, David C. *Wilderness of Mirrors.* New York: Harper & Row, 1980.

Moorehead, A. "Klaus Fuchs: He Gave Stalin the A-Bomb." *Saturday Evening Post*, 224 (50), 1952.

Moss, Norman. *Klaus Fuchs: The Man Who Stole the Atom Bomb*. London, UK: Grafton, 1989.

Radosh, Ronald, and Joyce Milton. *The Rosenberg File : A Search for the Truth*. New York: Holt, Rinehart & Winston, 1983.

West, Rebecca. *The New Meaning of Treason*. New York: Penguin, 1985.

Williams, Robert Chadwell. *Klaus Fuchs, Atom Spy*. Cambridge, MA: Harvard University Press, 1987.

HENRY WALLACE AND HARRY TRUMAN: DUBIOUS DEALINGS

Davis, Michael A. *Politics as Usual: Thomas Dewey, Franklin Roosevelt, and the Wartime Presidential Campaign of 1944*. Ithaca, NY: Cornell University Press, 2014.

Ferrell, Robert H. *Choosing Truman: The Democratic Convention of 1944*. Columbia: University of Missouri Press, 2000.

Fink, Leon. *Major Problems in the Gilded Age and the Progressive Era: Documents and Essays*. Boston, MA: Cengage Learning, 2015.

"Four Freedoms." Wikipedia, January 29, 2020, https://en.wikipedia.org/wiki/Four_Freedoms.

Greenfeld, Jeff. "The Year the Veepstakes Really Mattered." *Politico*, July 10, 2016.

Masur, M. B. "Century of the Common Man." *The Society for Historians of American Foreign Relations*, 2014, https://shafr.org/teaching/draft-classroom-documents/century-of-the-common-man.

"1940 United States Presidential Election." Wikipedia, January 26, 2020, https://en.wikipedia.org/wiki/1940_United_States_presidential_election.

Ross, Alex. "Uncommon Man." *The New Yorker*, July 9, 2019.

FREDERICK JOUBERT DUQUESNE: PASSING INTELLIGENCE

Breverton, Terry. *Breverton's First World War Curiosities*. Stroud, Gloucestershire, UK: Amberley Publishing, 2014.

"Duquesne Spy Ring." FBI Records: The Vault, US Department of Justice, vault.fbi.gov/Duquesne Spy Ring/Duquesne Spy Ring Part 1 of 1/view.

Evans, Leslie. "Fritz Joubert Duquesne: Boer Avenger, German Spy, Munchausen Fantasist." *Boryanabooks*, April 1, 2014, http://boryanabooks.com/?p=4355.

"Fritz Duquesne: The Spy Who Never Came In from the Cold." Reprobate Independent Views for Freethinkers, *Reprobate*, October 14, 2013, https://reprobate.co.za/fritz-duquesne-the-spy-who-never-came-in-from-the-cold.

"History of Bills and Resolutions." *Congressional Record* (Bound Edition), vol. 45 (1910), https://www.govinfo.gov/app/details/GPO-CRECB-1910-pt9-v45/GPO-CRECB-1910-pt9-v45-4.

Love and Ruin: Tales of Obsession, Danger, and Heartbreak from The Atavist Magazine. New York: W. W. Norton, 2016.

"Frederick Joubert Duquesne—Scout, Hunter, Soldier, Spy." *African Hunter Magazine*, December 1, 201, vol. 20 (1), vi.

Ronnie, Art. *Counterfeit Hero: Fritz Duquesne, Adventurer and Spy.* Annapolis, MD: Naval Institute Press, 1995.

Tunney, Thomas Joseph. *Throttled! The Detection of the German and Anarchist Bomb Plotters (1919).* Boston, MA: Small, Maynard & Co., 1919.

Wood, Clement. *The Man Who Killed Kitchener: The Life of Fritz Joubert Duquesne.* New York: W. Faro, Inc., 1932.

INDEX